$5 3 -

KNOCKABOUT FISHING SCHOONER "HELEN B. THOMAS" OF BOSTON
Photograph by W. B. Jackson

AMERICAN SAILING SHIPS

Their Plans and History

by
Charles G. Davis

With an Introduction by
IRVING R. WILES

Dover Publications, Inc.
New York

Published in Canada by General Publishing Company, Ltd., 30 Lesmill Road, Don Mills, Toronto, Ontario.

Published in the United Kingdom by Constable and Company, Ltd., 10 Orange Street, London WC2H 7EG.

This Dover edition, first published in 1984, is an unabridged republication of the work first published by The Marine Research Society, Salem, Massachusetts, in 1929, under the title *Ships of the Past*.

Manufactured in the United States of America
Dover Publications, Inc., 31 East 2nd Street, Mineola, N.Y. 11501

Library of Congress Cataloging in Publication Data

Davis, Charles G. (Charles Gerard), 1870-1959.
  American sailing ships.

  Reprint. Originally published: Ships of the past. Salem, Mass. : Marine Research Society, 1929.
  Includes index.
  1. Sailing ships—United States.   2. Sailing ships—United States—History.   I. Title.
VM145.D28   1984   387.2'2'0973   83-20612
ISBN 0-486-24658-2

INTRODUCTION

THE charm that exists for those of us who are ship-minded in anything that pertains to man's work or play upon the sea is difficult to explain. Nevertheless, anyone of us who has unexpectedly come upon a fine model of an old-time vessel, or what is perhaps as rare, a really good sea picture, knows well the excitement, the elation, that instantly possesses him, and to those of us who have seen the square-riggers at their wharves, or the last of the sailing vessels of war memory, adds a thrill that is ours alone.

A model takes on in our imagination the size and importance of the ship herself and we can wonder at the ponderous anchors and fairly smell the tar and bilge-water. Perhaps because these are memories of our youth we are in a measure blinded to any charm of the kind that may exist in modern ships, for in these days beauty of appearance has with designer and builder given place to the practical alone, and a beam-trawler is made to appear top-heavy or a dreadnaught is given the snout of a pig.

The writer of this book is not of this breed. Davis has always loved beautiful vessels. Seaman, designer, builder of ships, and crack skipper of racing yachts he is an artist in his soul and loves the sailing vessels of all times. They have been an absorbing interest of his life and this volume will place before us many of the results of his years of research. Aided by his knowledge of marine architecture he has found in libraries, old letters, or manuscripts a word or sentence here and there which solves some knotty problem of design or construction. Again, in faded writing is a table of "offsets," just dry figures to most of us, but from which he can draw the plans of some old vessel known only by name in the histories.

This book, a joy for him to write, will be for us a source of pleasure and profit, and we hope there will be others of the kind to follow.

IRVING R. WILES

New York City, June 1, 1929

CONTENTS

Block Island Boats and Pinkys 3

The Fishing Schooner 24

The Baltimore Clipper and Other Southern Craft 37

The Packet Ship "ISAAC WEBB" 56

The Frigate "RALEIGH" 77

The Frigate "CONGRESS" 121

Masts and Spars of United States Naval Vessels 139

List of Plans of Ships 159

Plans of Ships 165

Index 191

PLATES AND PLANS

On or facing page

Knockabout Fishing Schooner "HELEN B. THOMAS"
of Boston . . . . *(Frontispiece)*

Block Island Boats 4

Model of Chebacco Boat "LION" 5

Sail Plan of Block Island Boat "ISLAND BELLE" 7

Plans of Block Island Boat "ISLAND BELLE" 9

Sail Plan of Block Island Boat "DAUNTLESS" 11

Model of New England Pinky "GLOUCESTER" 12

Model of Quoddy Boat "YANKEE HERO" 13

Plans of Block Island Boat "DAUNTLESS" 13

Stern Views of Pinky from Yarmouth, Nova Scotia 16

Views of Pinky from Yarmouth, Nova Scotia 17

Sail Plan of Pinky from Yarmouth, Nova Scotia 19

Model of New England Pinky "TIGER" 20

Schooner "POLLY," built in 1805 21

Pinky "MAINE," built in 1845 21

Model of Marblehead "HEEL TAPPER" 24

A Knockabout Fishing Schooner 25

Gloucester Fishing Schooner "JAMES W. PARKER" 28

Provincetown Fishing Schooner "ROSE DOROTHEA" . . . 29

Sail Plan of Knockabout Schooner "HELEN B. THOMAS" . . . 29

Plans of Knockabout Schooner "HELEN B. THOMAS" . . . 31

Gloucester Fishing Schooner "METAMORA" 32

Model of Gloucester Fishing Schooner "COLUMBIA" 33

Details of Rigging on a Gloucester Fisherman 33

Baltimore Clipper Schooner of 1820 (Marestier) 36

Baltimore Clipper Schooner of 1820 (Marestier) 39

Baltimore Schooner "MILDRED ADDISON" 40

Hull of Baltimore Clipper Schooner "MILDRED ADDISON" . . . 41

Baltimore Clipper Schooner of 1820 (Marestier) 41

Plans of Baltimore Clipper Schooner (Marestier) 43

Primitive Dugout Canoe at Panama, 1928 44

Chesapeake Sailing Canoe 44

Chesapeake Bay Buckeye 45

Plans of Baltimore Clipper Schooner (Marestier) 45

Sail Plan of a Bugeye 47

Deck Views of Florida Red Snapper Fisherman
  "OVER THE WAVES" 48

Deck View on a Gloucester Fisherman 49

Sponge Boats at Tarpon Springs, Florida 49

Old Style Sponge Boats at Tarpon Springs 52

New Style Sponge Boats at Tarpon Springs 53

Packet Ship "ISAAC WEBB" of New York 56

Ships "ROUSSEAU" and "DESDEMONA" at New Bedford . . . 57

Model of Black Ball Line Packet Ship "MONTEZUMA" . . . 62

Deck Plans of Packet Ship "ST. DENIS" 63

Details of Packet Ship "MONTEZUMA" 65

South Street, New York City, in 1880 74

Clipper Packet Ship "RACER" of New York 74

Model of United States Frigate "RALEIGH," 1776 75

Model of United States Frigate "RALEIGH," 1776 82

Drying Hammocks on a United States Frigate 83

Sail Plan of United States Frigate "CONGRESS," 1841 . . . 120

Sailors Telling Yarns on an Old-Time Frigate 122

A Frigate of 1750 131

The Round Bodied Ship of 1750 135

A Pinky of the Year 1800 166

Plans of the Pinky "EAGLE" of 1820 166

Sail Plan of Pinky "EAGLE" of 1820 168

Plans of a Yarmouth, Nova Scotia, Pinky 170

Fishing Schooner "HENRY FORD" Ashore on Cape Ann,

    Mass., in 1922 172

Plans of Fishing Schooner "COLUMBIA" 172

Deck Arrangement of the "MARY E. COONEY" 173

Sail Plan of Fishing Schooner "COLUMBIA" 174

Plans of Chesapeake Bay Log Canoe "MAGIC" 176

Plans of Chesapeake Bay Buckeye 176

Plans of Very Old Chesapeake Bay Bugeye 178

Plans of New Orleans Oyster Lugger 178

Plans of Packet Ship "ISAAC WEBB" 180

Rigging Plan of Packet Ship "ISAAC WEBB" 182

Plans of United States Frigate "RALEIGH," 1776 184

Sail Plan of United States Frigate "RALEIGH," 1776 186

Plans of United States Frigate "CONGRESS," 1841 188

AMERICAN SAILING SHIPS

Their Plans and History

CHAPTER I

BLOCK ISLAND BOATS AND PINKYS

TO the man who really loves boats there is no greater enjoyment than to cruise along the coast and anchor in every little out-of-the-way nook and corner. There he can see some of the local craft, swap yarns with the hardy men of the sea, and learn many things about boats of all kinds, not to be found in books.

It is well-nigh impossible to accomplish this in any other way than by boat. To reach the haunts of these men and see their craft, as one should see them, in use and not abandoned or hauled up for the winter, is impossible by auto or any shore conveyance, for some of the best specimens may be found where there are no passable roads. Some are on islands or are found when you bear up for a harbor behind some breakwater, on the approach of a storm, and there discover some of the oddities of the sea—craft you couldn't find in any other way than just by chance.

Many years ago (in 1894) when we dropped our hook in the salt pond at Block Island, landlocked amid green rolling hills, marked off into farms by snake-like stone walls; to us, the chief characteristic of the landscape was a fleet of scoop-sheered, wide, lap-strake, two-masted sailing boats huddled along the shoreline. Moored to poles almost as big as their masts, the spars of these boats made a maze of sticks like that seen at the famous catboat dock at Newport, Rhode Island. We were interested in all kinds of boats and wanted to see those in Pole Harbor on the eastern shore, and after tramping across the island we found three of them. They were real old Block Island

Fig. 1. Catboats at Newport, R. I., in 1894

double-enders, bilged, busted and rotting and half full of sand. We had a good opportunity to study the lines of these wonderful sea boats that could cross Nantucket Shoals when no other craft could live. In the outer

3

basin rode a dozen or more of these hardy little craft moored to tall stakes in the cove sheltered by a newly-built stone breakwater.

Later, when we sailed across to the mainland and dropped anchor in Newport harbor, what should we see, close aboard of us, but a peculiar little schooner, the *Island Belle*, the most famous Block Islander ever built. Her skipper, in years gone by, had the contract from the Government to carry the mails to Block Island and carry them she did, winter and summer, blow high or blow low. Some of her trips were made when seamen declared no boat could live outside Newport harbor.

FIG. 2. THE *Island Belle*

I made a sketch of her just as she was then rigged, with all the top-hamper of a full-fledged, two-masted schooner, topmasts, crosstrees, backstays, triatic stay and all, like a Gloucesterman; but the plank lashed under her stout bowsprit, with its pulpit and spear, and the line-wound casks aft on deck, showed that she was then being used as a swordfisherman. With such a complicated rig she never would have carried the mails as she formerly did. When she was in her prime, she had two long, unstayed, tapered masts with very short-headed gaff sails, the rig known as the Block Island rig. The *Rhode Island*, another fishkiller that rounded to and anchored near her, carried this rig.

We lay nine days, fog and storm bound, in Newport harbor, with a fleet of twenty-eight Gloucester fishing schooners anchored around us. I sketched

FIG. 3. BLOCK ISLAND BOAT
Rhode Island

several and we visited many of them, their skippers only too glad to have company to relieve the monotony of enforced idleness. Three times the fleet attempted to leave. Sail was hoisted and anchors hove up to such an accompaniment of flapping canvas, clanking windlass pawls and merrily sung chanteys as only a fleet of sailing vessels can produce. Each schooner's crew, vying with the others, jumped to its work. It seemed like the start of a yacht race; one of the old-fashioned kind where boats started from an anchor. The schooners looked like a flock of swooping sea gulls, their white sails brilliant with rounding shadows in the bright sunlight, the deep blue sea water rolling over into

BLOCK ISLAND BOAT IN WEST HARBOR

BLOCK ISLAND BOAT AT NEW HARBOR, 1913

Model of Chebacco Boat "Lion" in the National Museum

white soapsuds under each schooner's bow as they tacked and retacked, careening gracefully under the puffs of a brisk new so'-west wind. As they beat out through the narrow, rock-bound channel, past the Fort and past the Dumplings light, they met an impenetrable bank of gray fog that came rolling in from sea and the whole fleet turned tail and sailed back with lifted sheets; back to the anchorage where they came from.

At the third attempt, we, too, ran out to sea, but it wasn't long before we were swallowed up by fog, that clung, wet and clammy, until we were almost up to the old whale dock at New Bedford, where we ran out into beautiful sunshine with a deep blue sky overhead. There we anchored and rolled up our sails just as the sun set in a shimmering mass of gold. Here we found four old whale ships, stripped of their gear, lying tied up at the dock and although we went ashore and spent a day looking them over —at their huge anchors and big casks of whale oil stored on the rickety old wooden pier—we didn't then consider it worthwhile

FIG. 4. GLOUCESTER FISHING SCHOONER *Kearsarge*

to record their names. They were only old "blubber hunters," anyway. But I made a sketch of them as seen from the deck of the old cutter *Pelican*, owned by my friend Commodore C. M. Connelly of New Rochelle, N. Y.

At Edgartown, on the island of Martha's Vineyard, we found an old whaling schooner rotting away at the pier, the clumsy wooden davits that disfigured her side undeniably denoting her vocation.

And so it is with each locality along the coast, from Maine to Texas, each producing different types; a model that has either proved by experience best adapted to the work it has to perform and the waters it has to work in or else a type which the settlers in those

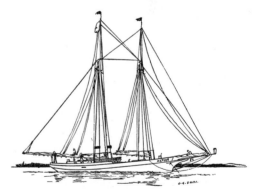

FIG. 5. *Active* AT NEWPORT, 1894

regions had used in the land from whence they came. Down in the Gulf, at Pensacola, for instance, the fleet of red-snapper fishing schooners are nearly all Gloucester fishing schooners that have been purchased by the Bluenose fishermen who have settled there and they are intermixed with a few little schooners that were built at Key West or Nassau. At Tarpon Springs, Florida, there is a large settlement of Greeks who use a double-ended boat, very similar in model to the old Block Island boat. They are sponge fishers, which is the sole industry of this place. It is one of the sights that tourists go miles to see on a Sunday when there will be a fleet of nearly fifty of these high-sheered, brilliantly painted boats tied up with their bows butted in to the long wooden pier built along the shore of the river.

In the Watercraft Collection in the United States Museum at Washington, D. C., are scale models of many of the various types of vessels used along the seacoast and it makes a most interesting collection to a lover of

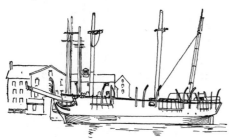

Fig. 6. Old Whale Ship at New Bedford in 1894

nautical affairs. There, side by side, one can compare the sharp Chesapeake "pungie" and "bugeye" with the clumsy looking, high-sided, blunt-ended "heel tappers," "dogbodies," Chebacco boats and pinkys of the New England coast.

Fortunately the lines showing the model or shape of the hull of some of the Block Island boats have been preserved to us by two enthusiastic fellow yachtsmen, long since dead. John Hyslop, who for years was the official measurer of the New York Yacht Club, made a special visit to Block Island in the summer of 1881 and took measurements and from the builder at Newport, R. I., he obtained the lines of the *Island Belle* which are here reproduced. In the summer of 1906 Martin Coryell Erismann took off the lines of the *Dauntless* and in 1911, after buying the old *Lena M.* of Block Island and finding her too far decayed to repair, after sailing her up to Marblehead, he took off her lines and had a new boat built from them which he named the *Roaring Bessie.**

Though these boats were all built by "rule of thumb," a strong family resemblance is noticeable. Most of them, in later years, were built at Newport, R. I., by Benjamin Caswell, and prior to his time Deacon Sylvester D. Mitchell, at Block Island, turned out between 1850 and 1875, such successful craft as the *Active, Dauntless, Sappho,* and the former mail boat *Thomas Lynch* and many others. Prior to his time, away back in Revolutionary days, John Rose was the principal boat-builder on Block Island, and he was succeeded by Lemuel B. Rose.

* See *Rudder* for April, 1912.

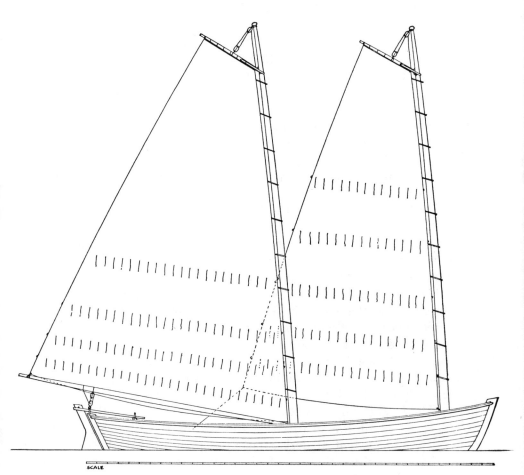

SCALE

Sail Plan of BLOCK ISLAND boat ISLAND BELLE.

The lumber for building these boats was obtained from the mainland for there were not trees enough on the whole of windswept Block Island to build half the fleet that tied up in Pole Harbor. Fifty-five boats were owned there in 1857. These boats were ballasted with stones and on the approach of bad weather they could be lightened by throwing out this ballast. They would then be dragged up on the beach by a yoke of oxen, for Block Is-

FIG. 7. BLOCK
ISLAND BOAT

land is so exposed, to the open ocean, that its shores get a terrible pounding during a gale.

In fair weather these boats tied up, bow and stern, to oak poles sunk about six feet into the sand, their tops standing above water ten to fifteen feet. There were over a thousand of these poles at one time and though many of them were pulled up when the Government built a new stone breakwater at the old or east harbor, as late as 1876 there were still remaining seven hundred and fifty of these poles.

Mr. Hyslop's description of the Block Island boat, as printed in 1884, is as follows:

". . . About sixty fishing boats are owned on the island; they vary in length from about twenty feet to a little short of forty feet and, with one exception, no Block Island boat has been lost during the present century. The only recent instance of loss occurred a few years ago by a boat striking a sunken rock near Point Judith. The next preceding loss was that of a small craft under twenty feet long, and occurred over ninety years ago; she left port and was not heard of again.

"Until 1877 these boats carried the mails and furnished the only means of communication with the mainland. The *Island Belle* was engaged in this service and through winter and summer the trips were made in regular course. The *Island Belle*, like the rest, is entirely open, with the exception

FIG. 8. BLOCK
ISLAND BOAT

of the small space forward of the foremast, a similar extent of deck aft, and a space between the second and third thwarts of about six feet, fore and aft, which is boarded in to form a cabin. The space between this and the next thwart is vacant, with a dividing partition running fore and aft, and is available for cargo. The next space has also a partition in it, and contains the ballast, which consists of large stones picked off the beach; this can, of course, be very readily shifted to windward or thrown overboard if required, though it is not often that either of these things is done.

"The gunwale of these boats is about 4½ inches wide by 2 inches deep,

8

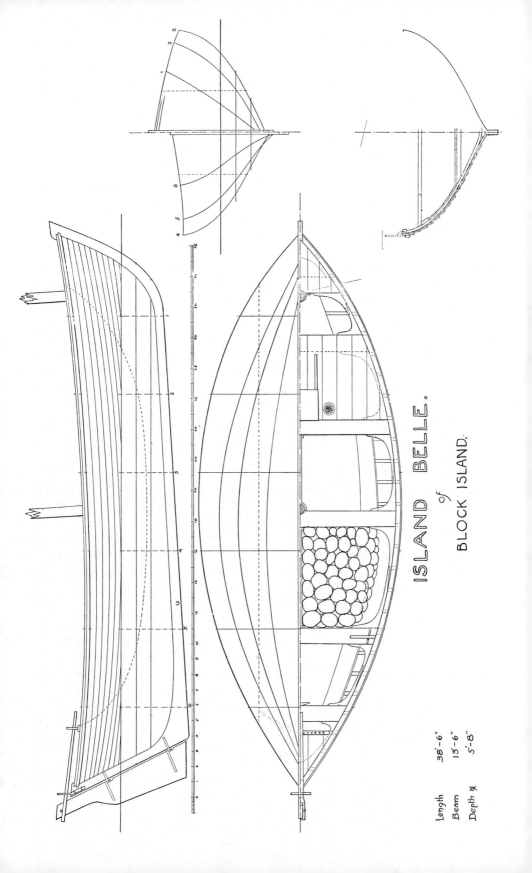

ISLAND BELLE.
of
BLOCK ISLAND.

Length   38'-6"
Beam   13'-6"
Depth &   5'-8"

and has holes or sockets in a line near its outer edge, and about 1½ feet or 2 feet apart. When they are being sailed gunwale to, or when spray is coming in to windward, light boards, one inch by twelve inches, and in sections about ten feet long, can be used in the waist or as far along as may be desired, to build up the sides and keep water out. These boards have bolts or pegs set off from the inner sides. The boards are bent round on the outside of the gunwale and the pegs are driven down into the sockets which are indicated by dots on the gunwale lines in the accompanying drawing.

"The boats are all lap-strake, of ⅞ inch cedar, on two inch bent oak frames, spaced about 13 inches from centers, with bent floors put in between, and extending halfway up the sides. They are all keel boats. In this and in some other points to be named, they differ from prevalent American custom. [Mr. Erismann also noted the fact that these boats and those used by the natives of the Isles of Shoals, off the New Hampshire coast, were of the same type.]

"The sails are very narrow in the head. The mainsail has a loose foot, the foresail is without a boom and the mainsheet has a traveler across the sternpost or the little deck aft. The sails are liberally supplied with reefs, namely, five rows of points in the foresail and four in the mainsail, but the running gear is reduced to a minimum — one halyard for each sail.

"Block Island boats are handled by from two to five men and even by a man and a boy. There is a rack carried across the after-deck with pinholes a few inches apart. With sheets flat aft and a full press of canvas, the craft jumps to windward in a very lively fashion. The helmsman would then stick a wooden peg or pin into the midship hole of this pin rack, put the tiller on the weather side of it and go into the waist (the middle of the boat) and with a boy's help, pick up a weather-board, adjust it to the gunwale quite deliberately, and resume his steering when he was ready. When he wanted to go about he would put his helm down, jam it upon the chafing strake and behind the gunwale and go forward to help the boy to haul the foresheet; the mainsheet would, of course, travel over without attention.

"These boats can be worked to windward under the foresail alone or under part of it and when caught in a hard blow on the fishing grounds, ten or fifteen miles off shore, they will get under sail and make their way into harbor, leaving schooners (much larger vessels) lying to and unable to follow them until the weather moderates. [This is where the double-ender or pink-sterned boat excels, as the sharp stern presents a shape, sharp like the bow, to the oncoming sea and parts it without the boat being pushed ahead at a mad, racing speed as it would be if the stern presented a flat transom to the sea.]

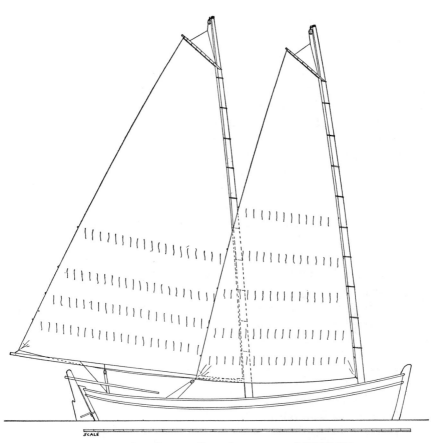

SCALE

SAIL PLAN of BLOCK ISLAND BOAT DAUNTLESS.

"The masts are all made very small at the top and with a straight taper. Those of the *Island Belle* measured nine inches in diameter at the foot and about three inches at the head, or top. They are made of spruce and are without shrouds or stays of any kind.

"The nearest customhouse or port of entry being Newport, these Block Island boats all have to register there and that is why, though owned at Block Island, Newport is painted on the stern as their hailing port."

The *Dauntless*, when Mr. Erismann took her lines off in 1906, was partially decked and his description of her is as follows:

"The boats are decked from the bow to about two feet aft of the mainmast, this deck being about eight inches below the waterway, which is six inches wide. The deck is pierced by a sliding hatch, which gives access to a cuddy about ten feet long with about four feet of headroom. The after end of the cuddy is shut off by a bulkhead and the compartment forms a hold about five feet, fore and aft, with a square hatch in the deck.

"Aft of the break comes the cockpit, fitted with two heavy thwarts acting as braces and tying the boat together. The construction is fairly simple, the boats being lap-straked planked with cedar about ¾ inch thick. The frames are laid on the flat and are 1⅝ x 1½, about ten inches center to center. There are no bilge keelsons, but the main strength lies in the gunwale. The shelf is of yellow pine, 6 x 2½ inches, and to this are kneed the thwarts, which act as mast partners; and hanging knees are also fitted. Outside, heavy rubbing strakes of oak and pine take the wear. The keel is about 3½ inches thick with a 3 x 3 inch keelson and floors, five inches deep. A fish well is fitted in the cockpit, in which the ship's pump empties."

The dimensions of the *Dauntless* were as follows:

Length on deck	33 ft.	6 in.
Length on water-line	30 ft.	9 in.
Breadth over gunwales	12 ft.	10 in.
Breadth at water-line	10 ft.	0 in.
Draft	4 ft.	6 in.
Least freeboard	2 ft.	0 in.
Freeboard at bow	4 ft.	9 in.
Freeboard at stern	3 ft.	3 in.
Sail area	702 sq. ft.	

The *Dauntless* was evidently an open boat, built with the same arrangement of thwarts as was the custom, but at some later date she had been decked over at the forward end. Today, summer visitors to this quaint old island see nothing but motor-driven boats with, maybe, an apology of a

Model of the New England Pinky "Gloucester," of 1843
In the National Museum

MODEL OF THE QUODDY BOAT "YANKEE HERO," 1889
IN THE NATIONAL MUSEUM

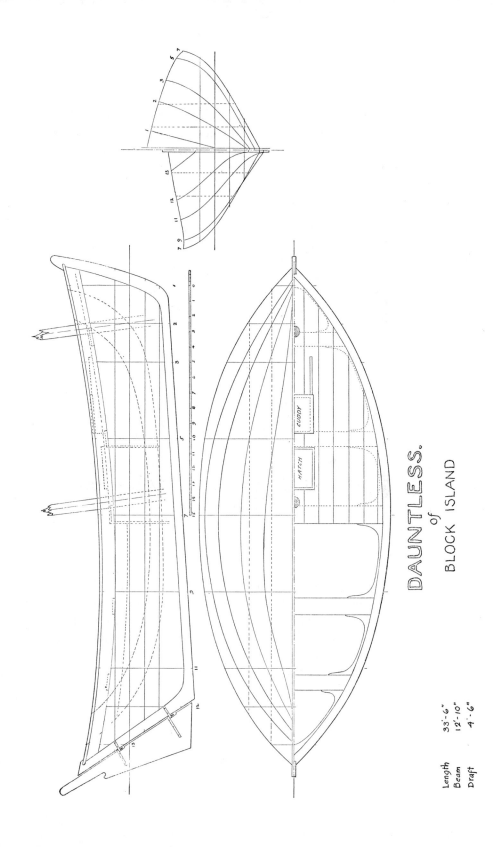

DAUNTLESS.
of
BLOCK ISLAND

Length	33'-6"
Beam	12'-10"
Draft	4'-6"

mast used primarily as a derrick post to swing a derrick boom for hoisting baskets of fish.

The pink-sterned Block Islanders were descendants or near relatives of the Massachusetts Chebacco boats, also double-enders, and the Quoddy boats of the Maine coast, also pink-sterned and about 35 feet in length. These boats were partially decked with a large cockpit and a cuddy forward, and were used extensively, up to 1873, in the herring fishery. The Quoddy boat usually had only one mast and sail, though a few essayed the

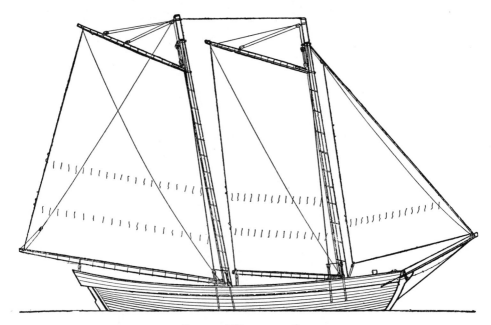

FIG. 9. A PINKY OF 1800

schooner rig; but the Chebacco boats were rigged with two spars and sails very much the same as the Block Islanders.

The pink is by no means a new type of vessel. In a little pamphlet published by the Bank of the Manhattan Company, in 1915, entitled "Ships and Shipping of New York," mention is made of the fact that pinkes from the Barbadoes, with sugar and molasses, came into the port of New York, as early as 1650. We find the pink *Bonetta*, a craft, ship-rigged, of 398 tons, described in "A Treatise on Shipbuilding" by Mungo Murray, a book that was published in London in 1765; and pinks and feluccas were common types on the Mediterranean, years ago. The plans of this *Bonetta* show a big, round-sectioned ship with bow and stern both pointed, the bulwark extending aft of the stern post above the deck. The same feature as shown in the Down East pink.

Pink-sterned boats were built in America in the parish of Chebacco* in the town of Ipswich, before the Revolution and were used by the fishermen alongshore and in going to nearby banks where the fish were plentiful. After the Revolution, so impoverished were these hardy people that the larger schooners, the old high-sterned, apple-bowed, "heel tappers," as they were nicknamed, that had been laid up to prevent their being captured or destroyed by the British cruisers, could not be financed for the offshore fishing and instead of using them they used the smaller Chebacco boats in which the fishing industry was carried on until the War of 1812 again created a disturbance, so that the fishermen turned to privateering.

The first privateer to fit out from Salem was the new Gloucester-built Chebacco boat *Fame*, of thirty tons, owned jointly by her master William Webb, and her crew of twenty-four ex-shipmasters. She put to sea on July 1, 1812, and returned eight days later with two prizes—a three-hundred ton ship and a two-hundred ton brig, both taken off Grand Manan without firing a shot.

Many of these Chebacco boats were home-built, with high, bluff bows, considerable sheer, and a rudder hung on a sternpost similar to an ordinary ship's lifeboat. The smaller boats of about five tons burden, had open hatchways or standing rooms in which the men could stand on a floor built just above the boat's keelson, waist high, and comfortably fish over the side. In rough weather or when sailing home to market with their catch, hatchcovers were fitted over these standing rooms which made them practically decked boats and kept out the weather. Aft, there was a similar well for the helmsmen, in which the crew could stand when the other hatchways were covered. Forward, the boat was decked over forming cramped living quarters below. Rude bunks were built along the sides and cooking was done on a brick fireplace, the smoke finding its way out through the open hatch above, as best it could.

The larger Chebacco boats, those approaching twenty or thirty tons burden, had wooden chimneys plastered with clay, to carry off the smoke. They were decked with hatchways smaller than the five- and ten-ton open boats. Around the deck-edge a more pretentious bulwark was built with a handrail on top. The waist was kept up off the planksheer of the deck, an inch or two, to give ample scuppers to carry off any water that came on deck.

On both large and small boats the waist was carried out away from the

* Now the town of Essex, Massachusetts.

sternpost to leave room for the rudder head to swing and were united aft of it with a V-shaped transom, somewhat like the stern-board of a dory. The sheer up aft was very abrupt which was characteristic of the pink.

Like the Block Island boats they were two-masted boats, the mainmast stepped about amidships, and the foremast, of the same length as the mainmast, placed well up in the bows of the boat. They had no standing rigging, carrying simply halliards, downhauls and sheets and a topping-lift to hold up the outer end of the main boom. Both sails were fitted with gaffs and booms and had two rows of reefs in each sail.

The peculiar stern of these boats was well balanced by an equally original stem. The stem-head was painted a bright red and carried up so that it formed a natural mooring post over which the eye-splice in the mooring rope could be slipped. The waist and rail ended at a timber-head, on either side, leaving an open space, level down to the deck, where the anchor could be hauled in and left with the flukes outward.

The dimensions of the *Lion*, a typical ten-ton Chebacco boat, are as follows: length over all, 34 feet; beam, 9 feet 6 inches; depth of hold, 4 feet 6 inches; length of foremast (above deck), 23 feet; mainmast, 23 feet 6 inches; foreboom, 12 feet; main boom, 18 feet 6 inches.

FIG. 10. HERRING FISHER QUODDY BOAT OF 1873

A boat somewhat distantly related to the old Chebacco boat is the "Quoddy" boat of the Eastern Maine coast. These clean-lined, little double-ended boats are used principally in the herring fisheries of eastern Maine, around Eastport and Lubec. The name is a contraction of the old Indian name given to Passamaquoddy Bay. Generally cat-rigged, of twenty to thirty tons, the later boats have added a small bowsprit and jib to their rig as speed is essential in getting their catch quickly from the fish weirs to the factories or packing houses. Now-a-days, of course, all or most of them, are equipped with motors. A cat-rigged boat, 35 feet long, with 12 feet beam, would have a mast 39 feet 6 inches long.

The sloop *Yankee Hero*, built at Lubec in 1889, was a typical Quoddy boat. Her dimensions were: length, 33 feet; beams, 11 feet 3 inches; and depth, 4 feet 6 inches. Her mast was away up forward with a small cuddy built on deck just abaft of it, with companion-slide on top giving access to the cramped living quarters below. Aft of this she had a large, open cockpit fitted with washboards 15 feet long and 5 feet 9 inches wide, with a small, narrow, steering well, aft of this. Her

Stern View of Pinky, Yarmouth, Nova Scotia

Stern of Pinky at Yarmouth, Nova Scotia

BOW OF PINKY, YARMOUTH, NOVA SCOTIA

STERN OF PINKY, YARMOUTH, NOVA SCOTIA

mast, above deck, was 39 feet 3 inches long; the bowsprit outboard was 6 feet 6 inches; the boom, 29 feet; and the gaff 10 feet long.

The "pink," as the Chebacco boats were called when they developed into larger boats, was rigged as the schooner, with a bowsprit. Pinks became such an institution on the New England seacoast, between 1800 and 1850, that the memory of them lives yet, years after most of them have disappeared. There are still one or two afloat, carefully preserved by their owners. The excellent reputation of the pink was due chiefly to its crudeness and simplicity (it was a poor man's boat) and to the fact that with all its cheapness it had the sterling qualities that endear any vessel to the heart of a seaman, namely, seaworthiness and weatherliness.

In 1851, when a hurricane destroyed Minot's Ledge lighthouse, a fleet of fishermen were anchored in Bay Chaleur, on the west side of the Gulf of St. Lawrence, between Gaspé Point and New Brunswick. When the storm came on, the only craft that was able to beat out against the terrific wind and sea was the pink *Ocean*, of Kittery, Maine.

The old pinks, such as the *Pink* of Edgartown, Mass., measured, according to the records of 1810 in the Plymouth registry, as follows: length, 42 feet; beam, 12 feet 6 inches; depth, 5 feet 3 inches; tonnage, 24½ tons.

In shape of hull they were very full-bodied, bluff-bowed craft with bows standing high out of water forward, their keels much deeper aft than at the forefoot, having considerable of what sailors term "drag," a feature of the fast-sailing Baltimore clippers. Pinks had quite a bit of sheer and the peculiar upshoot to the bulwarks, aft, accentuated the sheer to a marked degree and gave them a decided scoop to their sheer-line.

The feature that made these boats such weatherly craft was their heavy displacement, being very burdensome for their length, though not so very wide, and while bluff forward, their runs aft were clean and sweet and tapered so prettily to a sharp stern that aft they were just like a fish. Ordinarily a double-ended craft lacks stability to stand up and get the push out of her canvas. This was true of the Block Islanders which had their sails fitted with five rows of reef points. But just enough sail was exposed to the pressure of the wind and they were so easy-lined of hull they would slip through the water and make headway no matter how rough the seas might be. Block Islanders were sailors. They understood the peculiarities of their boats and could get all the speed out of them they were capable of. Too much sail would smother their boats and they would flounder about; but give them just the right amount of canvas and they would go to windward like a porpoise.

The pinks of New England were different and were ballasted with stones; like small deep-water ships they stood up better under their canvas. Their hulls were clean as a fish aft and as buoyant as a barrel forward. They rode the seas like a duck and made no fuss nor performed any of the wild antics a vessel with wider quarters aft would go through when climbing a sea, breaking through the crest, and sliding down the back of it. And they would do this with a minimum of strain on both hull and rig. They were fast for their day, but when the schooners were hipped-out with wider sterns, and powerful, big mainsails were put on them, and their bows were sharpened to a wedge so that they could be driven in from the Grand Banks under a press of sail like a racing yacht, then, the pink became a back-number. Schooners were built and racked to pieces by hard use until it was unsafe to venture off shore in them. They would then be laid up and new ones built to die an equally rapid death. The pink, meanwhile, outlasted a dozen of them.

But it became a question of a drive for dollars and as pinks were built more for the purpose of bringing their men home in safety, they fell into disuse and big Gloucesterman, big enough to carry a pink on their decks, took their places as "bankers," and the pink was relegated to a use alongshore in the lobster trade or in junking cargoes of anything they could get.

The pink *Mary*, of eight tons register, built at Portsmouth, N. H., in 1811, was still afloat and owned at Damariscotta, Maine, in 1907. She was then the second oldest vessel in the United States, the schooner *Polly*, built in 1805, at Amesbury, Mass., being the oldest.* For that matter, there is one of these craft still in use in Maine waters or was only a few years ago and that craft is the pink *Maine*, built at Essex, Mass., in the year 1845. Mr. C. H. Mansfield of Jonesport, Maine, purchased this interesting old craft and is keeping her afloat as a reminder of olden times. Her dimensions are: length, over all, 45 feet; beam, 13 feet 7 inches; depth of hull, 6 feet 6 inches. In the fall of 1927 a friend of mine was at St. Johns, Newfoundland, and made some enquiry for old pinks. None were owned in the southern part of the island but one or two were said to be in the fishing trade at the north, near the Straits of Belle Isle.

An old pink that came into Halifax harbor, a few years ago, was described to me by Mr. Irving R. Wiles, who went aboard of her and looked her over, as having a hull so full-bodied that it reminded him of one of the little, old-time, stub-ended brigs. She had all the ear-marks of a very old craft, the hull being built very heavy and crude. He measured her and found her to be forty feet long, not counting a figurehead; thirteen feet, beam; draft aft, loaded, seven feet; draft forward, four feet. Her sides

---

* The frigates *Constellation* and *Constitution* built in 1797 excepted being men-of-war.

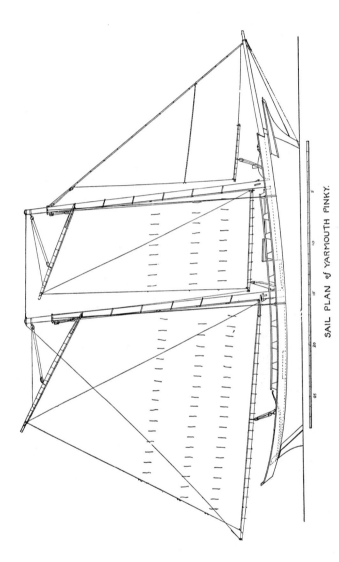

SAIL PLAN of YARMOUTH PINKY.

were just about plumb, up and down from the rail to the water, amidships; while forward, abreast the windlass, there was just a slight "tumble home." She only showed six inches of freeboard from her planksheer to the water when loaded. Her deck was laid out differently from most pinks it being flush fore and aft with an old-fashioned log windlass fitted across the deck at the inboard end of her bowsprit, the post there serving as a pawl post for the windlass. Her bowsprit was 8½ inches square, inboard, coming just under the throat knee that united the bulwarks and served to form a cap over the two hawse timbers through which the chain cable passed which formed the knight heads to steady the bowsprit.

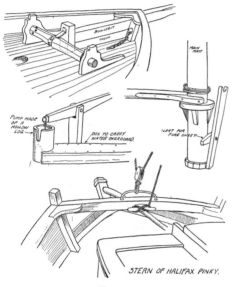

STERN OF HALIFAX PINKY.

FIG. 11

The space beneath the bowsprit, about six inches, was filled in solid with a bed-piece that formed a brace between the pawl post and the stem-head, to take the thrust from the windlass. Aft of the windlass was the foremast; then a clear space to the main hatch, with an open space where there was no bulwark amidships on either side, for about three feet, to facilitate launching and hauling a skiff aboard; then came the mainmast. A round saddle encircled the mast, supported by three small chocks to hold the main-boom jaws up at a proper height above the deck, and up the forward side of the mast was a board, its top cut to form a saddle or crotch for the fore-boom to rest in; its lower end notched down into the deck and held in place about a foot and a half up from the deck by a bolt through the mast. To keep this crotch away from the mast, to clear the jaws of the main-boom, was a block of wood set horizontally and shaped to form a rude cleat for belaying the foresheet.

Wherever ironwork, which costs money, could be dispensed with, it was done on these home-built boats. Even the ship's pump, just abaft the mainmast, was a hollowed-out log, the wooden pump handle being pivoted by a bolt through the notched end of an upright plank secured to the deck, and the water was carried off to the port side in a shallow, flat, wooden box. A small, raised cuddy was built just aft of this pump. It was about two feet

MODEL OF NEW ENGLAND PINKY "TIGER," BUILT AT ESSEX, MASS., 1830-1840
IN THE NATIONAL MUSEUM

Schooner "Polly," 48 Tons, Built at Amesbury, Mass., in 1805

Pinky "Maine," 24 Tons, Built at Essex, Mass., in 1845

high, and square, except for the bevel given to the sides that ran parallel to the rails, so that the after end was that much narrower. A sliding hatch on the roof, at the after end of this cabin or cuddy, gave access to the living quarters below. Aft of this cabin, and extending across the boat from rail to rail and butting against a staunchion on either side and kneed to the rail, was a stout timber as large as a deck-beam, characteristic of all pinks. It had the main-sheet horse and traveler on top and a cleat on its forward face. The tiller, a round stick, came through the rudder-head and bent down so that it projected forward under this beam.

This old pink was built in the days when seaworthiness was preferred to speed; when boats, being built for carriers, were shaped to hold all the cargo possible within their dimensions and yet be able to navigate the seven seas. But as time went on they were gradually sharpened a little under water and in consequence became faster sailers.

The customary deck lay-out, of nine out of every ten pinks built, was a forward deck extending aft to the main-hatch which was four to six inches higher than the deck aft of it and which had a low deck-house entered through a door covered by a companion slide in the roof at the after end, giving access to comfortable living quarters in the bows. The after end of the craft was used for cargo. The cuddy or living quarters had a regular brick fireplace built at the after end and cooking was done in pots hung over the fire just the same as it was done on shore. The smoke was carried up through the roof in a wooden, clay-lined chimney. The more modern pink naturally discarded this primitiveness for the new-fangled iron stove, with its iron smoke pipe going up through the usual iron water-ring set in the cabin roof.

The older pinks were painted outside, below the water-line, with pitch put on hot, copper paint not having been put on the market in their day. It was used, however, when painting with it became customary and the fisherman could afford the money wherewith to purchase. Above water the hull was painted green generally relieved with a white or yellow band. Green we find used extensively on the older ships, where economy was practiced, for the very good reason that it is the best wearing color that can be put on a boat. The old Western Ocean packets all used green on their deck-houses, and inside of the rails, etc., because of this fact, and only changed when the competition for the patronage of tourists demanded a more attractive color. White or some light tint was then used in place of the homely green.

There are two pinky models in the Watercraft Collection at the United States National Museum, at Washington, that show very clearly all the little peculiarities of this type of sailing craft. The first model is of a typical pinky, 45 feet long; 14 feet beam; 6 feet 6 inches depth and 8 feet 6 inches extreme draft. Her bowsprit extended 14 feet outboard; the foremast, above deck, was 34 feet; fore-boom, 19 feet; mainmast, above deck, 38 feet; main topmast, heel to truck, 13 feet 6 inches; and main-boom, 30 feet.

Such pinkys were used extensively in the general sea fisheries. They were employed on the banks and in the waters of the Gulf of St. Lawrence as well as off the coast of the United States. Few have been built since about 1850. Several large ones were built in the "forties," some of which carried flying jibs in summer, when engaged in mackerel fishing. Probably no more seaworthy vessels were ever designed. A few of them sailed well for the period in which they were built and in rough water sometimes outsailed the clipper "sharpshooters" of the early "fifties."

Another model in the National Museum is that of the pinky *Tiger*, built at Essex, between 1830 and 1840. It represents one of the larger boats of this class and one that was under the command of Capt. James Patillo, who distinguished herself when England sent men-of-war in an endeavor to break up the fishing industries of the United States in Canadian waters. On one occasion she was chased by a British brig-of-war, in the Bay of Fundy. A sudden lifting of the fog disclosed to the British officers the little pinky not far off and within the three-mile limit where it was claimed American fishermen had no right to go. All sail was crowded on both sides. The Englishman fired a gun for the Yankee to heave to and soon the blank cartridge was followed by round shot as the pinky continued on her way, one or more of which passed through her sails. But the undaunted Patillo sent his crew below, after the sails were set and trimmed, and lying on his back on deck, he steered the little vessel which showed a clean pair of heels to her pursuer.

On another occasion the *Tiger* was frozen in while in Fortune Bay, Newfoundland, after a fare of fish in winter. The local authorities determined to capture her, and an armed party, far outnumbering the crew of the pinky, went out near her on the ice. Captain Patillo had a few old muskets on board and defied them. He was a giant in size and his appearance and reckless courage intimidated his enemies, who returned crestfallen to their homes.

The dimensions of a typical New England pinky of 1840 are as follows:

Length between perpendiculars . . .	45 feet
Beam	14 feet
Depth of hold	6 feet 6 inches
Extreme draft	8 feet 6 inches

Bowprit outboard	14 feet
Foremast above deck	34 feet
Fore-boom	19 feet
Mainmast above deck	38 feet
Main-boom	30 feet
Main-topmast (heel to truck) . . .	13 feet 6 inches

The dimension of the pinky *Tiger*, built at Essex, Mass., between 1830 and 1840:

Length over all	52 feet
Length on waterline	48 feet
Beam	13 feet 3 inches
Depth of hold	5 feet
Bowsprit outboard	14 feet
Foremast above deck	40 feet
Fore-boom	17 feet 6 inches
Fore-gaff	16 feet 6 inches
Mainmast above deck	42 feet
Topmast	18 feet
Main-boom	33 feet
Main-gaff	18 feet

The pink *July*, built at Essex, in the month of July, 1837, was 52 feet long; 16 feet beam; 7 feet depth of hold; and drew 8 feet of water aft and 5 feet forward.

A Halifax, Nova Scotia, pinky, measured: length, 40 feet; beam, 13 feet; draft aft (loaded), 7 feet 6 inches; forward, 4 feet.

The pink *Maine* measured: length, 45 feet; beam, 13 feet 7 inches; depth of hold, 6 feet 6 inches.

Another pink measured: length, 42 feet; beam, 12 feet 6 inches; depth, 5 feet 3 inches.

The pink *Trenton*, built at Trenton, Maine, in 1840, was one of the last of these vessels built. Her dimensions were: length, 47 feet; beam, 14 feet 2 inches; depth, 6 feet 4 inches.

CHAPTER II

THE FISHING SCHOONER

THE development of the fishing schooner model may be traced from 1800 to the present day by means of a series of small models preserved in the National Museum at Washington, and its history has been printed repeatedly.* One of these models is a typical "heel tapper," and permits us to visualize just what those schooners looked like. My impression of her is shown in the two accompanying sketches. Her rails were painted white and the rest was as indicated in the sketches: cream or white, with a slight yellow tinge to it below the wales. The wales, to the plank-sheer, were a pea green and the bulwarks above a dark brown. The poop was green and brown repeated; while on her high, flat, transom a white arch enclosed a brown field with the outer, upper part black.

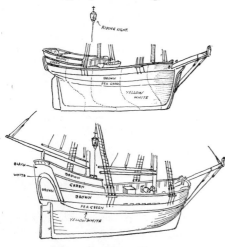

FIG. 12. HEEL TAPPER
FISHING SCHOONER OF 1770

She was a tubby little packet, with low bulwarks around the forward-deck and a high, raised poop-deck aft, reached by a ladder on each side leading up from the main-deck with a handrail, on stanchions, across the front of the poop. The bulwarks around the sides were solid. She steered with a tiller and had a companion slide, just forward of it, that gave access to the living quarters below. She had a main-hatch. Her log windlass went athwartships just abaft the foremast and was worked with handspikes and handled rope anchor

* See "Yachting" for May, 1910 — an article by Albert Cook Church. Unfortunately the captions under the cuts are mixed. The "Dogbody" is the "Chebacco" and the low, quarter-deck schooner of 1830 is really the "Pinky." The cut marked "Pinky" represents a "Heel Tapper." "Outing," page 334 to 349, date unknown, has a good illustrated article by Joseph Williams Collins. For pictures and descriptions of schooner models, *see* "Bulletin 127: Catalogue of the Watercraft Collection in the United States National Museum," Washington, 1923.

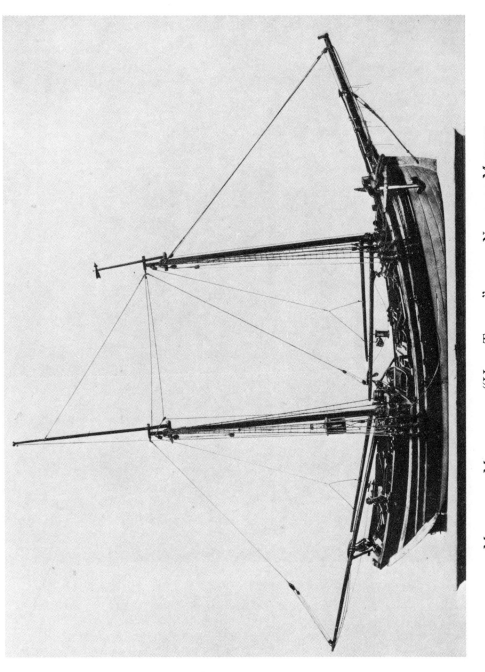

Model of a Marblehead "Heel Tapper" in the National Museum

A Knockabout Fishing Schooner

From a photograph made about 1890

cables. Two wooden pumps were fitted on the main deck at the break of the poop.

Her dimensions, or those of the real schooner that she represented, were: length over all, 52 feet; on waterline, 47 feet; beam, 15 feet; depth of hold, 7 feet 6 inches; bowsprit, outside of knighthead, 19 feet; total length, 25 feet; foremast, above deck, 33 feet; mainmast, above deck, 34 feet; main-topmast, heel to truck, 22 feet; main-boom, 32 feet; main-gaff, 16 feet 6 inches; fore-boom, 22 feet; fore-gaff, 16 feet.

This is very much the same type of craft as the original schooner built at Gloucester by Captain Robinson in 1713 for the banks codfishing. These little schooners varied from forty to eighty tons, old measurement (equal to twenty-five to fifty-five tons new measurement). Many of them had no bulwarks around the main deck, only an open handrail on the timber-heads, so there was nothing to hold water and the deck could more easily free itself of water. In bad weather the crew fished from the higher, drier quarterdeck. This was quite a common feature of most of the small sea-going craft up to about the year 1800.

The old "heel tappers" of pre-Revolutionary times were succeeded by Chebacco boats and pinkys when the impoverished fisherman started anew to build up their business and as they made money enough to afford larger schooners, they built full-bodied, bluff-bowed craft with the cabin aft. These later craft were of more pretentious appearance and had carved fiddle-heads and painted ornamentation to relieve the heavy, flat-looking transoms and solid bulwarks that were carried the full length of the deck. Jib-booms and topmasts were added to the schooners of the mackerel fleet to help them along in the light summer breezes, and the high-sheered sterns were done away with.

The schooners built about 1800 were bluff-bowed, keel schooners with their greatest beam abreast the foremast, the sides running aft almost flat and straight to a slightly narrowed transom. The beam across the taffrail was almost the same as at the foremast. Their sides extended down to a hard bilge that came up only a foot or so above water at the counters, aft. Forward, they were moulded into an apple-shaped bow, the rabbet rounding under almost to the heel of the foremast. The bottom swept aft with straight floor timbers and with but little or no deadrise. The keel had considerable drag, that is, it was deeper aft than forward which necessitated a hollow in the floors to give a clean run, for shipbuilders well knew that a boat like a fish had to narrow in quickly to permit the water to flow aft and unite at the stern without undo drag.

The schooner *Polly*, built at Amesbury, Mass., in 1805, and used during the War of 1812 as a privateer, was such a schooner, as were hundreds of the fishing schooners used on the Banks and off the Atlantic coast.

These bluff little schooners were much improved in 1848 by the introduction of a new type now known as the "Romp" model, a schooner of that name having been launched in 1847, that was very much sharper and finer-lined, low aft and high out of water at the bow. A straight-sheered, straight-sided, box-sterned craft that would be considered a tub today but at that time was such an innovation as to cause a sensation — the beginning of a new era in fishing schooners.

The sharp or relatively sharp bow of this craft caused old fishermen to shake their heads in doubt and to express the opinion that she was liable to dive into a sea and never come up. Many men would not risk their lives in such a diving machine as she was thought to be. But use proved her to be both weatherly and fast. She made the voyage around Cape Horn to engage in the Pacific fishery, and in later years she came through the same stormy weather that the full, apple-bowed craft did and sailed away from them, being the first to get fares of fish to market; and little by little, the builders and advocates of the old type began to sharpen the bows of their new boats and as usual the sharpening was carried to the extreme. Baltimore boats from the Chesapeake were purchased, and boats were built shoaler and sharper, though the deck forward was carried out to a full, rounded rail-line, giving excessive flare forward to keep them from diving too deep. The fault that developed, as the boats increased in size and tonnage, was in making the schooners too lean-waisted — too shallow, wide and flat.

These "sharpshooters," as they were called, had great initial stability, but when knocked over by a sudden squall, their stone ballast was stowed so high they had no ability to right themselves and many were lost at sea with all hands.

It takes a real "he boat" to stand the mauling a schooner gets when caught in one of those fierce squalls in the Gulf of St. Lawrence, or when a whole gale of wind comes down on them in the shallow waters over the fishing banks. A wave rolled up by a gale of wind is high enough in deep water but when waves are crowded up over the shoals that form the feeding grounds for innumerable fish, they break and form cross-running seas that toss a schooner about like a football and unless she has an excess of stability and bulk enough to have sufficient hull left in the water to keep her steady, when being thrown about by the seas, she is apt to be tripped and thrown on her beam's end and swamped.

To build a schooner to stand this tossing about and yet able to carry sail enough to give headway in seas when she had to claw out to windward to weather a shoal, was the problem various designers and builders had been working on for years. Sable Island, a veritable death trap for ships, has taken a large toll from the fishing fleet and many have gone down with all hands, swamped by the seas.

Samuel Hall, at East Boston, built a great many fishing schooners, mostly mackerel fishermen, that in the winter season freighted oysters from the Chesapeake to Boston. They were large vessels, close to one hundred tons burden. The *Express* and the *Telegraph* were two of his first schooners, and they undoubtedly were fast, carrying a big rig; but they were not deep enough to be the ideal Gloucesterman. His models were extensively copied, however, much more so than the few fishermen Donald McKay produced, such as the schooner *Frank Atwood*, which was famous for her speed.

Capt. Joseph William Collins advocated an improvement in the offshore, cod fishing fleet, beginning in 1882, when he published a series of articles in the Gloucester newspapers that culminated in his designing his ideal in the schooner *Grampus*, built for the United States Fish Commission. She was deeper and her stern frames were more V-shaped than those of other schooners of her time. Several changes were made in her rig. The large jib was done away with and the modern staysail and smaller jib substituted; the fore-topmast and foremast were both made considerably shorter than the main, and wire rigging was substituted for the hemp that had been universally used before that time.

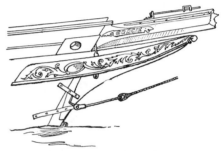

FIG. 13. SCHOONER *Gracie*

When the *Grampus* appeared on the fishing grounds, in 1886, and sailed away from the fleet, close hauled or reaching, other designers were found to build schooners to beat her. This brought out a fleet of schooners of the *Fredonia* type, from the draughting board of the celebrated yacht designer, Edward Burgess of Boston, and schooners were designed and built by D. J. Lawlor of Boston, noted for fast pilot boats and fishermen. Outside ballast, bolted to the keels like the racing yacht, was resorted to in some cases, the *Massasoit* of 1898 being so built; but most of the new boats used pig iron stowed low against the keel, between the frames, with boiler punchings poured over, bedded in cement.

The bows were carried forward in a long overhang. Some schooners, such as the *Helen E. Thomas*, built in 1902, had no bowsprit, their jibs coming to the stem-head as in the knockabout rig. A moderately long overhang, aft, was pulled in to a narrow, raking transom so that the hull had long sailing lines, in her topsides, when heeled over, and a heavily ballasted, canoe-like body of considerable bulk and much stability. The large, flaring topsides preventing their being smothered up or drowned out by a sea and they carried a proportionally large rig, which could always be shortened down to a snug sail area in bad weather.

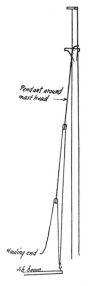

Pendant around mast head →

Hauling end

Jib boom

Spanish burton used to top up staysail boom also to hoist anchor up over bows. One of these on each mast to swing out dories with.

FIG. 14

The fishermen were proud of the superiority of their new craft, and sailed them with a daring that has spread the fame of the Gloucesterman around the world just as in the days of the sailing ship, the Yankee clippers were noted for their speed and superior models. These new schooners could sail the old fleet hull-down, in an hour or two, and great rivalry soon began to prove which was the fastest. James B. Connolly, a Gloucester boy, has written many stories that most ably portray the spirit that prevailed in the fishing fleet and show what it was that made the Gloucestermen so famous.

Away back in 1846, when the New York Yacht Club was holding its second year's racing, the contest was open to working boats and the race to and around Five Fathom Bank lightship was won in the yacht class by the schooner *Enchantress*. Pilot boat No. 1, the *T. S. Negus*, was winner in the pilot boat fleet and the working schooner, *W. H. Van Name*, and the fishing schooner, *Wallace Blackford*, won in their respective classes.

There also was great rivalry between the big sloops that used to sail on the Hudson River. The *Liberty* of Port Chester, was around in the Hudson and the boatmen were anxious to settle the question as to whether she was a faster sloop than the celebrated *Victorine*, then owned by some Quakers who were in the foundry business, making sugar machinery, and who disapproved of racing.

MAIN BOOM JYBER

FIG. 15

With her captain's consent, while he went ashore to have a friendly drink with a confederate of theirs, these Hudson River sloopmen stole the *Victorine*, on July 4, 1866, and sailed a race twice around a course from Sneed's to Croton Point. The *Liberty* was winning the race when her captain, to make her sails set better, sent two men up on her gaff to dump buckets of water on her mainsail. Those on deck hoisted them up on whips

GLOUCESTER FISHING SCHOONER "JAMES W. PARKER"
Photograph by W. B. Jackson

PROVINCETOWN FISHING SCHOONER "ROSE DOROTHEA"
Copyrighted photograph by W. B. Jackson

SAIL PLAN OF KNOCKABOUT FISHING SCHOONER HELEN B THOMAS.

rove for the purpose. But the weight of the men broke the sloop's gaff and so the *Victorine* won the race.

Boston has made a feature of the fisherman's race for years, as part of its annual Old Home Week celebration. In 1901 the schooner *Harry Belden* was the winner. These races have given hundreds of civilians who live the year round cooped up in pigeon-hole offices, a chance to see how these hardy, outdoor fishermen live and how they can handle the fine little schooners in which they ply their trade. During these races the fishermen enter into the spirit of racing with great zeal and carry on sail in a way to tickle the heart of any water dog. They are watched by hundreds from passenger steamers that follow them around the race course.

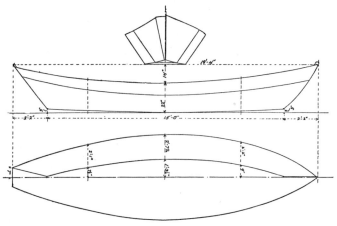

LINES of A DORY.

FIG. 16

Sir Thomas Lipton put up a perpetual trophy for this race in 1906, and this trophy has stimulated the building of fast sailing fishing schooners to a point where they have become more a yacht than a real fisherman.

Off Boston harbor, in 1907, the *Rose Dorothea*, a typical out-and-out Gloucester fisherman, with no frills or pretense at yachting features about her, sailed a close race against the *Jessie Costa* and won. She was the first to have her name engraved on the Lipton trophy. Both boats hailed from Provincetown. The *Rose Dorothea* was big, burdensome, yet clean-lined schooner, with the typical fishing schooner rig, an outline of sails, by the way, that looks like a big brother to a pilot boat. A third contender, the schooner *James W. Parker*, hailed from Gloucester. In the second class the *Francis P. Mesquita* of Provincetown, and the knockabout schooner *Helen B. Thomas* of Boston, one of the Wharf fleet, raced, the *Mesquita* winning.

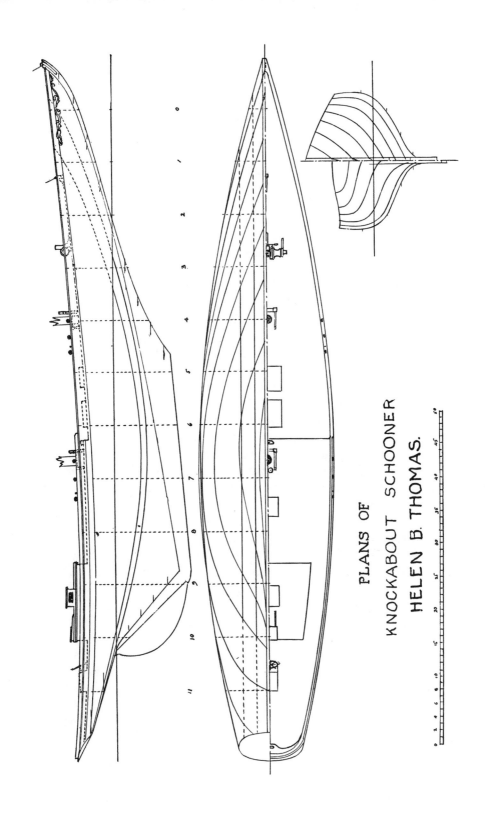

PLANS OF
KNOCKABOUT SCHOONER
HELEN B. THOMAS.

For several years this fisherman's race continued and then the Canadian fishermen, naturally anxious to show the ability of their men and schooners, arranged a contest for a trophy put up by Mr. H. W. Dennis of Halifax, Nova Scotia. This contest was open to bonafide fishermen, boats that had made a trip to the fishing banks, and so keen was the rivalry between Canadian and American fishermen, that committees had to be appointed and visits of inspection made to some of the boats to pass upon their eligibility as fishing vessels. Mere racing yachts built for speed at a sacrifice of safety were excluded and one schooner, the *Mayflower*, was disqualified on this score.

The schooner *Esperanto* of Gloucester, won, in 1920, in the first year's series of races. The prize was $4,000 and the Dennis cup. The *Bluenose*, in 1921, defeated the schooner *Elsie* of Gloucester, and in 1922 she again beat the schooner *Henry Ford* in a series of races.

The *Bluenose*, a sailor's nickname for the men and boats hailing from Nova Scotia, was the outstanding champion on the Canadian side. She was a schooner 142 feet in length, over all; 110 feet in length on the waterline; 27 feet beam; and drew 15 feet 8 inches of water. She hailed from Lunenburg and was built from designs by W. J. Roue of Halifax. She carried 9,770 square feet of canvas.

In 1923 the *Bluenose* raced with the *Columbia*, the contest ending in a dispute, the Canadian schooner having been disqualified in the second race for cutting inside a buoy which the race conditions called for keeping outside of and also for fouling the *Columbia* in the first race. The *Columbia* was awarded the victory, and the skipper of the *Bluenose* squared away for Halifax, which ended this series of races.

The *Columbia* was designed by Messrs. Burgess & Paine, naval architects of Boston, and was built by Arthur Dana Story at Essex, Mass. She is the last word in the development of the Gloucester fishing schooner, and is of the following dimensions: length over all, 135 feet; length on the waterline, 105 feet; beam, 25 feet; draught of water, 14 feet 9 inches. She carries 7,228 square feet of canvas in her four lower sails, divided as follows: mainsail, 4,110 square feet, foresail, 1,529 square feet; jumbo (staysail), 756 feet, and jib, 833 square feet.

The measurement of the *Columbia's* spars is as follows: mainmast, 95 feet, total length, and stands 84 feet above the deck; the masthead measures down from the upper cap 12 feet. This spar is 19¾ inches in diameter at the deck; 19¼ inches, half way to the crosstrees and 18½ inches just below the crosstrees where the cheeks are fitted. The main-topmast stands above the upper cap 32 feet, three feet of this being tapered into a

GLOUCESTER FISHING SCHOONER "METAMORA"
Photograph by N. L. Stebbins

MODEL OF GLOUCESTER FISHING SCHOONER "COLUMBIA"
Made by Charles G. Davis for C. R. Patterson

Details of Rigging on Gloucester Fisherman.

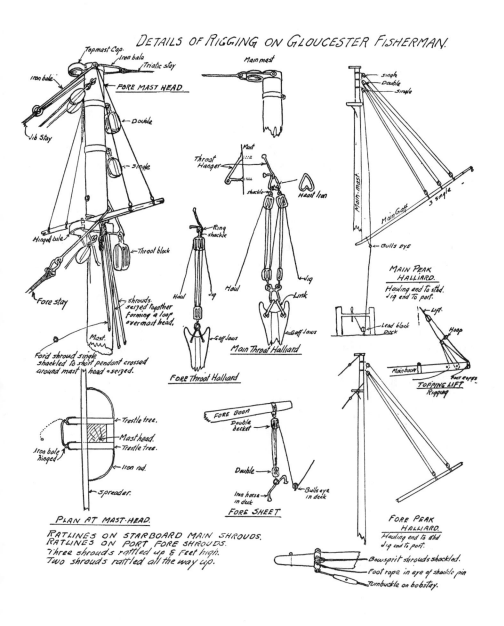

FORE MAST HEAD.

Topmast Cap.
Iron bale
Triatic stay
Iron bale
Double
Jib Stay
Single
Hinged bale
Throat block
Fore stay
shrouds seized together forming a loop over mast head.
Mast.
Ford shroud single shackled to short pendant crossed around mast head seized.

Main mast

Mast
Throat Hanger
shackle
Head Iron
Ring shackle
Haul
Jig
Haul
Jig
Link
Gaff Jaws
Gaff Jaws

Main Throat Halliard.

FORE Throat Halliard.

single
Double
Single
Main-mast
Main Gaff
3 single
Bulls eye

MAIN PEAK HALLIARD.
Hauling end To stbd
Jig end To port.

Lead block Dock
Lift
Hoop
Main boom
Foot ropes
TOPPING LIFT Rigging

FORE BOOM
Double becket
Double
Iron horse in deck
Bulls eye in deck
FORE SHEET

Trestle tree.
Mast head.
Trestle tree.
Iron bale Ringed
Iron rod.
Spreader.

PLAN AT MAST-HEAD.

RATLINES ON STARBOARD MAIN SHROUDS.
RATLINES ON PORT FORE SHROUDS.
Three shrouds rattled up 8 feet high.
Two shrouds rattled all the way up.

FORE PEAK HALLIARD.
Hauling end to stbd
Jig end to port.

Bowsprit shrouds shackled.
Foot rope in eye of shackle pin
Turnbuckle on bobstay.

pole at the top. It is 11 inches in diameter at the upper cap, tapered to 7¾ inches at the fid and is the same at the shoulder and at the pole.

Her foremast is 85 feet, total length; and stands 76 feet 6 inches above the deck with a masthead 11 feet long, measured down from the top of this spar. This spar is 18½ inches in diameter at the deck and 18 inches just below the crosstrees.

The fore-topmast stands 30 feet 3 inches above the upper cap, with a pole 2 feet 9 inches included in this length. It is the same diameters as the main, 11 inches at the cap and 7¾ inches at each end.

Her bowsprit extends 17 feet 7 inches outside the gammon-iron on the stem. The shoulder of the pole on the outer end being cut 19 inches back from this end. The bowsprit is 14 inches in diameter at the stem, 13 inches at the shoulder.

The main-boom is 78 feet, total length; 14 inches in diameter at the slings, 10 inches at the outer end and 11 inches at the mast.

The main-gaff is 47 feet, total length; 10 inches in diameter at a point two-thirds from the inner end; 7½ inches at the outer end and 9½ inches at the mast.

The fore-boom is 33 feet, total length; 9½ inches in diameter at the slings; 8 inches at the outer end and 9 inches at the mast.

The fore-gaff is 32 feet, total length; 8½ inches in diameter at a point two-thirds from the inner end; 7 inches at the outer end and 8 inches at the mast.

At Pensacola, Florida, one comes down Palafox street, the main street, on to a miniature T wharf, with Gloucester fishing schooners lined up along the pier. And they are the real "bankers," built up North and sailed down to this port to engage in the red snapper fishing on the Campechee Banks out in the Gulf. Designer B. B. Crowinshield laid down the lines of the boats for this trade and a rival fish company, for there are two of them engaged in this business at Pensacola, sent up North and purchased boats for its fleet. Here I came across such names as the *Mary E. Clooney*, *Meneola*, *Osceola*, etc., painted on the schooner's bows, some smacking of Down Easters and others evidently built for the red snapper trade and given southern names or renamed.

Much as one may know about a craft from having been aboard of her or even from having made a voyage in her, when you sit down to make a miniature model of her, there are things you will overlook notwithstanding your former close association. I found this to be the case when I began to make a model of a fisherman. I was repeatedly bucking up against some little detail of rigging or deck equipment, so I went down to Palafox street dock and sketched about every detail there was on the *Clooney*; all her deck fittings, dories, spare anchors, ice and chain boxes, the windlass, with one barrel padded out to take a rope cable, the other side using chain; the rope cable coiled down on a grating abreast the port fore shrouds; her hatches, pumps, travelers, wheel and wheel box; even the little bottle of oil in beckets on the side, I noted down; and up aloft, the peculiar heart-shackle into which the two, double main-throat-halliard blocks were shackled with the links and U-thimble with two eyes to take the lower blocks and those at the gaff jaws. The reeve of each halliard was diagramed, so that when I came to make the little model, she was a real little schooner and not a toy. These sketches are here reproduced for any who care to make a similar model.

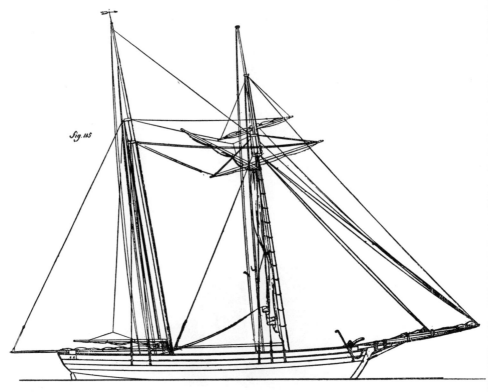

BALTIMORE CLIPPER SCHOONER OF 1820
From Marestier's "Mémoire sur les Bateaux à Vapeur"

CHAPTER III

THE BALTIMORE CLIPPER AND
OTHER SOUTHERN CRAFT

THE Delaware and Chesapeake Bays are historic cruising grounds where much ancient ship lore still abounds but it is so scattered that it requires a lot of time to investigate. Chesapeake Bay is like a tree, the Bay being the trunk, with innumerable limbs and branches stretching out on either side — inlets and rivers on which there are seaports ripe with historic interest.

The boats of these waters are peculiar. The Swedes who settled in this region were shipbuilders and farmers and they modified their national types of schooners to suit the shallow water conditions of this new country. The world-famous Baltimore clippers are said to have originated at St. Michaels, in Talbot County, where shipbuilding has been carried on since 1670 and developed from the pinnace of Capt. John Smith.

The boats that here claim our attention are the dugout canoe chopped out of three logs, the pieces doweled together, making a long double-ender or canoe; the "bugeye," a larger type of double-ender, built up in the regular way; "pungies," as the shallow schooners used in oystering are called; and the famous Baltimore clippers in use all over the world where speed was paramount. They were used in China, as opium smugglers; in the African slave trade to Cuba, where speed meant life or death; and even the American Navy used them to hunt down these very slavers and also to put to rout the bands of pirates that infested the tropical seas.

A trim-built, clean-lined little schooner would be launched at Baltimore or some nearby locality, and her builder, satisfied with cash, would see her sail away. That would be all he would ever know of her history, unless, perhaps, when contracting for another schooner, her story might leak out. She might turn up at Havana, probably with another name painted on her bows and stern, and there receive all the paraphanalia of a slaver. A Spanish or Cuban captain would ship a nondescript crew, though sometimes the men who sailed her down south would stay in her, tempted by the promise of big wages. She would then disappear out of Havana harbor to fetch up at some slave depot on the west coast of Africa. Here, playing hide and seek with the men-of-war of the various nations that were trying to suppress slavery, these schooners would hurriedly pack a human cargo between decks only four feet apart and spread every stitch of canvas of every conceivable shape, size and texture, until clear of the watch dogs. Many a wild sail has taken place with a man-of-war astern, crowded with studding sails to her royals, hot on the schooner's trail. Sometimes sail was carried too long and the fleet of little schooners, unable to stand the heavy press of sail, have been driven clean under and foundered. But under ordinary circumstances, so clean-lined and powerful were these little schooners, they usually ran away from their pursuers, to fetch in on the south side of Cuba, at some uninhabited key, there to hurriedly land their slaves, when the schooner would be burned and sink a charred hulk, destroying all evidence of "the run." The slaves, ever welcomed on the plantations, would be secreted and afterwards delivered to their purchasers with but little trouble.*

The south side of Cuba is a veritable ship's graveyard of sunken slavers and also of many vessels that were not slavers, for it was a convenient and safe place to get rid of an undesirable ship. Building new schooners for this trade kept the shipyards of the Chesapeake humming for years.

I had read about Baltimore clippers from the time when I was a boy and often wondered what manner of craft they could have been. My curiosity grew with the years and yet I could never find an authentic model or plan of these boats. Friends from Baltimore, to whom I appealed, promised to send me a model as soon as they returned home. They were sure they knew just where they could get one — but I never yet have seen one. One day while searching in the New York Public Library for a certain book, I was helping the lady librarian lift a pile of big books from off the shelf, when the telephone called her away and while awaiting her return, I idly opened a book entitled *Mémoire sur les Bateaux à Vapeur des Etats-Unis d'Amerique*, by M. Marestier, published in Paris in 1824. It was a book about steamboats, machinery and all sorts of monkey wrench stuff that didn't interest me at all, but I opened the book and purely by accident turned to a page of plans of schooners which immediately excited my curiosity, and upon investigating I found that I had before me the plans of six Baltimore clipper schooners, with sail plans and all, that were built away back in the 1820's. These plans had been sent to France, as the report about them read, to show to the French Admiralty what these clippers were really like (Marestier was a French spy, then in America), the French officials having often spoken with great admiration of the American schooners.

* For a full account of this trade see *Slave Ships and Slaving*, by George Francis Dow, Salem, 1927. Publication Number 15, Marine Research Society.

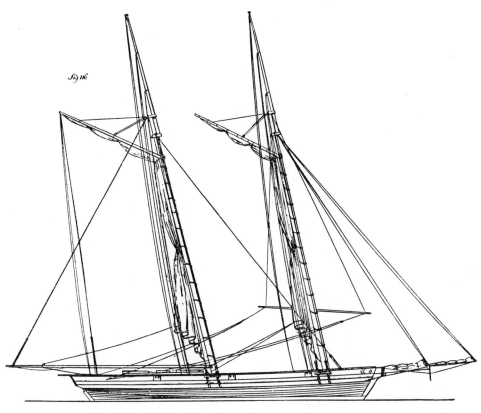

BALTIMORE CLIPPER SCHOONER OF 1820
From Marestier's "Mémoire sur les Bateaux à Vapeur"

While no two of these plans were exactly alike, each boat apparently having been set up to please the eye of her builder, with the rake of the stern post varying from 15 to 25 degrees and the stem from 25 to 45 degrees of rake forward, yet, in general form and proportion of their hulls, they were much alike. They all had an excessive rake or drag to the keel, being nearly twice as deep aft as they were at the forefoot of the stem. Their greatest beam was away forward, about a quarter of their length from the bow, and all had beautifully clean runs aft. Contrary to common belief they were not so wide and flat as usually represented. In proportion to their length they were narrower than other schooners. The secret of their speed lay in the fact that their bows raked under, though showing full curves in their waterlines, so that a diagonal line, such as a ribband bent around nearly square to the surface of the frames would make, would be very sharp and form an easy entrance that would crowd the water down as much as it spread it apart. They were described as long, low, rakish craft and they were low, very low-sided, and that is why they looked wide to those who saw and so described them. They had very little freeboard when compared with pinks, or the old "heel tappers," or any of the high-sided New England craft. A comparison of dimensions of the various boats will prove this.

Years ago there was in England a fast-sailing craft known as the Penzance lugger which was used for fishing. It was noted for its seaworthiness and speed, qualities that came in very handy when there was a cargo of brandy to be smuggled across the Channel from France. France, too, had a great many of these handy vessels, some of which visited American ports during the Revolution, and were no doubt carefully examined by the local shipbuilders. Whether they were copied exactly or somewhat modified it is impossible now to say, but certain it is that a comparison of the body plan of the Penzance lugger *Colleen Bawn,* one of the fastest luggers of her day, built by J. R. Wills, and that of the Baltimore schooner, shows a strong family resemblance. More than likely the French luggers were even more like the clipper schooners than this English lugger.

Another feature of the lugger was the absence of useless top-hamper and gear that offered so much windage to retard a vessel's speed. The luggers had no shrouds at all, just two naked poles of masts with a single halliard for hoisting the yard rove through a dumb-sheave in the masthead, and yet they were very fast sailing craft. During the gold rush to Australia one of these little luggers sailed there from England and beat the regular mail packet in spite of having to ride out a gale to a sea anchor made by rafting her spars and paying them out on the end of a cable. This simplicity of rigging was a noticeable feature of the clipper schooners and with their

Baltimore Schooner "Mildred Addison"

Baltimore Schooner "Mildred Addison"

Baltimore Schooner "Mildred Addison"

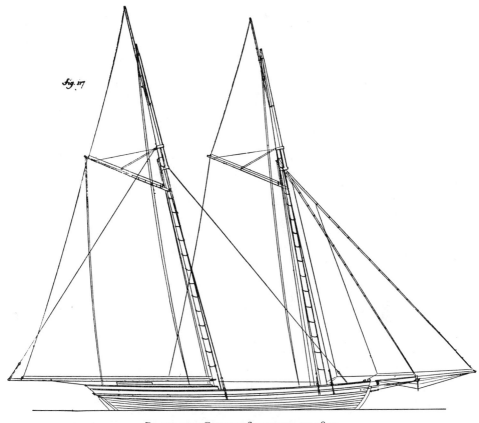

fig. 117

BALTIMORE CLIPPER SCHOONER OF 1820
From Marestier's "Mémoire sur les Bateaux à Vapeur"

large sail-spread was partly the reason for their speediness and weatherliness.

The famous little schooner *Enterprise*, the pet of the early American navy, was a Baltimore schooner carrying square topsails, a typical clipper built in 1799. She served in so many engagements and came through unscathed that she seemed to bear a charmed life. She captured nineteen vessels in the West Indies and went through five engagements at sea in 1800

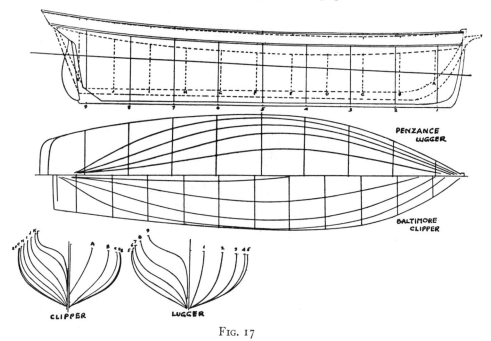

FIG. 17

and when war with Tripoli was declared in 1801 she went over to the Mediterranean, and did good work. She was rebuilt in 1809 and rigged as a brig and served throughout the War of 1812 and after that was used in the West Indies to help exterminate the bands of pirates that infested those waters. She was finally wrecked in 1823 on Little Curaçoa Island.

Under her original schooner rig she was a wonderfully fast craft and the seamen who had to use the various vessels regretted the conversion of this boat to a brig rig. One officer has written of her: "Official wisdom had changed her so woefully that only an expert would have recognized in her the trim, fleet-winged schooner of 1801. Her tall and raking masts had been taken out and the squat rig of a brig substituted."

The navy men fully appreciated the superior sailing qualities of this

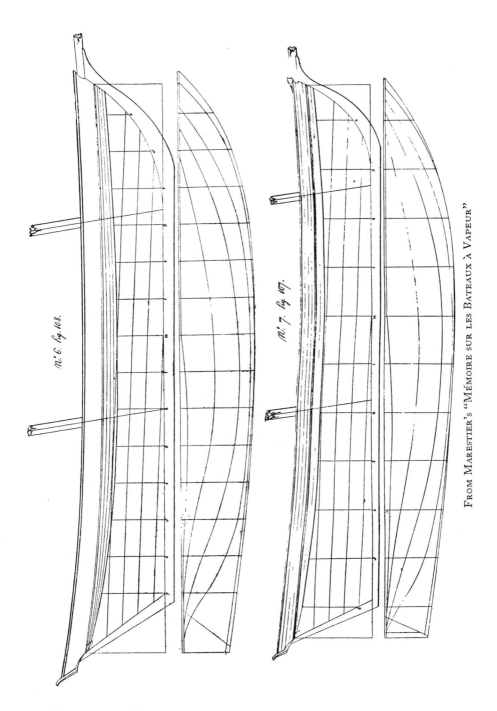

N.° 6. Fig. 108.

N.° 7. Fig. 107.

From Marestier's "Mémoire sur les Bateaux à Vapeur"

Baltimore clipper and though more of them were added to the fleet they never had as fast a craft as she, because they rigged the later boats man-of-war fashion. Five or six men would hoist the mainsail on a merchant clipper schooner but when she was crowded with a host of bull-like, husky men-of-war's men and thirty or more men walked away with a halliard, there was weight and strength enough in their combined effort to pull the eyebolts out of the deck or part a halliard, and so it became the custom at all navy yards, when fitting out a vessel for war, to make everything fool-proof and heavy enough to be unbreakable. Where a $\frac{3}{4}$ inch eyebolt would ordinarily stand all the necessary strain, $1\frac{1}{4}$ inch eyebolt would be used and the same principle prevailed all through the ship. This led to the adoption of such a large margin of safety that everything about a man-of-war became massive and heavy. This, alone, was enough to kill the fast-sailing qualities developed by this fast little clipper schooner built by Baltimore men and taken into the naval service.

As rigged at the builder's yards there would be two shrouds to the foremast and only one on the mainmast, except on very large schooners when some had two. The strain was carried by the masts. They bent and gave a little, thus easing the strain and giving a springiness that imparted life and speed to the boat and the shrouds only came into play to stop the masts after they had received strain enough to give them a decided bend. One reason for this was that with hemp rigging it was impossible to set the shrouds up to a piano-wire tautness as is now done when steel hulls or wooden steel-strapped hulls and screw turnbuckles are used. In those days the spars had to carry the bending strains and they were made large enough to do so. To-day the mast is only a compression member of a steel truss and it is made so light that it is even smaller at the deck than midway between the deck and spreaders, a scientific, steel, spindle-shaped affair, and the whole strain of the sail pressure is now carried by the wire shrouds. To prevent the sides of the vessel from being pulled up, steel straps go down under the heel of the masts.

These modern craft — we are now referring to yachts — may be faster even than the old clippers but what an expensive craft it has taken to beat them. Many tons of lead bolted on to an excessively deep keel and the ship herself when sailing, has no initial stability, or very little, and is merely a canoe-shape imposed between the capsizing thrust of the wind on the sails and the down-pull of the lead ballast trying to right the ship. The hull between these two forces gets a terrific straining and is generally heeled over so that living aboard is anything but enjoyable.

There has been many a controversy over the good and bad points of slack or taut rigging, but as I see it, it all depends upon the boat. It is like a vio-

Primitive Dugout Canoe at Panama, 1928

Chesapeake Sailing Canoe

Chesapeake Bay Buckeye

Chesapeake Bay Buckeye

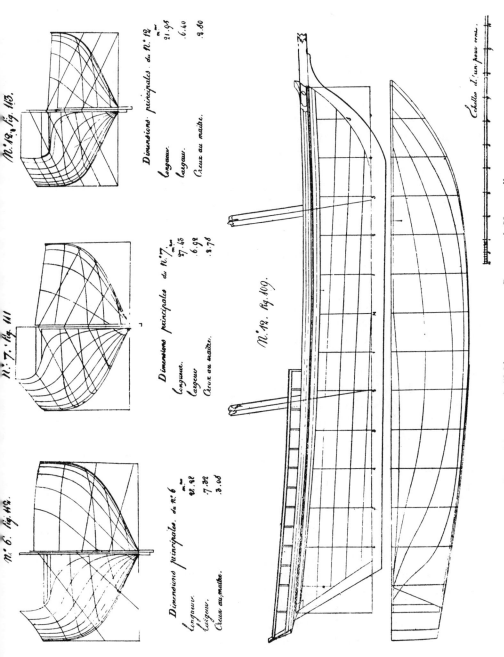

FROM MARESTIER'S "MÉMOIRE SUR LES BATEAUX À VAPEUR"

lin. Each string in a violin has to be pulled to a certain tension, the bass string not so taut; but the treble must be stretched to the breaking point to produce certain sounds. And so with boats. Many of us, especially old-timers, have seen an old oyster boat or one of those big, clumsy, North River sloops, with sails half-hoisted, the boom on the saddle and the mainsail luff hanging in bights, keep pace, hour after hour, coming down Long Island Sound, with a spick and span racing yacht on whose wire luff rope of the mainsail you could play a tune with a handspike. You couldn't set up that old sloop's shrouds so the lee one would not sag off slack and she wouldn't sail as fast if you did.

The navy did that very thing with all their little schooners. They added more shrouds and hove them up like fiddle strings, as if they were line-of-battle-ships, but fortunately some commanders knew enough to slack them up a bit.

A sailing craft is a most whimsical concoction. One man will take a schooner and make her eat out of his hand. He will make her outsail other boats and for no apparent reason. Yet there are, to those who know, many reasons that influence a boat's speed. Another man will take the same craft and everything afloat will pass him. Some boats can be pinched up almost into the wind's eye, while others won't move, if so treated, but will pay their heads off a point when they are moving fast and will fetch as high as the other yacht that looks up higher but sags off in doing it. In some breezes the canvas should be stretched taut as it can be hove up, while in other breezes it should be slack and soft. The men who sailed these little schooners were past masters of all these points and the captains who had a reputation for getting speed out of their craft were the men who were eagerly sought after when it came to running cargoes of black ivory, in "the Middle Passage," in days gone by.

For the oyster trade in the Chesapeake, similar schooners were built and by the same men who turned out the slavers; but for knocking about in home waters they didn't need the immense rigs slavers carried, for oystermen sail short-handed.

There is another very interesting type of craft which is a native of the Chesapeake and that is the dugout canoe and its enlarged contemporary, "bugeye." The dugout is perhaps as old as civilization in these waters. In Panama, today, one can see the same primitive dugout canoes hewed out of a tree trunk, being paddled in from the outlying districts by a negro seated at each end with a cargo of bananas piled up amidships.

The Chesapeake canoe was probably just as primitive years ago, but later it was made larger by using three logs, one for the central part and one for

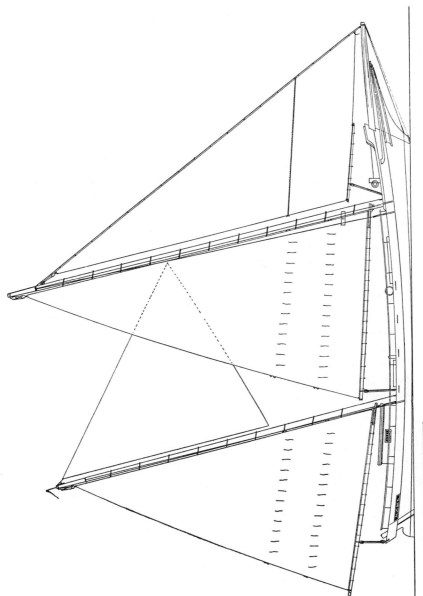

SAIL PLAN of BUGEYE

each side, doweled together and making, as in the case of the old *Magic*, whose plans we show, a canoe 34 feet 6 inches long; 6 feet 7 inches wide; and 2 feet 1 inch deep. The stem was generally carried away out forward under the bowsprit, only a board in thickness, but in outline making a most elaborate, elongated figurehead. Its end generally was carved to represent an eagle's head. A washboard about a foot wide and supported at intervals on brackets or knees was the only deck, and thwarts, fitted across below this washboard, completed the accommodations. A rudder hung on the stern post with a long, slender tiller extending forward to within reach of the rear seat. In the forward third of the boat a centerboard was fitted which was only used in beating to windward. A long, slender mast, stepped away forward, raked back over or past the middle of the boat, on which a leg-of-mutton sail was set with a sprit for a boom to keep the sail flat. The after corners of the sail were clipped and a short club was lashed and laced to it, thereby increasing the sail area.

When fully rigged as when fitted for racing or as the larger craft, such as the *Magic*, were usually rigged, these boats carried another smaller leg-of-mutton sail whose mast was stepped in a thwart about amidships, and a jib laced to a light boom on the foot. The *Magic* was 33 feet 4 inches long on deck; 6 feet 6 inches beam; and only drew about a foot of water with her centerboard up.

The "buckeye" — the fishermen pronounce it "bugeye" — is a craft peculiar to the Chesapeake and is like an enlarged dugout canoe. So long as tree trunks could be procured and three of them doweled together would give sufficient wood to chop out a "buckeye," they were built in that way; but when large timber became scarce they were framed and planked up the same as other boats.

Long, low-sided and pointed at each end, with a very easy midship section, these peculiar little flush-decked schooners could be recognized at a glance by their rig which consisted of two long whip-like spars, the larger one forward, both raking aft at an extreme angle, and a jib forward.

The bowsprit, heavy enough in itself to serve as a battering ram, was emphasized, when the vessel was viewed broadside on, by an extremely long figurehead that carried forward under and half the length of the bowsprit — a clipper bow indeed. Oyster hatchways occupied the middle of the craft and just aft of the small mainmast was a crude cuddy over the crew's sleeping, eating and living quarters below.

These craft originally had a large circle or eye painted on either bow and from this practice the name "buckeye" was given to them. After seeing one afloat it is a surprise to see one hauled up out of water as there is practically

FLORIDA RED SNAPPER FISHERMAN "OVER THE WAVES"
From a photograph made in 1927

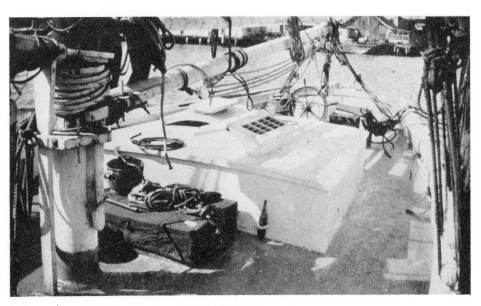

FLORIDA RED SNAPPER FISHERMAN "OVER THE WAVES"
From a photograph made in 1927

Deck View on a Gloucester Fisherman

Sponge Boats at Tarpon Springs, Florida

From a photograph made in 1927

nothing under them when compared to the pink and other New England craft of heavy burden.

"Buckeyes" were made both keel and centerboard. If no board was to be put in them they would have a little deeper false keel or shoe added under their keel to give them some grip for sailing to windward.

The little "buckeye," whose plans Martin Erismann drew, after taking the measurements off a boat that was hauled out at Sparrow's Point, Md., in 1902, was of the following dimensions: length, overall, 53 feet 6 inches; length on waterline, 48 feet 9 inches. Her figurehead was 8 feet 9 inches long; beam, 15 feet and draft, aft, 3 feet 9 inches.

In all small boats, where the tiller swings across above the deck, there is trouble in belaying the mainsheet so it will not interfere with the tiller and this difficulty becomes particularly acute on double-ended boats where the stern is so narrow. Some form of horse or traveler, to take the sheet-block, has to be provided and many a queer contrivance has been the result. The simplest and most usual way was to bend a round bar of iron into an oval loop and flatten and bend each end down so they could be bolted fast, one each side, to the stern post with the tiller swinging inside this loop and the mainsheet-block traveling across over it on this iron. For those who could afford the added expense the "buckeye" builders would build on a little box-like affair that brings to mind the pink-stern of our little Maine fishermen. This contrivance would take the mainsheet travel aft of the rudder head. Sometimes they would build a stubby little bob-tail of an overhang, aft, to accomplish the same object in a more stylish manner. Such a stern is shown on the plan of the *Cynthia*, a "buckeye," 49 feet long; 14 feet wide, with 3½ feet draught. She was built by Capt. James L. Harrison, at Tilghman's Island, Talbot Co., Maryland.

A comparison of the dimensions of several of the old-time "buckeyes" will show that there was no standard of proportion, each one being built as the builder pleased or as his materials at hand permitted.

BUCKEYE	Length	Beam	Draft
Cynthia	49′	14′	3′ 6″
Raven	48′	13′	3′ 10″
Anonyma	50′	12′ 6″	3′
Minnehaha	56′	11′ 2″	2′ 9″
Virginia G. Holland	60′	10′	5′
Lily Sterling	45′	13′ 6″	3′ 6″
Unknown	53′ 6″	15′	3′ 9″

In the short seas kicked up by a strong wind in the shallow waters of the Chesapeake, these "buckeyes" are in their element; wide and flat, with fine ends, they cut through the waves and make good weather of it, whereas, if they had to ride out a deep-water sea and gale off the Maine coast they would not do half so well as the native craft. They fit their environment perfectly. They are easy to handle and as they are shoal and low-sided, it is a small matter to lift the clam rakes aboard. They belong to the Chesapeake.

After living for a long time where northern types of boats were constantly before my eyes, on making a trip down along the Atlantic seacoast and into the Gulf, it was quite a surprise to see how different were the types of craft used in various localities, to the hardy little craft of the rock-bound New England coast. I mean the fishing-craft.

In Lake Ponchatrain, where the New Orleans yachtsmen have a fine, large club house, the Southern Yacht Club, and where they do their yacht racing, I came across several of the old sandbaggers that were once the crack racers in New York Bay and on Long Island Sound, boats that had been purchased and taken south. But of greater interest to me were the famous fishing luggers that in the 1880's made the levee banks at New Orleans look like the old Pole Harbor at Block Island. These boats were in model like an enlarged ship's long-boat, decked, with a big cockpit in the after half, fitted with light hatch-covers to keep the oysters fresh. A barren pole of a mast was stepped well aft of the stern with only one shroud, on each side, and a halliard to hoist the yard on which the single lugsail was set. On the deck, between the mast and the stern, was a low cuddy or companion-slide giving access to dingy, unventilated, living quarters down in the eyes of the craft, just as in the old Chebacco boats of New England.

FIG. 18. NEW ORLEANS LUGGER "LADY OF THE LAKE"

I made a sketch in 1914 of the lugger called the *Lady of the Lake* which, with the plans, will give a good idea of what these boats were like. The craft whose lines we show, thanks to Mr. L. D. Sampsell of New Orleans, is the *Giacomo*, and was modeled by Giacomo Cruti of the firm of Cruti Brothers of New Orleans, who hold an enviable reputation among lugger people as builders of superior boats. She is 39 feet long on deck; 12 feet beam; and is 4 feet deep at the point of greatest beam which is 12 feet from the bow. Her lugsail contains 755 square feet of canvas and is fitted with five rows of reef points. When a "black norther" sweeps down across the Gulf, it blows, and while these boats are broad and have good bearings to stand up and take their medicine, especially when deeply loaded with a cargo of oysters, there are times when it pays to reef, as they carry no ballast whatever.

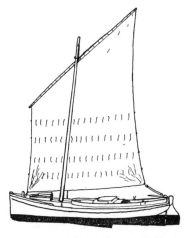

They are centerboard boats but are sweetly modeled and very fast sailers as many a yachtsman has found out who has had a scrub race with them. They have to stem the swift current of the Mississippi and twist and turn up the many inlets and bayous that lead up back of the city of New Orleans in a veritable network of waterways. This requires a minimum of draft to pass over the shoal places and to operate on the oyster reefs and yet they have to go off into deep water and negotiate all kinds of waves.

FIG. 19. NEW ORLEANS LUGGER

These luggers have a short traveler across the forward deck for the tack of the sail and a wide traveler across the stern for the sheet. On either side of the bow is a block hooked to an eyebolt in the rail to haul over the fore-tack of the sail. They have one shroud on each side, set up with a lanyard and one halliard to the sail rove through a single becket-block hooded to the masthead; and a single block at the yard which spar is held close to the mast by a single, stout, mast hoop. Two men are a crew for these boats which are very easy to handle. The sail is not dipped in beating to windward but lays against the mast on one tack.

This does not injure the draft of the mainsail as much as one might suppose because the tack is hauled snug over to the windward rail. The rudder is hung outboard, as in an ordinary rowboat, with the tiller swinging under the traveler or "horse." Strictly speaking, the traveler is the ring and block that slides back and forth across on this iron

FIG. 20

horse — but by common usage and due to the usual laxity in the matter of accuracy in the use of sea terms, this "horse" has become popularly called the "traveler."

A characteristic of these luggers is the short, stout pole or staff set up in cleats on the transom. This serves a variety of purposes; to fly the ensign from; to lash the end of the yard to keep it up off of the deck when the sail is lowered; or to hang a basket of bait to when the latter becomes over

ripe and so carry the odor off to leeward when close-hauled. Sometimes an orange branch, laden with fruit, is lashed to this pole or a bunch of bananas or branch of magnolia buds, for the sons of sunny Italy, who operate these craft, have tastes peculiar unto themselves.

FIG. 21. NEW ORLEANS LUGGER

At Tarpon Springs, on the west coast of Florida, a few miles up the Antioch River from the Gulf of Mexico, there is a colony of Greek sponge fishermen who operate a craft that is unique. The boats are double-enders with excessive sheer and are painted in the red, yellow and blue so dear to the Greeks. The raised decks, at either end, are painted blue;

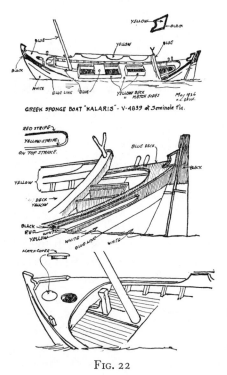

FIG. 22

their spars and hatch-covers are blue; the king-plank down the middle of the deck is blue; while the deck itself is a brilliant yellow and so are the sides of of the hatchways. The head of the stem and stern posts are yellow outlined with black. The sheer strake is black with a long, round-ended panel in it ruled with the top edge in red and the bottom edge or outline in yellow. The sides of the boat above water up to this sheer strake, are white, but at each of the three scuppers, along her side where the dirt would ordinarily stain the side, brilliant triangular patches of red are painted with the apex at the scupper hole. The edge of the third strake down from the deck is beaded and ruled with a fine blue line that still further accentuates the high sheer of these boats. Below water they are painted an anti-fouling copper red paint.

It is claimed that the original of these boats was brought from Greece, and I was told the first reproductions were built by Merrill Stevens of Jacksonville, Florida. The Greeks build their own boats now, at Tarpon Springs,

OLD STYLE GREEK SPONGE BOAT, TARPON SPRINGS, FLORIDA
Photograph made in 1926

OLD STYLE GREEK SPONGE BOAT, TARPON SPRINGS, FLORIDA
From a photograph made in 1926

GREEK SPONGE BOAT "KALARIS," SEMINOLE, FLORIDA
From a photograph made in 1926

NEW STYLE SQUARE STERN SPONGE BOAT BUILT BY GREEKS
AT TARPON SPRINGS, FLORIDA
From a photograph made in 1926

and several of the newer ones are departing from the original model and have square sterns. The decks are down about nine inches below the top of the gunwale, with a short piece of raised deck flush across either end. A circular hatch in the forward one, gives access to a small locker for the storage of lines and grapnels. There is a stout mooring post, braced by a knee, extending forward on the deck between the raised forward deck and the mast. The latter is stepped so that it rakes sharply forward and is only a short, stubby affair. A long yard has its heel becketed in what old-timers called a "snotter," in the days of spritsails. The surf boatmen who had the Jersey beach boats so rigged, taught me this, back in 1880. A piece of rope about two feet long had a long loop of an eye-splice in one end and a small eye-splice in the other, the long loop was doubled around the mast, the small eye end was passed through the big eye and the whole pulled taut, fastening the rope or "snotter" to the mast and when the sprit was stuck into the becket in the head of the sail at the peak, the yard was shoved up extending the spritsail to its full area and the shoulder or tapered lower end of the sprit was put into the small eye of the "snotter" with play enough to permit the sprit to swing freely. To peak up the sail, the "snotter" was shoved up on the mast and by the simple process of wetting with a handful of water kept from sliding down again.

On these Greek boats this sprit (some used to call it a "spreet"), was kept standing and its heel was toggled into a short tackle at the mast instead of a "snotter." Its upper end came about over the boat's stern and was steadied aloft by a vang or rope leading down to each quarter. A wire runner spliced over the masthead and the end of the yard, with hanks on it, acted as a curtain pole for the sail to slide out on, it being hauled out by a rope through a sheave in the outer end of the sprit and hauled in (clewed in, as it were) by another rope that returned through a block at the masthead and down to the decks.

Two shrouds, a side- and a head-stay, completed the rig. There was no boom on the sail. It was loose footed and while this sail made a fine square-sail, when slacked out, it was at best but a poor sail for beating to windward. Now-a-days they all have "pushers" (motors) in them and the sail is only used to save fuel when there is a strong, fair wind blowing.

In a raised hatchway, amidships, there are two compartments each reached by a companion slide. The after one gives access to where the motor is installed and the forward one houses an air pump to supply the diver who puts on a full diving suit and goes over the starboard bow, just forward of the rigging, on a ladder, the lower part of which is hinged so it can be raised out of water when sailing or dropped down about four feet under water when the diver is operating. So many accidents have happened in getting the air hose afoul of the boat's propeller, that cages of iron rod are built around the propellers to keep the hose from becoming entangled or cut.

Though the boats have excessive sheer they are so picturesquely painted they do not look at all unsymmetrical. Their hulls in shape somewhat resemble the Block Island boats and are smooth planked and beautifully modeled; as clean as a whale boat, fore and aft, though of course much more burdensome. The stern post is straight and rakes under with the rudder hung on it. The stem is curved and rakes under quite decidedly, its head above deck curved on the back side to hold a mooring rope thrown over it. The sides, amidships, are built up with a high waist-board and across the boat, just forward of the steersman's cockpit, is a square timber, about six by six inches in dimension, whose ends extend out about a foot beyond the boat's side. In a hole near each end the forked end of a limb from some tree is stuck and supports the after end of a small spar that extends forward to the rigging and acts as a handrail to keep one from falling overboard. Three irons with rings welded to the top, are spaced along each side to hold this spar and generally a bundle of miscellaneous poles, as well.

The Key West spongers hook up their sponges from the bottom in about thirty feet of water, but these Tarpon Springs spongers go down in over a hundred feet of water, on the reefs out in the Gulf.

This short review describes only a few of the many types of schooners used in the waterways of the Atlantic Coast. There were pilot schooners whose story alone would make a book; coasters, from two masts up to six and even one that had seven masts — the *Thomas W. Lawson,* wrecked on the English coast. There are the little pug-nosed, apple-bowed, Rockland lime schooners; the wide, flat, Sound and river brick schooners; sand schooners; bluestone carriers; and so on, almost without limit in variety.

I once made a West Indies voyage in a schooner just to see how these "telegraph poles," as deep-watermen termed them, when I was at sea, behaved, and I found out, for I was caught south of Hatteras, in the blizzard of 1894, in an overloaded, well-deck schooner, with no deck load. Some of the craft we fell in with were historic old packets, but the insight one got by living as a sailor among sailors proved there is a real brotherhood of the sea among men who sail ships that is unmatched on land. The common danger that is always present and the shoulder-to-shoulder hardships men go through when there's real work to be done in a gale of wind, weds them into a bond of fellowship that is true manhood. When a man will take off his pea jacket in cold, wet, winter weather, and put it on the shoulders of a mate who lacks a proper coat, knowing it may, like as not, come back to

him soaked through by a sea; or when one sailor will forego a mug of **hot**
coffee, badly as he may need it himself, and hand it to a more needy **mate**
— that's the spirit that true sailors are made of and will show when **the**
emergency arrives.

CHAPTER IV

THE PACKET SHIP "ISAAC WEBB"

THE ship *Isaac Webb*, of the famous "Black Ball Line" of Western Ocean packet ships, running between New York and Liverpool in the 1850's, was a fine example of perfection attained in the construction of this type of vessel. She was one of the largest of her class, registering 1800 tons, and was built at New York, in 1850, by William H. Webb, who has left a complete record of her, in the way of plans, by which this interesting craft can be reproduced.

It was before the days of steamships, when communication between Europe and America was carried on wholly by means of sailing vessels, that the "Black Ball Line" was established. The King's packets, little brigs of only about two hundred tons, sailing every month between Falmouth, England, and New York, had carried the mails since early in the seventeen hundreds. This service was maintained up to and during the Revolution, after which these brigs made Halifax, Nova Scotia, their destination.

For several years after the Revolution, ships were sailing to and from England, but there were no regular packets. The French government tried operating a subsidized line between 1784 and 1792, the management being vested in a private company though the ships were handled by French naval officers, but it was not a success.

As early as 1805, when the Boston Importing Company was formed, an effort was made to operate a packet line between Boston and Liverpool, and Thomas P. Cope, in 1807, began running a line of ships from Philadelphia to Liverpool. The War of 1812, however, put a stop to these undertakings.

Peace was declared on the 18th of February, 1815, and packets again began to ply across the Atlantic, but their date of sailing was dependent upon when they obtained sufficient cargo to fill their holds. Freight was what the shipowner then relied upon to supply an adequate return on the money he had invested in his ship; the passengers were carried more as an accommodation to them and they had to put up with meagre fare and such quarters as the ship afforded. It was not at all an uncommon event for persons who had engaged a passage to Europe, sailing on a certain day, to be obliged to put up at a nearby tavern for some time to await the day when the ship actually sailed.

PACKET SHIP "ISAAC WEBB" OF NEW YORK
From a photograph in the Marine Collection, Peabody Museum, Salem

Ship "Rousseau," Built in 1801, and Ship "Desdemona," Built in 1823, Lying at a New Bedford Wharf

Ship "Rousseau," 305 Tons, Built at Philadelphia in 1801; and the Ship "Desdemona," 236 Tons, Built at Middletown, Conn., in 1823, Lying at a New Bedford Wharf

THE PACKET SHIP "ISAAC WEBB"

Ship's cabins have always been provided with a couple of spare staterooms and as the passenger trade increased more staterooms were fitted up. The extreme after-hold of a ship, due to her shape, is necessarily a shelving, V-shaped compartment where the stowage of cargo is difficult and uneconomical when compared to the square, box-like sections of the ship nearer amidships; thus, very little available space was lost to the storage of cargo in taking enough to fit up a few extra rooms in this part of the ship.

When Capt. Benjamin Marshall was returning to New York, in 1816, from a tour of European cities, and had put up with all the inconveniences and uncertainties attending the sailing date of a ship, he met as fellow passengers, three Quakers, William Francis Thompson, his brother Jeremiah Thompson, and Isaac Wright. The enforced leisure of such a passage gave these four men, all of whom were engaged in shipping ventures of one kind or another, ample time to discuss the evils of the situation, and to suggest remedies. The outcome of this accidental meeting was the formation of the famous "Black Ball Line" of packet ships to ply between New York and Liverpool. They advertised that their ships would sail, regardless of cargo, on the first and sixteenth of each month.

This was a great accommodation to prospective passengers for whose patronage the Line was striving and it taught consignees to hurry up their cargo shipments. Busy scenes were enacted as a result. Last minute cargoes were crammed into the ship's hold at a heretofore unheard of speed. Night gangs of stevedores, working by the dim glow of lanterns, made the waterfront a hustling scene of activity at all hours. Sweating teams waited in line or tugged at their harnesses as they moved up dragging heavily-loaded trucks through the mud and mire of South Street down on to the wooden pier.

Man power and horse power performed all the labor, for hoisting engines and donkey-men were yet to come. Cases were swung from the truck on a lowering fall, when it was low tide, and the ship, nearly loaded, was low in the water; but at high tide and when starting to load a light ship, whip purchases were rove through cargo-blocks, hooked to pendants from the topmast-heads, leading down through a lead-block on the dock where a big, heavy "hoisting horse" walked away with the fall, hoisting the cases, bales or barrels, up the skid boards protecting the ship's side until they swung inboard over the rail.

Ships of fair size, particularly the deep ones, were constructed with another deck below the main deck, termed the "'tween decks," a contraction of the full name "between decks." On some vessels this deck was only about four feet below the main deck and at best there was only headroom. Small schooners and craft of only six or eight feet depth inside the hull, usually only had one deck, but the early "Black Ballers" and vessels of four hundred tons register, were nearer fifteen feet in depth, permitting a height of a little over six feet between the main deck and the 'tween decks, with over eight feet hold for cargo, less, of course, the thickness of the intermediate decking and the supporting beams.

The four ships forming the nucleus of this Line were the *Amity, Courier, Pacific* and *James Monroe,* to which were soon added the *William Thompson, James Cropper, Orbit, Nestor, Albion* and *Canada,* all ships of about four hundred tons. They were flush-decked fore and aft, with the housed-over long-boat securely lashed in chocks just forward of the main hatch. Outside they were painted black above the waterline with bright varnished bends, as the five or six planks just below the deck-edge were termed. They were copper-bottomed below water. On deck, the inside of the bulwarks, the deck-houses and boats were painted green, and the planks of the deck were kept bright and clean, bare wood, scrubbed daily and holystoned once a week with sand.

The *James Cropper,* launched in 1822, was the first of this fleet to be fitted with a central deck-house and a house at the stern over the wheel, a custom other builders were quick to imitate. The deck and cabin plan of the four hundred and twenty-five ton ship *Dover,* built by Thatcher Magoun, at Medford, Mass., in 1828, for the "Boston and Liverpool Packet Line," shows clearly how these ships were arranged, with the main saloon aft and the ladies' cabin forward of it, instead of aft against the transom as in the early "Black Ballers" of 1818.

Evidently this location was preferable as the motion of the ship's plunging would be felt less there than away aft. The *James Cropper* was so arranged and another packet ship of which we have the cabin plan, the *St. Denis,* built by A. T. Westervelt, at New York, in 1848, to ply between Havre and New York, a ship of a thousand tons, was also arranged in this manner. Like the *Isaac Webb,* she had a forward deck-house, where the galley and crew were housed, leaving the entire 'tween decks open to the steerage passengers.

Let us first look at the way the deck of the first little four hundred ton "Black Ball" ships was arranged and then compare it with the two thousand ton ship *Isaac Webb,* of 1850. The first four ships of this Line measured about four hundred and twenty-five tons each, with a length of about 121 feet over all; 110 feet, length of keel; 28 feet beam; and 14 feet depth of hold. These are the *Dover's* dimensions.

Beginning forward there was always some kind of figurehead beautifying that end of the ship. They were bluff-bowed, straight-sided, square-sterned craft utilizing about eighty-five to ninety per cent of the parallelogram enclosed within her length and breadth dimensions. The body, under water, was sharpened up just a little finer than the old cargo-boxes of merchantmen and these ships, therefore, were considered at that time marvels of speed. The *Dover's* floors had a dead-rise or upslant, of 12 inches in seven feet or about double what most ships had. The head-knee would be

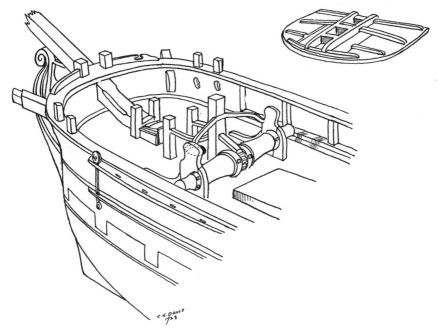

FIG. 23. BOW OF AN EARLY PACKET SHIP

either capped with a beautifully carved billet-head of design similar to the head of a violin—a volute or spiral scroll such as is used in the Ionic, Corinthian or Composite capitals in architecture.

The stem might be capped with a sculptured image of the person the ship was named for, either a bust or full-length figure, and the braces which extended back against the ship's bluff bows, to steady this part of the head, would be worked so their edges showed a fancy moulding. The greatest care was taken by the old shipbuilders to so curve each of these and to space them so that they radiated from this volute or figure, in lines pleasing to the eye. Like a fan, each of these head-rails should increase in size as they recede aft from the billet or volute head and the space between each should show a gradual increase.

One of the old packets showing this feature very clearly is the *Rousseau*, of 305 tons, built in 1802 for the "Cope Line" of Philadelphia. The photograph, here reproduced, shows her when she had degenerated into a whaler, and the beautiful bust of Rousseau, carved by Philadelphia's famous sculptor, Rush, had been replaced by a plain billet-head. The *Desdemona*, of 236 tons, built in 1823, laying at the right of her, shows how varied these head-rails were and how different were the shapes of the ship's heads. The latter still carries a figurehead, a bust of Desdemona, or some sculptor's conception of her appearance.

There was very little flam or flare outwards to the topsides at the bows of these old packets. The sides under the catheads had just a little slant outward, enough so the anchor bills would not dig into her planks as the anchors hung suspended at the catheads. The *Desdemona*, of a later date, shows a much more sharpened-up bow than the round, apple-bows of the old *Rousseau*.

On deck, the bowsprit came in between the two knight heads, its high steeve or slant causing the inboard end to go down through the deck where it butted into a stout Sampson post that was well braced by and bolted to heavy deck beams on both decks. Bowsprits, so fitted, were a necessary evil and caused a wet and leaky forecastle wherein poor Sailor Jack had to sleep, eat and live.

This same Sampson post or pawl post, as it was generally termed, had the pawl hung on its after side that engaged in the ratchet on the windlass barrel and prevented it turning one way. The windlass, one of the old, horizontal-log kind was supported at each end by stout posts set edgeways, fore and aft, and braced against the pull on the anchor chain by a large oak knee, one each side, securely bolted down to the deck beams. Half the circular score to receive the axle of the windlass was cut out of these windlass posts and when the windlass was put in place another, shorter piece, with the other half of the score cut out, was bolted to these posts on the after side completing the housing for the windlass.

Just abaft the windlass there was a small companionway with a vertical ladder beneath, down which one had to climb to get into the sailor's quarters—the forecastle. Then came the foremast, with its topsail-sheet bitts and fiferails holding belaying pins for making fast the various ropes. Other ropes belayed to pins in the pinrail built on the inside of the ship's bulwarks, from bow to stern, about three feet above the deck. Aft of the foremast was the galley, a square box of a structure containing the stoves on which the cook prepared the meals. Then came the ship's long boat, stowed in chocks and lashed down securely to ring bolts in the deck. At the beginning of a voyage it generally was full of crates of chickens and live stock, to stave off for a while at least, the monotony of salt beef, salt pork and other salted foods.

Over the main-hatch, a booby-hatch was placed and lashed down to ring-bolts in the deck at each corner. This box-like affair had companionway slides and doors giving access to the ladders leading down to the steerage deck.

Then came the mainmast with its bitts and fiferails around it and just abaft of it were the ship's pumps. These were iron-chambered, plunger pumps with the plunger rods hooked up to a rocker arm pivoted between the pump chambers, with sockets on either side where long lever arms could be inserted so that two or more men could get hold of the oak cross-bar fitted at the end of each of these levers or heavers. When not in use the long levers could be removed and stowed out of the way.

There was a square, box-like well built from the deck down to the bottom of the ship in which the pipes of these pumps extended to the bilge. There were cleats or rungs nailed to the after side of this well so that the ship's carpenter could climb down and clear or repair the pumps. The entrance to this well was through a removable section of the pump-well in the 'tween decks. On small, single-decked boats there was a low, raised hatch on deck where the carpenter entered this compartment when it was necessary for him to do so. The water pumped out on deck found its way back into the sea through the scuppers.

A short distance aft of the pumps was the forward companionway, a raised hatch with glass windows in the sides and after end and doors in the front with a slide on top. A square-topped skylight, a good seating-height above the deck, came next, going aft; then the mizzen mast with its bitts and fiferails; another after companionway, behind the mizzen mast; and from there to the stern was only the binnacle and steering wheel.

This deck furniture, as it was called, was in a row, fore and aft, extending from bow to stern, and it left the decks clear and unencumbered for the crew to run, fore and aft, in manoeuvering ship, to get at quickly and haul the necessary braces, brails, etc., along her bulwarks.

These packets were small ships and the captain's voice could be heard bellowing out his orders without using a speaking trumpet even in a gale of wind. Tidy ships, the old shellbacks called them, because all their gear was so easy to get at. When forecastle heads, poop decks and large deck-houses made their appearance there was much discontent among the crews, who objected to such unnecessary deck encumbrances, and to the unhandiness of having to scramble up and down ladders, from one deck to another, in order to handle the ship's gear. Such foolish top-hamper would affect the ship's sailing and seaworthiness, besides, these exposed surfaces would offer a great deal of wind resistance and slow up the ships, so the sailors argued. "Growl you may, but go you must," is an old axiom of the sea and though the men growled, the new ideas prevailed.

The *James Cropper*, built in 1822, initiated the style of carrying deck-houses and it was never given up. They were enlarged, from year to year, until they encumbered the deck as in the *Isaac Webb*. In the bows of this ship there was a raised platform or deck, about six feet above the level of the main-deck, with the bowsprit going in through the ship's bows below this forecastle head. Instead of being a round spar, as on the old *Dover* and other ships, the *Isaac Webb's* bowsprit was a square stick and continued so for a couple of feet forward of the bows when it was chamfered off on the corners to an eight-sided stick, for about fifteen feet, and then rounded off. Instead of going down through a housing or narrow hatchway made for it in the deck, her bowsprit was hewed out of a stick with a crook so that it stayed above the main deck until it butted into a pawl-bitt into which its heel was morticed to steady it against the side strain.

The *Isaac Webb* was a large ship, for her day, dwarfing the little four hundred and five hundred-ton pioneer ships into insignificance. She was registered at 1800 tons; was 185 feet long on deck; thirty-eight feet and ten inches moulded beam, that is to the outside of the ship's frame, inside of her planking; and had a depth of hold of twenty-seven feet and three inches. When loaded to a draft of twenty-two feet, her main deck was still nine feet above the water level. Her poop deck, aft, was sixteen feet and her forecastle head at the stem was eighteen feet above the water. The distance from her main truck down to the water was 172 feet and from her knight heads to the end of her flying jibboom was eighty-nine feet. Her main yard was eighty-four feet long and she looked like a frigate on the water. Her forecastle head measured thirty feet in length and was thirty-two feet wide across the after end inside the bulwarks. Forward she was almost square across, there being just a slight curve with a quick round, aft, to the cathead. A measurement taken nine feet aft of the stem, gave a width across the forecastle head of twenty-seven feet.

The *Isaac Webb* carried a capstan, away forward, ten feet from the bow, and the center of her pump-brake windlass was twenty feet aft. Only the windlass, pawl-post, with its crank, to receive the windlass heavers, and the catheads, were on this forecastle head. A ladder, on each side, led down to the main deck. Under the forecastle head, just aft of the windlass, was a companionway down which the crew went by means of ladder into their living quarters in the forecastle, below the main deck.

Black Ball Line Packet Ship "Montezuma," Built by W. H. Webb in 1843

Model made by Charles G. Davis

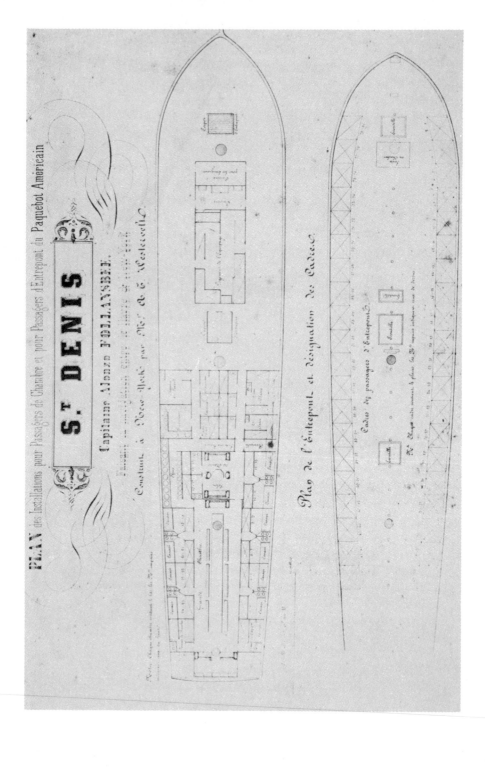

THE PACKET SHIP "ISAAC WEBB"

There was a space of sixteen feet between the forecastle head and a long deck-house, built just aft of the foremast, which was thirty-six feet long and sixteen feet wide. Its top showed just above her seven-foot high bulwarks.

The galleys, one for cooking the food for the steerage passengers and crew, and the other for the cabin passengers and officers, were in the forward end of this house. The after end was fitted with staterooms for the accommodation of second-class passengers.

Over the main hatchway, after the cargo was stowed, a small, square house was hoisted into place and lashed down to ring bolts in the deck. A window in each side furnished light and two doors in the forward end provided an entry to the ladders leading down to the steerage in the 'tween decks. Aft, the ship had a raised poop or quarterdeck extending from the stern, forward, ninety-three feet and ending in a bow-shaped curve so that at the center it went clear and forward of the mainmast. This quarterdeck had a handrail for protection. The housed-in part, below, came to a point eighty-five feet forward of the stern, so that eight feet of the poop deck overhung and furnished a short, sheltered space, on the main deck, where the doorways leading into the afterquarters were located. Ladders leading up through hatchways, on either side of this poop, gave access from one deck to the other. The ladders started on the main deck near the water-ways and slanted inboard as they went up to the poop, being set athwartships and not fore and aft.

Aft of the mainmast was another capstan; then a small companionway covered the gangways leading below used by the stewards and junior officers, and aft of this was a skylight over the ladies' room below. Then came the mizzen mast, with another companionway abaft of it, that gave access to the forward end of the dining saloon. At the extreme stern was the steering wheel, with a binnacle on deck, just in front of it.

From the day of a cargo ship, carrying passengers purely as an accommodation, to the time when emigrants in considerable number were anxious to get to the land of freedom and prosperity, the packet ship had developed into the highest class of passenger vessels. The accommodations were planned with every possible convenience and comfort that the naturally cramped quarters of a ship would permit and considerable elegance of finish was evidenced in the joinerwork. Mahogany, rosewood, satinwood, and bird's-eye maple were used with delicately carved pilasters and capitals, edged with gold leaf, and the upholstery of the comfortable divans or sofas was carefully selected with a view to making the saloons beautiful.

Both William H. Webb and Donald McKay were believers in flat-floored ships, that is, ships with a very small amount of deadrise to their midship section. They believed in fining away the ends in order to obtain speed, but to counteract the downward pressure of the wind on a ship's sails, they believed that the flat-floored ship made a better sea boat, a drier ship than one whose floor-frame was more angular. The *Gazelle* was built by Mr. Webb for a couple of old sea captains who insisted on a very sharp midship-section with a deadrise of 25°, almost as much as had the smaller Baltimore clippers. But he was skeptical of her success and in the *Challenge*, and *Flying Dutchman*, two of his best ships, their angle of deadrise was 17°, which was his limit. J. W. Griffiths' ship *Rainbow* had 8° deadrise, but his next ship, the *Sea Witch*, was sharper, having 14°. Samuel H. Pook, who designed many fast clippers, gave 10° deadrise to the *Red Jacket*. Donald McKay's *Flying Cloud* had 11° and the *Lightning* 8°. The Webb packet ships, *Isaac Webb*, *Guy Mannering* and *Joseph Walker*, all had only 4° to 5° angle of deadrise and the *Montezuma* and *Yorktown* 8°, showing the difference between clipper ships of later days and the old packet ships that preceded them.

Griffiths' little clipper, the *Sea Witch*, had a very rounded midship frame with more beam at the deck than anywhere else. He flared the topsides so that his ships increased their area as they heeled over, which surplus buoyancy in the topsides of the ship lifted them up when hard driven in a sea-way and carried them through much drier than the ships built more wall-sided amidships which, like the *Challenge* and other Webb ships, relied on obtaining speed by the sharpness of their extreme ends. They did obtain great speed but they were wet ships when hard driven in a sea-way, as was the *Flying Cloud* and the *Dreadnaught*. Their fine ends offered less resistance but they dove deeper and broke more sailors' bones than the big, bluff, top-sided packet ships, that were finely modeled below water but above water were buoyant as a barrel. They butted the tops of the seas and rolled them over into acres of white suds but rode drier than the racing clippers that sliced deeply into the seas. Their sides "tumbled home" as in the men of war, the old round ships that gave the oncoming sea less leverage to heel them over.

The sides of the *Isaac Webb* "tumbled home" about four feet, beginning away down at the turn of her bilge, under water; a typical kettle-bottomed ship, as they were called in those days. They were so built in order to avoid heavy tonnage charges and could carry much more cargo than their tonnage indicated. The measurement for calculating the tonnage measured for breadth at the deck which was the narrowest part of the ship. This is shown very plainly in her plans.

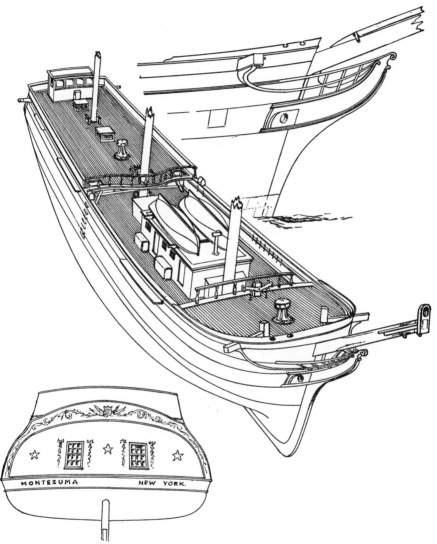

DETAILS OF PACKET SHIP "MONTEZUMA" OF THE BLACK BALL LINE
Built by Wm. H. Webb in 1843

The famine in Ireland, in 1846, due to the complete failure of the pota-to crop, caused a rush of emigrants to America that filled the 'tween decks of every west-bound ship. It was partly due to the need for sufficient room to house the large number pleading for passage to a land where they would not starve to death, that resulted in fitting up the entire 'tween decks with sleeping stalls for the emigrants. The first-class passengers were accommo-dated with quarters on the upper or maindeck over which a long quarter-deck was built and the crew were quartered in a house built on deck, abaft the foremast.

In 1852 there were 306,279 emigrants who left English seaports for America, 217,459 of whom sailed from Liverpool. During the month of April, 1853, alone, it is recorded that 27,000 embarked at Liverpool bound for America.

A very good description of how the *Isaac Webb* crossed the Atlantic with a load of emigrants is given by one of her sailors named Denis Kear-ney, in an article printed years ago in the *San Francisco Call*.

Crossing the Atlantic on the Emigrant Ship "Isaac Webb"

"Standing upon the pier at Birkenhead and looking across over the glassy surface of the Mersey toward the Princess Dock, the eye couldn't help but see a handsome-looking, freshly tarred and newly painted full-rigged ship swinging lazily to her anchor in the river. Her yards were braced square, and the cotton sails upon them were neatly stowed with bunts as smooth as the round bottom of a sailor's bag, and the yard-arm gaskets were passed harbor fashion and as close as the seizing on a mainstay.

"The tide was on the flood, and yet there wasn't a ripple on the water save where it broke against the ship's stem, and the few wrinkles that were made by the boatmen as they rowed to and from the ships.

"There wasn't a breath of wind. The starry banner at the peak of the monkey gaff hung in folds sluggishly, and the weather vane that was fas-tened to the mizzen royal backstay looked as limp and lifeless as a wet main-deck swab that lay on the windlass end.

"The white cotton sails, new manila running gear, the crowds of young women and men, dressed in homespun, about the decks and looking over the rail, all went to show that she was an outward-bound Yankee.

"'Look you here, young fellow, if you want to get on board this ship with-out trouble, put some more elbow grease into that there rag and make the top of that binnacle shine like a looking glass. We can't have any skulkers aboard this ship.'

"The coarse voice was Mr. Patton's, the chief mate of the *Isaac Webb*, and he was introducing himself to me as I was busy scouring the brass around the binnacle.

"Mr. Patton was a down-easter, tall, angular and rawboned. The color of his skin from long years of contact on the ocean with hail, snow squalls, fogs and sunny weather resembled the yellow shoes now worn by dudes. A severe cut which he once received below the right eye left an ugly scar, and a broken nose disfigured what was once a very handsome face. The knuckles of his right hand were all broken, and he carried a brass knuckle in the starboard pocket of his monkey jacket.

"I didn't like the blustering introduction. It made me feel very sheepish at the moment, for beside me there stood a young emigrant girl who was looking at the compass, and she asked me what it was.

"'We're-a-goin' to 'ave a breeze shortly,' I heard the pilot say to the captain, who had just come up out of the cabin and joined him in a walk on top of the after house. 'It's looking dirty way off there to the south'ard of east,' he went on. 'I've been watchin' it for some time, and it 'pears to me to be risin'.'

"'Get your men together, Mr. Patton,' said Captain Stowell, the ship's commander, 'and heave in the slack chain. Send a few of 'em aloft to cast off the yard-arm gaskets, and when the slack is all in we'll masthead the topsail yards to be ready for sheeting home.'

"The breeze that the pilot predicted came sooner than expected, and inside of half an hour after feeling its breath the anchor-fluke was in the grip of the shankpainter and the *Isaac Webb* was gliding down the Mersey and out toward the Irish Sea under a cloud of white canvas that reached from the upper rail of the bulwarks to the now mastheaded royal yards, and we were assisted by the tide which began to ebb.

"The breeze which canted the ship's big bows downstream when we tripped the anchor hung to us till we were well abreast of the northwest lightships, when it shifted to the east and stiffened, and, bellying the big topsails, sent us reeling along about ten knots, with a full cargo and seven hundred passengers, all bound for New York.

"We discharged the pilot at midnight, and two days later the rattling breeze, which sent us spinning down St. George's Channel and gave us such a splendid offing, chopped around to the west'ard and began to howl. Four days and nights we lay to under a close-reefed main and fore topsail, and part of the time we had her reduced down to a storm staysail. The sea lashed itself into a fury, and the big green waves, as they rolled up above us, broke and their curling crests leaped over the ship's bows, chased each other along the deck, smashed in the weather door of the galley, put the fire out in the range and drove the cooks away. The hatches were all battened down and the companionways closed up tight, making the 'tween decks the most miserable of places.

"All of our passengers were young, and the sexes about evenly divided. They had brain and brawn, and in their composition was the best blood of Europe. It was the soundest and the best looking of the family that emigrated. The dwarfs and cripples were kept at home. Seven hundred of these young people, with hopes high burning, braved the dangers of the wild Atlantic on the *Isaac Webb* and were stowed away in her 'tween decks with but little air or light, and all seasick. The wet, dirty and dismal 'tween decks with its seasick occupants mingling their moans with the creaking of the ship's joints as she plunged her knightheads into a sea that flooded the main deck above them, and, when she rolled, washed the waters in a wave that broke against the bulwarks, the fierceness of the gale as it shrieked through the shrouds and played upon the running rigging, the big ship under a storm staysail struggling with the immense combers that thumped her on the weather bow and threw her off into the trough of the sea when she'd roll and show her copper-covered keel to the hungry wild seabirds who were hovering above and about us carefully watching our every move, the cursing of the officers and the growling of the sailors as they were being washed from the pumps, made a scene which no brush could truthfully paint nor pen describe.

"These packet ships carried no waiters, not even a stewardess to look after the comfort of the female portion of the passengers. The provisions, too, were severely plain, the principal item being Indian (or yellow) meal, which was served out in the raw state to the emigrants themselves twice a week. The daily allowance of this food they used to carry to the galley and fetch away when cooked. The galley was located well forward on the main deck and a good distance from the booby hatch, the entrance to the 'tween decks.

"How often I have witnessed dozens of young girls saluted by a green wave as they tried to reach the galley that swept them off their feet, piled them in a heap on top of each other in the lee scuppers in a most helpless condition and washed the food which they were taking to have cooked into the sea to the delight of the seagulls, who would swoop down and carry it off.

"Drenched, discouraged, hungry and frightened, we used to come to their assistance, lift them out of the floating scuppers, soothe their fears, and after leading 'em down the companion ladder to their berths below, still the pangs of hunger by dividing with them our own hard but scanty fare, which consisted of bread skouse that was sometimes seasoned with too much salt water and a black wash called coffee, sweetened with treacle that tasted like a mixture of salts and senna.

"I have many times seen the poor creatures, when the ship was pitching, lose hold of the man-rope while trying to reach the steerage with cooked food, tumble down and lay prostrate at the foot of the ladder, with their yellow meal stirabout scattered around the decks and on their clothes.

"There is no comparison between the steerage of the ocean liners of to-day and the 'tween decks of the time of which I write. Those early day emigrants endured sufferings and hardships while crossing the Atlantic which only themselves can ever know. Both owners and captains were careless of their comforts, and I who saw the trials and the troubles of their every day life on board considered them the most miserable of wretches.

"Many times I went hungry, having shared with the girls that I knew were in want my last bite, and yet they appeared to be more courageous than the men, and despite their femininity made better sailors, for when the day broke and the Yankee pilot, who had just boarded us, gave the order to 'fill away the main topsail,' thirty or more of them who heard of his coming were about, and grabbing hold of the frosty braces rushed along the snow-covered deck singing:

> 'Hurrah, my boys, for Paddy's land,
> 'Tis the land that we adore;
> May the heav'ns smile on every child
> That left the Shamrock shore.'

"It took us six weeks to make the passage, and when we anchored off Castle Garden our passengers, now in groups, some dancing, more singing, had forgotten all about the long journey and their sufferings vanished as if it were but a dream."

Packet ships in model of hull were not like the slim, sharp racers, the clippers, that succeeded them. On the contrary, they were a modification of the big-bodied, heavy-displacement frigates that had been so much in the public mind in the preceding years of warfare. Packets were practically frigate-shaped ships fitted up for mercantile use after the War of 1812 was ended. In fact, some of them had been frigates and had seen service as such. They were deep, beamy and high-sided, their rails high above the water even when loaded; and they were as square and bluff of bows on deck as a canal-boat. Below water they were beautifully modeled. The *Isaac Webb* made the run from New York to Liverpool repeatedly in sixteen or seventeen days, whereas the early ships of this Line, the little four hundred tonners, required on an average of twenty-three days for the voyage across. Coming back to New York, sailing westward, the winds and currents were against them and the passages generally were much longer. Under favorable circumstances, during the winter months, the west-bound trip was made in twenty-four to thirty days, although there were instances when a ship was over fifty days in crossing.

Quick passage in those packets were only made by carrying on sail and driving and as they were ships with big, single topsails it took a tough and hardy lot of men to stand the hard work and the exposure necessitated by the continual reefing and sail-handling. They carried a full set of studding sails and carried them often until they blew away, for speed was what advertised a line of packets more than anything else and brought the cream of the trans-Atlantic traveler's patronage. A packet ship's captain had to be not only a fearless and skilful skipper but also a congenial host who could be a jolly good fellow at the head of the table during meal times and yet uphold the dignity of his position and command the respect of all in his ship.

The mates were the men on whose shoulders all the hard work fell. By untiring energy, quick initiativeness and ready fists, they made the tough gatherings of humanity, that formed a packet's crew, jump at the word of command and put the ship through every necessary evolution with a promptness that rivalled a man-of-war. A packet's crew consisted of the captain and three mates, the chief or first mate upholding the dignity of the quarterdeck while the second and third mates were the real man-handlers who drove the crew and worked with them; then came the carpenter, a steward, two cooks, one for the crew and one for the cabin, a cabin boy and about twenty sailors. This was actually the crew of the packet ship *St. Denis*, of one thousand tons burden, when she sailed on her last voyage January 4, 1856. She was dismasted and sunk two days later during a severe hurricane. The first and third mates and nine of her crew, taking to a small boat, were picked up twenty-nine hours later by the ship *Naples*, Capt. Lowell, of Leghorn, and brought to shore. The captain, Alonzo Follansbee, thirteen passengers, and the rest of the crew refused to leave the ship and went down with her when she sank at noontime.

One can imagine the daring with which American seamen handled their packet ships at the close of several years of warfare on the high seas. Their captains, bred and trained to life aboard frigates, exacted a discipline that was as rigid as iron; yet it was necessary in order to drive the ships and make the fast passages that made American packets famous the seas around.

The captain of the slow-going merchant ship could clew up his royals as a precautionary measure when nightfall came, but on a packet, with mail aboard and high-priced freight and often with distinguished persons registered on the passenger list, the captain and officers carried sail, night and day, to uphold the honor of the house flag they sailed under, and to win a reputation for speed.

These packet ships carried a full set of studding sails, not in the sail locker, but up aloft on bending yards and booms, and many times they carried them until booms began to break and they had to be hauled down to save the spars. It was a race against time, night and day, winter and summer, and under the hardest of conditions, from a sailor's point of view. The run was so short that the gang forward could only get well broken in and accustomed to working together when the trip ended and then it all had to be done over again with new hands. No self-respecting, deep-water sailorman would put up long with such conditions. The best sailors shipped on vessels that cleared for a year or two-years' voyage that took the ship out to the Far East where the men had time to grow accustomed to each other. When sail was carried with caution and freights were not perishable stuff there was no great hurry in delivery, and such ships became homes to sailormen.

The packet ship crews were recruited from the riff-raff of the waterfront dives. They were herded aboard, more or less drunk, by the unscrupulous boarding-house runners. Raw greenhorns were marched around a cow's horn in a dive kept by one Paddy Doyle, who then vouched for the men as seamen who had been around the Horn.

There were many tough characters in such a crew and they were a class of men that were appropriately termed "packet rats." Living in poverty, as a rule, they were as unscrupulous as they were untidy. Such men, half clad, with ragged clothes and few of them, would lay aloft on a freezing winter night when the wind cut to the very bone, their shirt and jacket minus buttons and held together by a peg of wood, a "Liverpool button," thrust as a toggle through the cloth that could be pulled through the buttonhole. Their shoes, worn out when they salvaged them from some ash can, would be razeed, or cut down, to low shoes — pumps — so that only two or three lace holes remained and these were tied up with rope yarns. There was no time on shipboard, to stop and lace up shoes, when the mate banged on the forecastle door with a belaying pin and bawled out — "All hands reef topsails!" A sailor then had to stick his feet into his pumps, grab his hat and coat and run, pulling on the latter as he went, and if he wasn't going fast enough to suit the mate he was expedited by the toe of the latter's boot. Mittens or any kind of protection on the hands were absolutely tabooed at sea. Bare hands, at all times, were a necessity, both for efficiency in pulling with all one's "beef" on a rope as well as a matter of safety; for often a tight grip on a rope meant life or death to a man aloft —a slight slip would mean man overboard and drowning.

Many famous old sea songs, "shanties," as they are called, such as "Whisky Johnny," "Blow Boys Blow," "The Black Ball Line," "Blow the Man Down," "Leave Her Johnnie, Leave Her," etc., originated aboard these famous Liverpool packets. On a man-of-war no such wild hilarity would be countenanced and there were men enough aboard to furnish abundance of power for hoisting sail; but on a merchant ship, with smaller crew, the only way of getting united action from an untrained gang of mixed sailors and hoodlums was by singing these ribald chanteys to the swing and tune of which a gang of men could all sway in unison on a rope.

Without a chantey it was like trying to dance without music. But let some little Cockney pipe up:

> "Oh! whisky is the life of man,
>   Whisky! Johnny!
> Oh! I'll drink whisky while I can,
>   Whisky! for my Johnny."

And the gang, catching the tune, would be ready to join him when he came to the next chorus. His shrill voice would pipe out the words of the song, "Oh! whisky makes me wear old clothes" and while he was singing, the gang, lined up along on the halliard lean forward, would get a fresh grip on the rope, all stiffening for the pull and join in drawling at the top of their lungs "Whisky!" At the word "John-ny!" which is emphasized as a signal, all hands would heave with all their strength and this united effort would send a topsail yard up the mast.

It is a tough game—seagoing. I know! I've been there! I've pulled my heart out on a topsail halliard all in vain, until the second mate, seeing that it was useless with the short-handed crew we had, started a chantey and got the gang swaying in unison until goaded to superhuman effort, then and not till then, did we masthead that heavy topsail-yard.

It is the swaying—the swing to the tune, that does the work, with any short signal word such as "Yo-o-o-o-o-o-Ho!" The "Yo'o" being long drawled out just as the word "Whisky" is drawled "Whiske-e-e-e-e," until the moment of action arrives and the "Ho!" short and sharp, is shouted just as in the other chantey the word "John-ny" is snapped out sharp.

The words of each line of the song are made up by the chanteyman with no sense whatever, so long as the last word of each couplet harmonizes.

THE PACKET SHIP "ISAAC WEBB"

Solo by chanteyman: "Oh the cook he's mixing up his bread!
Chorus of all hands: Yo-o-o-o-o-ho, heave the man *down!*
Solo by chanteyman: An when you eat it yo'll drop dead!
Chorus of all hands: Yo-o-o-o-o-ho, heave the man *down.*"

The words *bread* and *dead* complete that stanza and then the next two lines are composed. Maybe the chanteyman, in a hasty glance aft, sees the captain and mate getting ready with their sextants to shoot the sun, as taking the noon observation is termed. This would give the quick-witted songster an idea and he would pipe up:

"Oh, the old man's a-going for to shoot the sun.
All hands: Yo-o-o-o-ho, heave the man down.
       Ay' this here old topsail it must weigh a ton.
All hands: Yo-o-o-o-ho, heave the man down."

It was only by a liberal use of these chanteys that the mixed crews on the Western Ocean packet ever did the hard work they were put to. There were chanteys to enliven their souls and brass knuckles and belaying pins to hasten their bodies.

A landsman can't realize how near one can come to being worked actually to death as a sailor is when a ship starts out for sea. There's a thousand and one things to be done in a short space of time — to clear up the ship's deck and be ready for sea. All the dunnage accumulated about the decks during the period the ship lay alongside the dock, loading, has to be disposed of somewhere; coal, potatoes, fresh vegetables, crates of live stock, hawsers, fenders, ladders and so on. Anchors to be hove up on the forecastle head and lashed, cables unbent and hauled in through the hawser holes and the latter plugged, besides all the sails to be hoisted and sheeted home; cargo tackles stowed away, fish tackle falls to be taken down and stowed, etc. It is no wonder sailors got drunk just before sailing time. If they could stand on their pins and work they were so exhilarated by the whisky they didn't realize what they were doing. If it put them down and out they were unconscious and by the time they came to, the hard work had been done by others. Their drunken carcasses may have been kicked by angry mates, who didn't kick so hard as to stave in a man's ribs for that would only make the crew short-handed. But more than one man has received a kick in the face that disfigured his nose. That only marred his beauty and left him a workable animal that the mates could make use of in handling the ship.

Many a deep-water ship has started for sea and had to let go her anchors out in the bay and wait overnight until the next day to let some of the crew sober up so the ship could be worked. Not so on a "Black Ball Liner." They sailed from New York on the first and the sixteenth of each month

73

and sail they did. Their mates used such forcible persuasion that even the green crews performed the necessary work. Naturally when these men got ashore they told all their friends how badly they had been used and their stories lost nothing in the re-telling until the bucko Yankee mates and captains were rated as first-class demons. Many a landsman who crossed the Atlantic on a packet ship as an able seaman, would, under the most lenient officers, consider the work of sail-handling and trimming as a brutal, hard, man-killing job, and so describe it. That is why the packet ships received such a black name.

Those who were sailors and trained to the hard life, thought nothing of such trips and stayed in the service. They were the "packet rats," as hard and tough a crew as could be found in any quarter of the globe. Occasionally, whether by accident or design we know not, the whole crew would be made up of such men. It was such a crowd that endeavored to kill Capt. Samuel Samuels and his mates on the *Dreadnaught* in August, 1859, but with revolvers the mutineers were subdued and put under hatches for several days during which the officers worked the ship. When the mutineers were released, they were kept under close surveillance until the ship reached Liverpool. One can readily understand that life from day to day was not one round of pleasure for the officers of these packets.

The fare for first-class cabin passengers was $150 (£31) while the steerage fare varied from $25 (£5) to $40 (£8). Cabin passengers lived in staterooms opening into the cuddy or main saloon, which was built under the raised poop deck. A long, narrow, dining table, with benches either side, extended aft from the mizzenmast nearly to the stern where a library and lounge was built across the after end of the ship. A small room on either quarter served as a toilet and (bucket) bath room.

A ladies' parlor was partitioned off forward of the main cuddy and pantry and the stewards' and mates' rooms occupied the rest of the space covered by the poop deck. These after quarters were very handsomely paneled and decorated with mahogany, rosewood, satinwood and gilded carvings made of *papier mache*.

The steerage passengers slept in stall-like partitions in the 'tween decks and were packed in like sheep, being allowed on deck only in fair weather. When bad weather came, the hatches were put on and they were sealed below deck in a close, unventilated space.

Some idea of the way the cabin fared in the matter of food, is given in a record left of a dinner aboard the packet ship *Cornelius Grinnell*, while on her passage from New York to London, in 1858. The menu was as follows: soup, boiled cod with boiled potatoes, roast turkey, mashed turnips,

SOUTH STREET, NEW YORK CITY, IN 1880

CLIPPER PACKET SHIP "RACER" OF NEW YORK

From a wood engraving in "The Illustrated London News," Oct. 18, 1851

Model of United States Frigate "Raleigh," 1776

Made by Charles G. Davis

Model of United States Frigate "Raleigh," 1776

Made by Charles G. Davis

roast and boiled potatoes, stewed chicken with macaroni, pie, hot rolls, sea pies, pickles and plum pudding. The steerage passengers had to do their own cooking in a separate galley provided for them in the forward end of the deck-house, just abaft the foremast.

Each adult received weekly the following food, its disposition being entirely with themselves, viz.: 3½ pounds of bread or biscuit, 1 pound of flour, 1½ pounds of oatmeal, 1½ pounds of rice, 1½ pounds of peas, 1¼ pounds of beef, 1 pound of pork, 2 pounds of potatoes, 2 ounces of tea, 1 pound of sugar, ½ ounce of mustard, ¼ ounce of ground black pepper, 2 ounces of salt and 1 gill of vinegar.

Before steerage passengers were allowed on board each had to show that he or she had the necessary outfit with which to eat and cook their fare. These outfits could be purchased from waterfront chandlers near at hand, who also had sea-boots, oilers, sou'-westers, clothing, blankets, tin pots, pannikens and spoons and the straw mattresses (donkey's breakfasts they were nicknamed) for outfitting the sailors at prices by which they made a very neat profit as the purchasing of these supplies were only too often deferred to the last minute and there was no time for argument about the price so the victims had to pay what was asked.

THE BLACK BALL LINE

Amity, Capt. Pease, 400 tons, 18 feet draft; wrecked on Long Island.

Courier, 380 tons, length 116 feet, beam 27 feet, depth 16 feet 10 inches.

Pacific, 400 tons, built by Brown & Bell, in 1821, length 112 feet, beam 28 feet, depth 14 feet.

James Monroe, 420 tons, length 130 feet, beam 30 feet, depth 15 feet.

William Thompson.

James Cropper.

Orbit, built by Brown & Bell.

Nestor, wrecked on Long Island.

Albion, 360 tons, wrecked on Old Head of Kinsale Island.

Canada, Capt. Williams, 400 tons, built by Brown & Bell.

Oxford, 750 tons, built in 1836, length 180 feet, beam 36 feet 6 inches, depth 22 feet, draft 15 feet, wrecked in a hurricane, Jan. 6, 1839, at Liverpool.

Cambridge.

Burgundy.

Columbia, 1099 tons, built by William H. Webb, in 1846, length 169 feet, beam 37 feet, depth 21 feet.

Britannia, built by Brown & Bell.

New York, 860 tons, built in 1842.

Montezuma, 1070 tons, built by William H. Webb, in 1843.

Yorkshire, 1150 tons, built by William H. Webb.

Isaac Wright, built by William H. Webb.

Isaac Webb, 1800 tons, built by William H. Webb, in 1850, length 188 feet, beam 40 feet, depth 27 feet 3 inches, draft 22 feet.

CHAPTER V

THE FRIGATE "RALEIGH"

FRIGATES, in the language of the prize fighting ring, were middle-weights. The navy's heavyweight fighters were the cumbersome, high-sided, three-decked, line-of-battle ships, or ships-of-the-line, which, like floating forts, bore the brunt of the battle. They formed in line, single file, and sailing alongside the enemy's ships hammered them with shot. On the leading ship, the admiral's flagship, were hoisted the signal flags directing the rest of the fleet like a column of soldiers. Fighting ships strictly followed certain rules just as boxers fight according to a code. Frigates, however, were ships that operated single-handed and maneuvred and fought according to circumstances. They were originally used as fast-sailing, armed, dispatch boats to do scout duty and to attend, as handmaidens, on the portly ships-of-the-line. As fast sailers they became so useful that in later years they were improved upon and developed into real fighting ships.

All European countries formerly estimated the strength of their navies mainly on the number of their line-of-battle-ships, but in 1776, when America went to war with England, instead of trying to create a fleet of large ships, those in charge of naval affairs in the United Colonies, wisely built frigates. These could be built quickly and just how quickly is shown in the case of the frigate *Raleigh*, which was completed at Portsmouth, N. H., in sixty days. They also could do more damage to the enemy's commerce and at the same time be sufficiently strong in their armament to cope with the many English frigates that infested our coast at that time.

Congress ordered thirteen frigates to be built for its first navy and while they were being constructed, such merchant ships as were available, were armed and refitted at Philadelphia for fighting purposes. A fleet of vessels ranging from a 440-ton ship to a tiny sloop were accordingly sent to sea and succeeded in capturing some British merchantmen.

Five of the new frigates were 32-gun ships; five carried 28 guns and three 24 guns. Who designed these first ships it is now well-nigh impossible to determine; but from old records it would seem as if certain men in the ports where the ships were to be built, were called upon to submit designs for approval to the members of the naval committee appointed October 13, 1775, by Congress.

Sylvester Bowers who built the 32-gun frigate *Warren* and the 28-gun frigate *Providence*, at Providence, R. I., was ordered by this committee to "make a draught of the larger ship as soon as may be."

Joshua Humphreys no doubt designed the frigates *Washington*, 32 guns; *Randolph*, 32 guns; *Effingham*, 28 guns; and *Delaware*, 24 guns; which were built at Philadelphia, and at Portsmouth, N. H. James H. Hackett was undoubtedly the man who designed the *Raleigh*, 32 guns. The *Hancock*, 32 guns, was also probably of his design though built by Stephen and Ralph Cross, at Newbury, Mass. The slight variation in the dimensions of the various ships, information based upon such data as have been preserved, would seem to indicate this. England captured two of each of these larger vessels and took them into her navy and in so doing preserved the record of their dimensions, as follows:

	Length on gun deck	Length keel	Beam	Depth	Tonnage	Guns
Hancock	137' 1"	116' 6"	34' 3¾"	10' 11"	730	32
Raleigh	131' 5"	110' 7¼"	34' 5"	11' 0"	697	32
Providence	126' 6½"	104' 10¾"	33' 8"	10' 5"	632	28
Virginia	132' 6"	108' 0"	34' 7"	10' 7"	712	28
Delaware	117' 9½"	98' ¼"	32' 10½"	9' 8½"	563	24
Boston	114' 3"	94' 3½"	32' 0"	10' 3"	514	24

But what is of far more interest to Americans of this generation is the fact that the English naval authorities, who had been impressed by reports of the speed and handsome appearance of the American frigates made by British naval officers who had seen them in action on the American coast, after the capture of the frigate *Raleigh* had her put into dry dock at Portsmouth, England, in 1779, and a copy made of her model showing her lines or plans. These plans are here reproduced, showing exactly what kind of craft our first frigates were. They bear out the assertions often made by writers in the past that our vessels were largely copied from the French ships. If they were, it is a compliment to the judgment of the American commissioners, for France was then the leader in the development of naval ships and England studied and copied the ships they captured from the French.

James H. Hackett of Salisbury, Mass., was called to Portsmouth, N. H., to build ships for the Government and was not only associated with the construction of the *Raleigh* in 1776, but also with the *Ranger*, 18 guns, and the *Alliance*, 32 guns, built in 1777. In 1782 he designed the 74-gun line-of-battle ship *America*, the ship that was presented to France, in token of our appreciation of her coming to our aid, to replace one of her ships, the *Magnifique*, 74 guns, that was wrecked on a reef in Boston harbor. In 1794 Mr. Hackett was called to Philadelphia to consult with the Naval Committee on the construction of some new frigates, and in 1797 and 1799 he built the *Crescent*, 36 guns, the *Congress*, 36 guns, and designed the *Essex*, 32 guns, that was built at Salem, Mass., by Enos Briggs.

Our frigates of the Revolution were quite similar to the ships then in use in the British navy that rated as fifth- and sixth-rate ships-of-war. Fifth-rate British ships included those carrying 44 guns to 32 guns, while sixth-rate ships carried from 28 to 20 guns. The largest of the fifth-rates had two decks, the lower battery being of 18 pounders, and the upper deck battery 9 pounders.

Such a craft was the frigate *Phoenix*, 44 guns, length, 140 feet 9 inches on her gun deck; 116 feet 11 inches keel; 37 feet 1⅜ inches beam; 16 feet depth of hold and 856 tons burden.

The 36- and 32-gun ships had only one complete deck of guns, 12 pounders, with 6 pounders on their quarterdeck and forecastle head. The *Venus* was a fifth-rate of 36 guns; 128 feet 4½ inches length on gun deck; 106 feet 3 inches keel; 35 feet 9 inch beam; 12 feet 4 inches depth; and 722 tons burden.

The American frigate *Raleigh*, of 36 guns, measured 131 feet 5 inches length on gundeck; 110 feet 7¼ inches keel; 34 feet 5 inches beam; 11 feet depth, and 696 86/94 tons burden. The 44-gun frigates carried a complement of 280 men while the 36-gun frigates carried 240 men.

Frigates of the sixth-rate carried 9 pounders; those of 28 guns having 3 pounders on their quarterdecks and had 200 men, while those of 24 guns, carried 160 men. The *Carysfort*, a 28-gun frigate, was 118 feet 4 inches on her gundeck; 97 feet 3½ inches keel; 33 feet 8 inches beam; 10 feet 6 inches depth and of 586 tons burden. The *Dolphin*, a 24-gun frigate, was 113 feet on her gundeck; 93 feet 4 inches keel; 32 feet 1 inch beam; 11 feet depth and 511 tons burden. The American 24-gun frigate *Boston*, was 114 feet 3 inches on her gundeck; 94 feet 3½ inches keel; 32 feet beam; 10 feet 3 inches depth, and 514 tons burden. These vessels were all very similar except that the American ships were shoaler-bodied boats.

The outstanding feature wherein American frigates differed from the British vessels was in their lighter draught, their depth of hold being eleven feet while the Englishmen were twelve to thirteen feet and over in depth. The British ships were also slightly beamier.

The dimensions of some of the British frigates are given here for purposes of comparison:

	Length on gun deck	Length on keel	Beam	Depth	Tonnage	Guns
Solebay	129′ 0″	119′ 2″	35′ 4″	12′ 7″	710	28
Flora	140′ 8″	113′ 1″	38′ 0″	13′ 3″	868	32
Hague	129′ 0″	117′ 0″	34′ 9″	12′ 0″	663	32
Cleopatra	126′ 0″	104′ 0″	35′ 6″	12′ 2″	673	32
Thisbe	124′ 0″	99′ 6″	33′ 6″	11′ 0″	594	28
Glasgow	109′ 4″	91′ 2½″	30′ 6″	9′ 7½″	451	24

These are some of the ships that were stationed off the American coast operating against the Colonists during the Revolution.

The American ships, built of newly-cut wood and planked with yellow pine, were very much lighter in weight than the famous "walls of oak" — water-cured, too — oak that had lain for years under water in British dock-yards to season, as all British ships were built; and in consequence the American vessels were much faster craft under sail. They had as much stability to carry their canvas as the British ships and had tons less of water to push aside in getting through it as they forged ahead, so it is no wonder that the enemy referred to them as the beautiful and fast new frigates. They were built by men who had been born of seafaring people, who knew ships as a farmer knows horses and who could build a ship as well as sail her to the four quarters of the globe, men who, if wrecked in some far away land, could build a smaller vessel out of the wreck of the larger one and come home in her. When it became a matter of life and death, as in a battle on the high seas, is it any wonder that such men should resort to every expedient they could think of to make their ships better than those of their enemies?

Twenty years later, Joshua Humphreys wrote to Robert Morris, saying: "the ships should have scantling equal to a seventy-four and I believe may be built of red cedar and live oak for about twenty-four pounds per ton, carpenter's tonnage . . . beams to be of Carolina pine," etc. He was referring, of course, to the later frigates, the *Constitution, President, United States,* etc., that were so to be built.

Men like James H. Hackett were equally conversant with the various kinds of timber available for ship construction and it was the use of such light, strong timber, that made the first frigates of the American Navy such useful ships. They were, in model, the conventional type of that day — the old round ships, as they were termed, the bulk of their frames being laid out with a pair of compasses set to varying lengths of sweeps.

Compasses for sweeping circles, played an important part in the designing of old ships, but to thoroughly explain their utility requires a volume in itself. The reader who cares to study the formation of the shapes of these old vessels, should consult a book on shipbuilding, written by a man who worked in British shipyards all his life. Mungo Murray was his name and in his work, published in 1765, he explains the use of the shipbuilder's sector and he also gives an abridged copy of M. Duhamel du Monceau's treatise on shipbuilding which describes in great detail how the shapes of these old round ships were delineated. Sev-

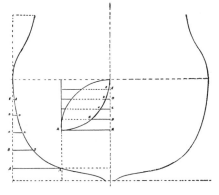

eral different shapes of midship-sections are projected, all so nearly inscribed within a circle that only an expert would note the difference and all drawn with arcs of a circle.

Deep ships, so called, were made slightly elliptical in their bottom timbers, but the topsides, above water, were all very similar. To show how these designers contemplated a ship we will here quote briefly from Murray. He writes: "We come now to consider the upper works or all that is above water, called

FIG. 24. FULL BUILT SHIP

the dead-works. And here the ship must be narrower, so that all the weight that lies above the load-water line will thereby be brought nearer the middle of the ship; by which means she will strain less by working the guns, and the main sail will be easier trimmed when the shrouds do not spread so much."

Other reasons were that when two ships came together, yard-arm to yard-arm, their fighting men could not jump from one ship to the other; they could

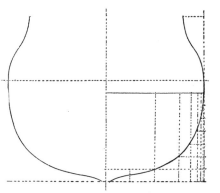

FIG. 25. VERY FULL SHIP

not "board" so easily and the round side received less impulse from the waves which tended to make the ship roll less and her decks in consequence would be a steadier platform to shoot from.

You may rest assured there were very good reasons for the old ships being modeled as they were and under similar circumstances, no doubt, those same ships would again be found superior to any other shape — but the point is that circumstances have changed. The development of larger and more powerful cannon was the principal cause of the change in ship models. To make effective the shot fired by the old 9 and 12 pounders, they formerly had to come so close, that it invariably terminated in one ship laying the other ship aboard and boarding parties then settled the dispute in a hand-to-hand conflict, with boarding pike and cutlass. Guns and pistols were good for one discharge only, as there was no time to reload the old "pepper pots" when boarding a ship and after the first discharge they were hove either overboard or in the faces of the opposing sailors.

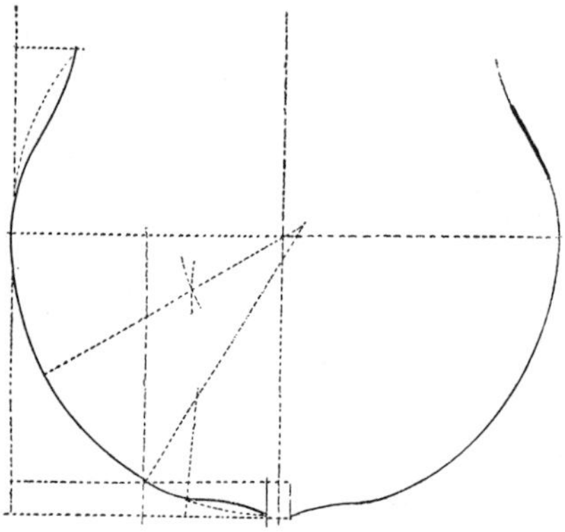

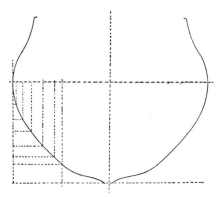

FIG. 26. CIRCULAR FLOOR SHIP

In the days of the *Raleigh* (1777-1779), there were no 18-pound frigates in the American Navy, but when the *Constitution* and her sister ships were built, in 1796, they were armed with 32-pound and 28-pound cannon. The weight referred to in speaking of cannon is not the cannon itself, but the weight of the cannon ball it thew. This rapid increase in the size of the cannon resulted in the ships staying farther apart and fighting at longer range, yet, for years, the call of "Boardaway" and "Boarders repel boarders," echoed above the din of battle as the engagements were ended in desperate hand-to-hand contests on deck. It was not until the late frigates of the Civil War that this excessive "tumble home" or rounding in to the topsides of ships was dispensed with.

FIG. 27. VERY SHARP SHIP

Recognizing the efficiency of frigates as fighting ships, due to their handy size and fast-sailing ability, when called upon, in 1793, by the Naval Board to design some new ships for the United States Navy, Josiah Humphreys recommended for the larger class of ships-of-the-line, heavily armed vessels built with much heavier timber than was usual at that time. To razee a ship is to take off one of her decks, to reduce her height out of water, and that is what the new frigates were equivalent to — a 74-gun ship cut down to a frigate of 44 guns.

So successful were these American 44-gun frigates, when pitted against the British ships, that the Englishman razeed several of their cumbersome, high-sided, 74-gun line-of-battle ships and made them into heavy frigates. The *Akbar*, a teak-built Indiaman, purchased in 1801 by the Admiralty for

Model of United States Frigate "Raleigh," 1776
Made by Charles G. Davis

Model of United States Frigate "Raleigh," 1776
Made by Charles G. Davis

Drying Hammocks on a United States Frigate

From an engraving by Baugean

a navy ship, was cut down to a 60-gun frigate, which, in later days, became known as the *Cornwallis*.

The old frigate *Constitution*, now (1929) being rebuilt at Boston, and over one hundred and thirty years old, and also the *Constellation*, a ship even older than the *Constitution*, bear testimony to how well these ships performed their mission.

The *Raleigh* and her sister ships were more lightly built as the small 9- and 12-pound cannon did not require such heavy construction as did the 32-pounders. Their displacement, or total weight, was only 696 86/94 tons as against 1576 tons for the *Constitution* — less than half — but while they then rated as frigates they were not much larger than the sloops-of-war of 1812 — 18- and 20-gun ships. The *Erie*, built at Washington, D. C., was 509 tons burden and she was the smallest. Most of the sloops-of-war of 1813 were 700 ton ships, of the *Vincennes* class.

The *Raleigh's* plans are most complete; every essential part is shown. The shape is clearly delineated by the three diagonals, the five waterlines or swimming lines, as the old timers sometimes called them, and by the sixteen vertical transverse sections. The midship or largest section being only 52 feet aft of the forward perpendicular. So 39½ per cent. of her length is bow and 60½ per cent. is stern. A typical cod-head and mackerel-tail model. Not only is the detail of the outside of the ship with the figurehead and stern ornamentations clearly shown, but each deck with its beams, hatchways and ladders are all traced in so that one could reproduce the ship in all its details.

There was only four feet of headroom under the maindeck beams, huge timbers, fourteen inches by eighteen inches, but that was quite common practice, as shot and ammunition had to be passed up to the men on deck. Even on the old 74-gun ship *Vermont*, I can remember this headroom was so low that it necessitated our crouching low and running crab-fashion when we were going through drills, gun practice, and executing orders such as "boarders on the starboard bow." Certain men from each gun would scurry away to that part of the ship and one or two bumps on the head against those beams and one would soon remember to run crouched over with head lowered. The upper deck of the *Raleigh*, where the guns were handled, had all the universe for headroom, except for a few guns forward and aft under the forecastle-head and poop.

The mast steps, the tiller, capstans, mooring bitts and pumps are all shown on the plans. The steering wheel, a double one, is shown aft and forward the ship's bell and galley range is indicated. The position of the masts and bowsprit with their angles of rake or steeve is shown. Both the foremast and the mainmast are stepped so they stand square with the keel, but as the ship sets sixteen inches by the stern, the keel being that much lower at the stern post than it is at the stem, below the upper waterline, it gives these masts just a slight rake aft. The mizzenmast is shown with a more decided rake — ½ inch to the foot from a vertical line.

Ship's masts always slanted or raked aft as they went up from the deck and each one, fan-like, spread apart from its neighbor at the top. Nothing looks so unshipshape and unseamanlike as to see the royalmast pulled closer to the adjoining mast at the top. Many model builders make this error. The rake of a mast is something often changed by the men of the ship to improve her sailing qualities after she has been fitted out by the mechanics at the navy yard. Sometimes the fore and aft trim of the ship would be changed for the same reason.

The 44-gun frigate *St. Lawrence*, did not carry her canvas satisfactorily to her commander in 1849 and the next year, Captain Paulding took on board at Bremen Haven, forty-four additional tons of ballast, which he subsequently reported had not only improved the ship's stability, but her sailing qualities as well. The 20-gun sloop-of-war *Jamestown*, that took a cargo of food to Ireland during the famine in 1848, had her masts upright, they having previously raked aft and in consequence she pitched violently and was recommended to be altered again. The log books of all the old frigates show numerous changes were made, both in trim and spars. When John Paul Jones took the *Ranger* to France in 1777, she had been hurriedly fitted out with a set of spars that had been made for a 400-ton Indiaman and when he arrived at Nantes, on December 11, 1777, he had all three masts shortened and their rigging set up anew, so it was not until February 12, 1778, that the *Ranger* was ready to go to sea and create havoc among British shipping around Ireland.

We have no authentic plans of the *Raleigh's* spars. They were evidently not considered important enough to require plans. Probably being rigged according to the then well-established rules of the time, she could easily be resparred by observing those rules. The lengths of spars on warships were more certain to be standardized than those on merchant ships, owing to the frequency with which they had to be replaced after an engagement. The ships themselves carried spare spars and all the dockyards kept a stock of them on hand.

There were certain characteristics by which sailors could recognize the nationality of a sailing ship almost as far as they could see her. The French vessels had shorter yards which gave a high-narrow, appearance to the sails on each mast. The Swedes generally had very short lower masts and fairly long yards, which gave a more squatty look. Such nationalities as the Swedes, Danes and Hollanders were referred to by seamen under the one general term of "Dutchmen." As one writer ably expresses it: "There was a great look of the Dutchman or Souwegian about these ships, distinguishable by short lower masts and unusually square yards." By square yards was meant long yards which gave a more square-block appearance to the sails on a ship's mast than the narrow look of one with shorter yards.

With the English in New England, the Dutch about New York, and the Swedes in the Delaware, America, in 1776, had a variety of rigs on its vessels that would be difficult to standardize; but as we know James H. Hackett designed the *Essex* and also built the *Raleigh*, it is a fair assumption to suppose there might have been a similarity in rig between the two and fortunately the size of the spars on the *Essex* has been preserved in Enos Briggs' own handwriting. He was the master-shipbuilder who produced her and as there was no great difference in the size of the two ships, the same spars would do for both, if reduced in proportion to this difference in size.

Here is a comparison of dimensions:

	Essex (1799)	*Raleigh* (1776)	*Constitution* (1797)
Length on gun deck	141′ 0″	131′ 5″	174′ 10½″
Length on keel	118′ 0″	110′ 7¼″	145′ 0″
Beam	37′ 0″	34′ 5″	43′ 6″
Depth	12′ 3″	11′ 0″	14′ 3″
Tonnage	850	697	1576

The masts and yards were a ratio of the beam, and by using the beam of the ships to find the proportional size we obtain the following suit of spars, as a proper set for the *Raleigh*:

Spars	ESSEX Length	Dia.	Head	RALEIGH Length	Dia.	Head
Mainmast	85′ 0″	27″	12′ 0″	79′ 3″	24¼″	11′ 0″
Foremast	75′ 6″	26″	11′ 6″	70′ 5″	23½″	10′ 9″
Mizzenmast	71′ 6″	21″	10′ 0″	66′ 5″	19″	9′ 4″
Maintopmast	65′ 0″	18½″	7′ 6″	51′ 4″	16½″	7′ 0″
Foretopmast	51′ 0″	18¼″	7′ 0″	47′ 6″	16¼″	6′ 6″
Mizzentopmast	40′ 0″	14″	6′ 0″	34′ 7″	12½″	5′ 4″
Main-topgallant mast	25′ 0″	12″		23′ 4″	10¾″	
Fore-topgallant mast	23′ 0″	11½″		21′ 5″	10½″	
Mizzen-topgallant mast	21′ 0″	9½″		19′ 6″	8½″	
Main-royal mast	15′ 0″	7½″		14′ 0″	6¾″	
Fore-royal mast	14′ 0″	7″		13′ 0″	6½″	
Mizzen-royal mast	12′ 0″	6″		11′ 0″	5″½	
Bowsprit	54′ 0″	26″		50′ 4″	23½″	
Jibboom	40′ 0″	14″		37′ 9″	12½″	

Spare	Essex			Raleigh		
	Length	*Dia.*	*Hand*	*Length*	*Dia.*	*Hand*
Main yard	80' 0"	20"		74' 6"	18"	
Fore yard	72' 0"	19"		67' 0"	17¼"	
Mizzen yard	52' 0"	14"		48' 5"	12½"	
Main-topsail yard	58' 0"	14"		54' 0"	12½"	
Fore-topsail yard	52' 0"	13½"		48' 5"	12"	
Mizzen-topsail yard	40' 0"	10½"		37' 4"	9½"	
Main-topgallant yard	37' 0"	10"		34' 6"	9"	
Fore-topgallant yard	35' 0"	9½"		32' 7"	8⅞"	
Mizzen-topgallant yard	28' 0"	7½"		26' 1"	6¾"	
Main-royal yard	30' 0"	7"		28' 0"	6¼"	
Fore-royal yard	27' 0"	6"		25' 1"	5½"	
Mizzen-royal yard	20' 0"	5"		21' 4"	4½"	
Spanker boom	57' 0"	14"		53' 0"	12½"	
Spanker gaff	46' 0"	11"		42' 9"	10"	

The rules for sparring a ship, that were in vogue at the time the *Raleigh* was built, were as follows:

PROPORTIONS FOR THE MASTS AND BOWSPRIT

The mainmast, two and five-eights; or two and a half times the breadth of the ship.

The head of the mast, one-tenth of the length.

The diameter of the mainmast, three-fourths of an inch to every foot of breadth of the ship. The diameter at the top, two-thirds of that at the partners (or deck).

The foremast, two and a quarter times the breadth of the ship, and its diameter, one-fortieth of the length, or one-tenth to one-twelfth the breadth of the ship.

The mizzenmast, one and three-quarters the breadth of the ship, and its diameter at the partners, in inches, the 48th part of its length in feet.

The bowsprit, once and a half the breadth of the ship and its diameter at the bed (or inboard end), the 27th or 28th part of its length; and at the cap (or outer end), one-half that diameter.

The main-topmast was the same length as the bowsprit; and the diameter was about the 44th part of its length.

The fore-topmast, one and three-eighths the breadth of the ship, and the diameter, the 43rd or 44th part of its length.

The mizzen-topmast, half the length of the main-topmast; and its diameter, half the diameter of the main-topmast.

The main-topgallant mast, five-twelfths the length of the main-topmast, and half its diameter.

The fore-topgallant mast, four-sevenths the length of the fore-topmast and half its diameter.

PROPORTIONS FOR THE YARDS

The main-yard, in lengths, two and one-eighth of the breadth of the ship.

The diameter at the slings, in inches, two-thirds of the breadth of the ship in feet. The diameter at the yard arms to be one-third as large as at the slings (or mast).

The main-topsail yard, in length, one and one-quarter of the breadth of the ship. The diameter at the slings to be half that of the mainyard.

The main-topgallant yard, in length, three-quarters of the breadth of the ship. The diameter at the slings, half of that of the main-topsail-yard.

The fore-yard, in length, twice the breadth of the ship. The diameter at the slings to be five-eighths of an inch for each foot of breadth of the ship.

The fore-topsail yard, in length, to be one-sixth the breadth of the ship. Its diameter to be seven-fifteenths of that of the fore-yard.

The fore-topgallant yard, in length, to be two-thirds the breadth of the ship. Its diameter to be half that of the fore-topsail yard.

The sprit-sail yard, in length, one and a quarter times the breadth of the ship, and its diameter at the slings, half that of the mainyard.

The spritsail-topsail yard, in length, three-quarters of the breadth of the ship, and its diameter seven-sixteenths of that of the spritsail yard.

The mizzen-yard (lateen), in length, twice the breadth of the ship and its diameter in inches one-third of the breadth of the ship in feet.

The crossjacket yard, in length, the same as the fore-topsail yard.

The mizzen-yard, a relic of mediaeval times, was just being dispensed with about the time the *Raleigh* was built. British East Indiamen are shown carrying this long yard and lateen spanker, as late as 1788, by which time that part of the sail forward of the mizzenmast had been abolished, the after end of the yard only being used to extend this important after sail so useful in heading a ship up into or towards the wind.

In America, the gaff-rigged sail had been in use since 1713 when Capt. Andrew Robinson rigged his first schooner with them and gaff sails were much in use on American vessels by 1776. So it is more than likely the *Raleigh* had a gaff-spanker or driver, which is the older term for it, brailing in to the mast and gaff and sheeted out to a boom, loose footed.

For some years after the adoption of the short gaff, in place of the long lateen yard, British ships carried no boom but sheeted the spanker, the same as a lug sail, with tackles hooked to deck eyebolts in the stern instead of out on the end of a boom.

Paintings of old ships show that the ship *Tom*, of the year 1800, was rigged without a boom and also the brig *George*, of 1793. The brigantine *Peggy*, of 1788, however, was rigged with a boom. Evidently it was a matter of personal choice. But on a vessel of war, where the ability to maneuver smartly meant victory or defeat, there is little doubt but that the spanker of the *Raleigh* had a boom to haul it well out aft, and no doubt this spanker was a sail of good size to enable her to luff quickly; just as the spritsail was carried on those ships — that square sail under the bowspritsprit, that could be set and canted to the breeze to pay the ship's head off quickly. As a steering sail, also, this spritsail was valuable, as it lengthened the baseline of the sail-plan so that when one of those fullbodied little vessels plunged and ascended in fairly heavy seas, with a stiff quartering wind bowling her along under a heavy press of sail, it prevented her from yawing and greatly decreased the labor of the men at the steering wheel in holding her to a straight course.

The spritsail fell into disuse little by little, as the jibs or headsails were made large enough to take care of that end of the ship. The headsails consisted of the fore-topmast-staysail, jib, and flying jib; the first coming down from the topmast-head to the outer end of the bowsprit; the jib came from the same place aloft down to the end of the jib-boom; the flying-jib came from the top-gallant-mast-head down to the end of the flying-jib-boom; and on some ships, such as the old 74-gun, line-of-battle ship *Ohio*, there was still another — the jib-of-jib (pronounced "jib-o'-jib"), that came to the end of still another outrigged spar called the jib-o'-jib-boom.

In the merchant service, the same headrigging was carried until about the time double-topsails came into vogue, along in the 1850's, when the jib was subdivided into two sails called inner and outer jibs. Ships had increased in size to such an extent that one big jib was getting unmanageable with an ordinary ship's crew. Yet I have it from good authority, my own father-in-law, Capt. T. R. Webber, who went out to China in 1863 as a sailor on the Westervelt-built clipper ship *Contest*, Capt. Lucas, that this ship carried a spritsail under the bowsprit which went by the nickname of the "bull driver" and was anything but a favorite sail with the men, for it was a mean sail to furl when the ship got into any kind of a real sea. Yet in those days when speed meant everything to a sailing ship and all sorts of sails were improvised to catch every breath of air, and "save-alls" and "watersails" were hung out, this spritsail acted as a counterbalance to the "ring tail," on the after edge of the spanker, and in that way also was useful.

The little Continental frigates of 1776 were pitted against great odds, for Great Britain had dozens of ships to every one of them, and the signing of a treaty of peace on Sept. 23, 1783, came very opportunely. Not one of the original thirteen frigates built in 1775 and 1776 were left in the navy when peace was declared. All had been destroyed or captured by the British. The 28-gun frigate *Trumbull,* built at Chatham, Conn., was the last one to be lost. She was captured off the Delaware Capes on August 8, 1781, by the *Iris* which was the new name given to the *Hancock,* by the British, after they had captured her and taken her into their navy. In fact, there were only two frigates remaining in the American Navy at the close of the war — the 32-gun ships *Alliance* and *Hague.* From 1785 to 1797 there was no regular navy.

On March 27, 1794, an Act was passed by Congress providing for the construction of six frigates but it was not until April 27, 1798, that a Navy Department was created. Benjamin Stoddart was made Secretary of this important department, relieving the War Department that had heretofore carried on this work.

Joshua Humphreys was commissioned by the government to design these new ships and James H. Hackett, who, some twenty years previous had designed the frigates that fought during the Revolution, was called to Philadelphia, April 1, 1794, to give his advice. The ships Humphreys designed were the 44-gun frigates *Constitution, United States* and *President* and the 38-gun frigates *Constellation, Chesapeake* and *Congress.* The 44's were all built from the same plan and this was also true with the 38's; in fact, these two sets of plans seem to have been used for the construction of many succeeding frigates, until a modification was made in 1821, producing vessels known as the *Potomac*-class of frigates. The *Congress,* a 44-gun frigate, built at Portsmouth, N. H., 1839 to 1841, was the first to show any radical departure in model and that was principally in the shape of her floors, which, instead of sweeping down to the keel, in an arc of a circle, according to the old established rule, was practically a straight line, the two sides forming a shallow V due to the angle of deadrise, her topsides above water being very much the same as in previous frigates.

There was never a handsomer spectacle presented to the sight of man than that of a man-o'-war, under a cloud of canvas, sailing in a smart breeze. To see one of these ships standing into the roads for an anchorage, with everything set even to royals, and to hear the shrill cheeping of boatswain's whistles warbling like the notes of a far-away mocking bird, echoing over the water; and then, in a twinkling to see every sail disappear as if by magic — it is a magnificent spectacle. It is almost unbelievable how quickly a well-manned frigate can take in sail, but there were always men enough aboard of her, as the deepwater merchant sailors used to say, "to eat her."

A first class frigate carries a complement of 470 men, while a merchant ship of the same tonnage would be handled by twenty. The men are tolled off according to what was called a "station bill," each man or group of men to handle a certain rope just as each man on a football team is given a position, and according to this "bill" each man jumps to his allotted position for whatever manoeuvre the ship may be called upon to perform.*

Hoisting the topsail-yard was always the heaviest job on a square-rigger—and on merchant ships, when this halliard was taken off the pin and passed aft along the deck so that man after man, one behind the other, could

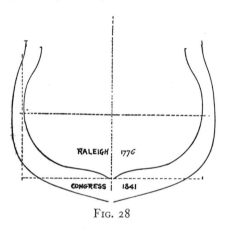

FIG. 28

get hold of it, and two or three more reach up and get a grip on the rope before it entered the leader-block hooked into an eyebolt down on the deck; on the "fore all," as this part was called, every one, even the cook, mates, captain and cabin boy, "tail on" to lend their bit and help in this heavy, pulling job.

But not so on a man-o'-war. There are more men stationed in each of the big, square tops than the whole crew of the merchant ship. The forecastle-head swarms with men and the deck is a mass of humanity that "tail on" to the topsail halliard. There are so many of them they don't have to bend their backs and strain their arm and leg muscles. They just "stomp and go!" They walk away with it, walking aft till the break of the poop stops them when they drop the rope. Other men behind them have taken hold so they return forward to get another grip on the rope in the line of men and so an endless stream of humanity walks the yard up the mast "two blocks," till the bosen's shrill whistle pipes up the signal to belay and the halliard is swung over to the rail and belayed.

By the way! That little operation of passing the turns around a belaying pin on a topsail halliard or sheet or tack, in fact, any rope that has a very heavy strain on it, is a most dangerous proceeding. Not so bad on a man-o'-war, where the strain is held by a large and sufficient gang of men, as it is on a merchant ship where the mate is frenzily urging the small crew to hurry to another job, for there's much to be done in a short time and few to do it. Sometimes the gang on the "fore all" will take it for granted that

* Totten's *Naval Text Book*, published by C. C. Little and J. Brown, Boston, 1841, gives nine tables with the watch-bill and station bills for each class of ship for various manoeuvres and shows in detail where each man was stationed about the ship (see pages 197 to 247).

the man behind them, who has to twist the stiff, wet, stubborn rope close around an iron belaying pin, has made fast and will let go before he calls out "All fast!" with the result that the rope tightens and sometimes catches his fingers, or the flesh of his fingers, in a grip like a vise and bites off a finger as clean as a surgeon could cut it. I never lost a finger, but I've come mighty near it, more than once. I've had a main brace tighten before the last turn was passed around the pin and bite a chunk of flesh out of my forefinger between the knuckle and first joint as if bitten out by a dog. While salt water is a good antiseptic for such a raw bite, it's a mighty painful one and makes a fellow set his teeth hard to withhold a cry of pain. But the sea and the ship keep a rough school and one can only grin and bear it. Sympathy is unknown. All one gets is "Hell, man! You're lucky you got your finger left!" Sometimes the mate will warn the gang, "Next time hold on till the man at the pin sings out 'All fast, sir!'" And you don't want to omit the sir, either, at sea.

It is easy enough to see how the small crew of a merchant ship can be accommodated on board. On "old timers" the crew's quarters were below the deck, up in the ship's bows, reached through a scuttle or companionway with a sliding hatch on top and a vertical iron ladder leading below. On the later, larger ships, the crew were housed in a deckhouse built just abaft the foremast. A fore-and-aft partition generally divided the first twelve or eighteen feet of this house into two rooms, one for each watch, and box-like stalls, two deep, were built around the four sides. There was a window and a door, the latter having a high sill to keep out deck water.

On a man-o'-war, like the *Raleigh*, for instance, with a crew of about two hundred and forty men, the housing problem was important. Only the officers enjoyed the privacy of a stateroom and even these were made with removable partitions so that all might be taken down when the ship was going into action so as to leave the deck free for the working of the ship's guns. The rank and file of the crew slept in hammocks swung from rows of hooks in the sides of the deck-beams on the berth decks, the deck below the gundeck. They were sandwiched in together, head and foot, like sardines packed in a box. In the daytime these hammocks were taken down and rolled up into a compact bundle with the blankets inside, each lashed with seven turns of hammock lashing and then stowed in the hammock nettings fitted on top of the ship's rail, there to act as a protecting bulwark against an enemy's small shot. A waterproof, painted canvas cover enclosed the hammocks and bedding and kept them dry as the flap on top folded over, inboard, and was laced down.

When a frigate started off on a long voyage, her decks would somewhat resemble a merchantship, for many of the upper guns would be dismantled and stowed away in the hold, and her maindeck, in the middle part or waist, would be packed with crates of chickens, ducks and geese, barrels and boxes of fresh vegetables to be stowed away, and pigs and even cows which were kept a while and then slaughtered to supply the crew with fresh meat. This mass of provender was taken care of by the men on deck, known as "waisters." The more experienced seamen, who were stationed in the tops or on the forecastle head, looked down upon the men on deck, with disdain, for they were the less experienced seamen, many of them raw recruits making their first voyage and doubtless many of them knew more about the care of cows and pigs than they did about the workings of the ship. The carpenter would build a shed for the cows and after the cables were stowed below and anchors secured, the porkers would be placed in the manger, up in the eyes of the ship, where the cables came in through the hawsepipes, a sort of breakwater scuppered to carry off the mud and water that came in on the cables, a natural pig sty. After the boats had been hoisted in and nested, with the spare spars lashed fore and aft close under them, they were stowed full of crates of chickens and other fowl, to get them up in the air so that water, slopping over the rail would not drown them.

An occasional meal of fresh meat was indeed a relish to men whose only food was salt beef and salt pork, so the nattiness of a man-o'-war's deck was willingly desecrated, for the time being, with such truck. On land, where farms abound, the crowing of a rooster is a common sound, but when heard at sea, under decidedly different surroundings, it is something that will live for years in one's memory. Doubtless it brings up thoughts of home and so makes a deeper impression.

The old sailing frigates were little floating principalities with all the various personalities from king to clown. The captain was "lord of all he surveyed," and the petty officers were his court, who adorned the quarterdeck. The "after guard," so styled by the crew, consisted of lieutenants, chaplain, master, purser, surgeon, professor of mathematics, clerk, midshipmen, lieutenant of marines, and so on, down through a long list of less favored subordinates, who respected the sanctity of the quarterdeck and kept themselves on the main deck. These were the boatswains, gunners, carpenter, sailmaker, cooper, yeomen, corporal, cook and what not, down through a list of a couple of hundred seamen, marines, landsmen, privates, to a drummer and a fifer.

Naturally the human needs of such a gathering of humanity demanded other artisans such as cobblers, tailors, barbers, etc., but these positions were acquired, not being positions of appointment by the captain, and often were found to be very lucrative. Every sailor was supposed to be his own tailor, cobbler, etc., failing in which he had to hire someone to do the work for him, which resulted in such artisans becoming attached to the ship and frequently they became bankers to whom the crew appealed for a loan when allowed shore leave.

The ship's cooper held a highly responsible position in those days when all the drinking water and grog was carried in wooden casks stowed in the bottom of the ship. Owing to the loss of much space between the casks, in later years, iron tanks, made to fit the shape of the inside of the ship, were used for stowing fresh water and in the days of sailing clippers, there was always a large, iron, fresh-water tank fitted away aft, in the run under the cabin floor, a place of little use for cargo stowage.

Dunnage is loose wood in various forms, generally about firewood size, used for chocking the casks as they are stowed in the hold, to keep them from rolling about. After the rock, pig iron or pig lead ballast was stowed in the bottom of a ship, it was covered with boards or dunnage wood and the water casks were then stowed, bung up and bilge free, in the ship's hold reaching from the main-hatch forward to the fore-hatch. Dunnage wood is used to take the chafe of these casks and jam all tightly together so there will be no room for them to shift. On top of the first tier was laid a second tier, the riding tier, and then provisions were stowed on top of the casks or forward of them. The casks of pork to starboard and beef to port, with flour, beans and rice in the wings or sides.

Right under the main hatchway, down in the bottom of the ship, the shot or cannon balls were stowed where their weight would be effective as ballast and so centrally located that when expended in action the diminution in weight would not affect the fore-and-aft trim of the ship.

On either side a grating, called the "cable tier," was built on which the heavy rope cables were coiled down and kept dry. The starboard cable was coiled on the port side and the port cable on the starboard side, with their ends made fast around the mainmast or to an orlop deck-beam. Inside of them were stowed smaller ropes such as the stream cable, hawsers, messengers, cat and fish hooks, pendant tackles, nippers, etc.

The spare sails were stowed on either side of the space abaft the mainmast, the shell room, with the pump wells, going through it and occupying the central part of the ship. Aft of this was the spirit-room where casks of whiskey, molasses and vinegar were kept under lock and key.

The daily consumption of food, carried in barrels and casks, kept the cooper busy knocking down or putting together hoops, staves and heads, for room was valuable on a craft packed so full of human beings. Even the space between the beams of the orlop deck was utilized, battens being nailed fore and aft, from beam to beam, and the space filled with boards, planks, oars, shooks, etc., and round, square and flat iron for the shipsmith to make repairs with and other miscellaneous gear.

There was some ironwork about the decks and rigging but the old sailing men-of-war used as little as possible. It was truly the day of oak and hemp. Oak was used because it was a wood of such tenacious grain that it gave off few murderous splinters when crushed by a cannon ball; and hemp was used because it could quickly be spliced and repaired. Iron hooks, bands and eyes on blocks or spars were as deadly as bullets when shattered and sent spinning through the air by a cannon ball.

My father, Theodore W. Davis, when Admiral Farragut's clerk on the old steam frigate *Hartford*, was wounded by being struck over the eye by a splinter knocked off a spar during the bombardment of Fort Powell off Mobile, Alabama, in 1863.

The frigate *Raleigh* was an oak and hemp ship with rope-stropped blocks, rope standing-rigging and rope anchor-cables. Her top-sail tyes were rawhide, chain not yet having come into vogue. She had that grace and beauty of rig and hull characteristic of the ships on which ornamentation formerly was lavished. The French and English ships sometimes overdid this ornamentation in a national rivalry. But there were enough ornamentation on the *Raleigh*, in the way of a beautifully carved stern, archboard, graceful mouldings and pilasters about the stern-windows and quarter-galleries, and a figurehead that was the work of a real sculptor, that lightened to the eye the otherwise massive ends of the ship. A full-length figure of Sir Walter Raleigh straddled the knee of the head with carved scrolls decorating the trailboards. All this detail is preserved for us in the case of this particular ship, by the draughtsmen who took off the lines of the *Raleigh* in 1779. It is such details that give value to the model of a ship and which in most cases have not been preserved though we may have the shape of the ship's hull. It is the accurate detail that gives to a ship's model its value and individuality.

I was born at Poughkeepsie, N. Y., where two of the Revolutionary frigates were built—the *Congress*, 28-guns, and the *Montgomery*, 24-guns, and as a child I often wondered what these ships looked like. They were built by Messrs. Lawrence and Tudor, on a beach just south of Kall Rock and taken up the river to Kingston to be rigged and there information seemed to end. The historical societies do not have much information as to the appearance of the ships as they are more interested in preserving records of civil affairs and personalities.

THE FRIGATE "RALEIGH"

Half a century later, to satisfy my curiosity, I built a little ship model, eighteen inches long, after the original plans of one of the frigates built at Portsmouth, N. H., in 1776 — the *Raleigh* — and the result was well worth the trouble I had taken. I will admit that I'm a crank on anything pertaining to sailing ships — so much so that I have made it a life's business, being a naval architect. In 1892, as one of a crew of eight, I helped to work the *James A. Wright*, an 880-ton bark, around Cape Horn and back just to see for myself how ships behaved and were handled. Capt. Charles H. Freeman gave me a deep-waterman's impression of how much of a crank he thought I was when, in reply to his query: "Whatever brought you to sea, Davis?" I said, "For the fun of it," and he remarked with apparent disgust, "A man that'll go to sea for pleasure will go to hell for pastime!"

Outside of its historical value this little ship model is almost priceless to me — just to have her and be able to turn her around slowly and admire the grace and beauty displayed in the form of the old-fashioned round ships.

For the same reason I have made models of some of the famous clipper ships to admire the clean lines of those racers with their beautiful runs and light sterns — as sharp aft as a racing shell. I also modelled the *Montezuma*, a big, bluff-ended packet ship, one of the old stately "Black Ball" liners. It is a most interesting comparison to set the little frigate alongside of a clipper or a packet and note the difference.

The little, round-sided frigate, ornamented with carving, fore and aft, in comparison with a packet ship, is like one of those old, intricate and highly ornamented, paper-lace, lover's valentines, that were the fashion in the 1880's, when compared with the stiff, square, plain post cards of today. The packet ship and clipper both have excessive flam or outward flare to the deck, forward, while the frigate was as round as an apple, and yet so delicately and appropriately were the rails of the head applied and moulded, that they beautified this end of the ship with their lines sweeping in graceful curves to the figurehead, a statue of Sir Walter Raleigh. The stiff, straight, sheer lines of the more modern ships look ugly when the eye catches the beautiful sweeping sheer of the older ship, rising high at the stern, with its picturesque little quarter-gallery and beautifully carved arch-board over the windows in the stern — framed like a picture.

The plans of the *Raleigh* give us the moulds by which the shape of the frigate may be carved out to the proper shape from a block of pine, either in one piece of wood, if it can be obtained large enough, or, from a block consisting of inch-thick layers glued together and held tightly pressed together until the glue has set. The cutting out of the shape of the hull may seem to be the greater part of the work but in reality it is the simplest part in the operation of building a ship model.

She is to be gouged out hollow, of course, and the lower decks must be fitted in, at least, around where one can look down the hatchways so as to appear to be complete. If it is to be a two-decked ship, the lower tier of

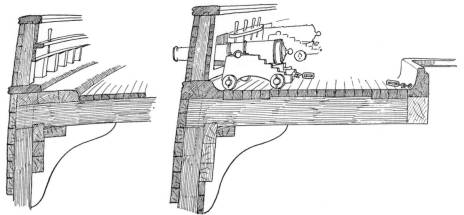

Fig. 29. Merchant Ship Bulwark   Fig. 30. Man of War Bulwark

guns must be put in and finished before the upper deck is put on. In a frigate, this means that the berthdeck must be put in, with its hatchways, and the gundeck also completed before the quarterdeck and forecastle heads are put on.

Men-of-war had solid bulwarks, the timber heads being planked up inside and outside. In merchant ships that carried no guns, the inside of the timbers were left exposed below the pinrail and bib piece under it. Another feature of the man-of-war deck was the waterways. On merchant ships they were wide, heavy strakes, sometimes a foot or more in from the bulwarks and were four inches or more thicker than the deck planking. On the war vessel the decks, including what was called the thin waterways, were all one level, to the inside of the bulwarks, where the thick waterways filleted into the corner and permitted the gun carriages to be run close up against the bulwark so as to get the muzzles of the guns as far out from the ship's side as possible, when they were discharged.

These are features that will show up plainly in a model and should be made correctly. Some of the old packet ships, those built soon after the War of 1812, were frigate-built ships and had the man-of-war or solid type of bulwarks.

A ship's deck at first glance may seem to be nothing but a plain flooring of narrow boards and in too many models it is so made, the seams being ruled in India ink on a smoothed, painted surface, and then shellaced over when the ink is well dried. Sometimes the plank lines are creased in with a sharp point, after the deck has been shellaced. It is then painted with burnt umber and after the paint has stood a couple of minutes and soaked into the scratches, the deck is then rubbed clear of paint which easily comes off the shellaced part and leaves seams looking as if they had been payed with pitch.

The same rule that governs the shifting of butts in the ship's outside planking, applies to the shift of butts in the deck. This rule does not allow the butts to be nearer than five feet from each other unless there is a strake worked between them, when this distance may be four feet. No butts are permitted in the same frame or deck beam unless there are three strakes between them. These butts are as much a part of the deck as are the seams and if put in, and not given undue prominence, add materially to the appearance.

At the ends, particularly the bow, where the planks snape off on a bevel, where they meet the thin waterways, they are never allowed to come to a shim or sharp point, but the end is cut off to a minimum width of two inches, in the real ship, that being as narrow as a caulking iron can be worked in. In the deck planking, butts were always made on a beam, for the beams of war ships were massive, necessarily so to support the weight of a battery of cannon weighing many tons.

The lower deck of a frigate was laid in three-inch thick fir, and the upper deck of four-inch fir, except nine strakes from the side where the gun carriages worked, which were of oak. The first three or four strakes of deck planking, clear of and alongside the hatch coamings that ran continuous, fore and aft, were termed binding strakes and were generally an inch thicker than the rest of the deck. These were scored down the extra thickness into the beams, although in some vessels the extra wood was allowed to stand above the rest of the deck. The nicety of slightly tapering the forward ends of the deck planks, forward of the foremast, so as to counteract the optical illusion occasioned by the meeting of straight lines against a side of considerable curvature, was resorted to in order to improve the appearance of the decks of old frigates. The older the frigate the more pains were taken in such details.

There was not much "round up" or "crown," as it was called, to the decks of men-of-war—only enough to drain off water. The forecastle head, quarterdeck and main-gundeck would only have a crown five inches in width of thirty feet and the lower deck would be much flatter, only crowning two inches, in a ship of thirty-foot beam.

The hatchways in a ship's deck are passages for free communication between the different decks and for permitting the lowering of supplies into the ship's hold. Heavy coamings were built around these openings to keep out any water that might be sloshing about the decks, for the coamings were from eight inches to a foot in height, their corners dovetailed together and all bolted down to the deck frame, leaving a ledge around all four sides for the ends and edges of the deck plank to be fastened to the beams. The outer edges of the coamings had a slight bevel and a ledge was cut around their inner edge for hatch covers or grating to be set in flush with the top of the coamings. These covers were made of material of the same thickness as the deck, with small cross-beams whose ends fitted into deeper notches cut on the inside of the coaming to receive them.

Deck scuttles are openings to permit access to certain compartments below that are only opened occasionally and were used principally on protected or covered decks. Some had a small coaming around them and a wooden cover that fitted over it. Those were known as "cap scuttles." Others were flush or nearly flush with the deck when the covers were set in and were called "flush scuttles."

In bringing up powder and cartridges from the magazine below, various scuttles were provided until they came to the upperdeck where the ammunition was then passed up one of the various hatchways. The shot was hoisted up at the main-hatch, from the shot locker, by small tackles termed "whips" — a single rope rove over a sheave in a block.

Bitts are upright timbers, in a ship's deck, used for fastening various ropes to. At the inboard end of the bowsprit there is also a pair of stout bitts to hold the bowsprit in place. Aft of the forecastle head, down on the main-deck, where it is nearly on a level with the hause pipes or holes in the ship's bow where the big rope anchor cables come through, are the riding bitts, the hitching posts, by which the ship is held, tied up, as it were, to her anchors. Large vessels generally had two pairs of these mooring bitts, to divide the strain, which would be too great for any one timber to bear. Small merchant ships used to ride to their windlass, which was a big, round log laid acrossways and turning in a saddle, each end cut into upright bitts braced with huge knees bolted to the deck, where other timbers distributed the strain forward, over the whole bow-frame of the ship.

Men-of-war sometimes had four anchor cables to take care of and a windlass would be too cumbersome; besides, the cables were so large it was impossible to bend them readily around a windlass barrel. Capstans, therefore, were used on war ships and a "messenger," which was a smaller cable-laid rope, about half the size of the anchor cable, was taken around the capstan barrel three turns in an endless loop, the forward end going around a roller under the bowsprit. The ends would then be lashed together. This was laid alongside of the cable, up forward, and lashed temporarily to it, the lashing nippers being cast off as the cable came aft where it was passed down the main hatch to be coiled down in the cable tiers, amidships. New lashings were added behind, as fast as the cable came in through the hausepipes.

Men with brooms and buckets of water, scrubbed off as much of the mud as possible as the big rope cables passed through the manger, on its way aft, but for all that it was often necessary to sprinkle sand on it to make the nippers hold, otherwise they would slide along on the slimy rope.

To secure the cable, to hitch it around the riding bitts, was both a difficult and dangerous operation when there was a heavy wind or sea on. To handle so large a rope, to form a loop in it and throw this loop over the bitt head, took the united strength of several men and it behooved them to be spry, for a pinch from a loop of that cable meant the loss of a hand or an arm.

To hold the cable forward of the bitts, while this was being done, there were several stout ring bolts in the deck or knees bracing the bitts, into which "deck stoppers," as they were termed, were hooked. Temporary seizings were passed around the cable so that the strain was held, permitting the slacking-up of the cable, aft, so it could be hitched around the bitts. The starboard cable was twisted inboard, with the sun, around the bitt head so that its end pointed aft on the outside of the bitt. The larboard, or port cable, was twisted just the reverse. Both cables led outside the bitts and had to be passed inboard and forward around the bitt head, against the sun, the end pointing aft, outside, or to port of the bitt head. Several turns were taken around the bitt head, in veering out the cable, so that considerable twisting strain was brought upon the bitt head. This might shear it off if it were not strengthened and held from turning by the heavy cross-piece or "bolster" that united the two bitts. On smaller vessels a single bitt was used, but there the strain would not be so great.

In this manoeuvring of hawsers or cables one great danger was the liability of a turn to ride up over another. This led to several inventions, one of which was the inserting of bars that kept each fake of the rope in its place. Another was a cast metal head, with flanges, like the worm on a screw, that guided each fake, or turn of the cable, so that it rode around the bitt head, while being slacked out, without jamming or riding one fake on top of another. Later frigates in the American navy, were fitted with such bitt heads when chain cables came into use.

Forward of each mast were other bitts to take the heavy pull of the top-sail sheets. They were known as the "topsail sheet bitts." Aft of these extended the fife rails in which were the belaying pins for making fast the many ropes composing what is called "the running gear." At the mizzen-mast these fife rails only ran fore and aft, on each side of the masts, but at

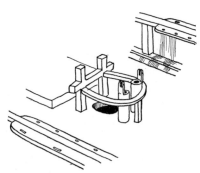

the fore and mainmast, to which so many of the ropes lead, there was a wide pin rail, athwartships, as well; and in the bottom of the turned stanchions which supported this rail, three sheaves were fitted so that gear could be rove through them and the crew run away with the hauling end. These fife rails were about eight inches wide and six inches thick and were prevented from looking clumsy, as they would have appeared had they been left plain, by being so moulded that they looked like two pieces, one laid on top of

FIG. 31. AROUND THE MAIN MAST
SHOWING OLD WOODEN PUMPS

the other, each with a rounded edge, which gave them a much lighter appearance. They stood about thirty inches above the decks.

The deck was so cut up by hatches and mast holes down the center line of the ship, that it became necessary to preserve the strength of the ship by extra bracing, and lodge-knees were worked into the deck frame at each corner of a hatchway, and the space between the beams where the mast went with its partners, was filled in solid, through-bolted and kneed. As there was no continuity of deck plank, a thicker material than the decking by one or two inches, was used and made of oak or teak forming a very stout reënforcement to take the heavy strain of the mast and to hold the bitts and fife rails.

Immediately abaft the mainmast the pumps came up through the deck. The pump well did not show on deck. It was a wooden box or well that extended from the deck on which the pumps were located, down to the bottom of the ship, with ladder rungs down one side, entrance being had through a door in the after side, so that a man could go down into the well, if necessary, to fit sheaves on the pump chains. The suction pipes led down this well and were get-at-able, their whole length, in case of trouble.

At the time the *Raleigh* was built, chain pumps were much in favor, for they could throw out a continuous stream and discharge more water than any plunger pump. A chain, with a series of washers at intervals along its length, was rove over a sprocket wheel, working in brackets fastened to the deck beams above, on the starboard side. It passed over a similar wheel, on the port side, from which it went down a pipe to the bottom of the ship where it rove over a guide wheel and crossed to the starboard side in an open space left between two frames. It then went between the keel and keelsons under another guide wheel and so up another pipe where it was shackled to the other end of the chain. The water flowed in the pipe between each washer, while at the bottom of the pump well, and was brought up to the deck where it poured out and was led in a wooden trough to the scuppers, to drain overboard. The crew turned the upper sprocket wheels by means of long crank handles hung or pivoted in brackets from the beams above. These cranks could be made as long as desired, so that many men could lay hold of them and assist in the work. To rig up the second pump, all that was necessary to

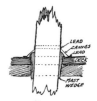

FIG. 32

do, was to key the sprocket wheels on to the shafts, otherwise they would turn idle.

Where the masts went through the deck or rather, through the mast partners, they were octagonal in shape and held snug by wedges. These wedges did not show as a mast-coat covered them. This coat consisted of a piece of canvas fitted around the mast and made watertight so that rain water would not run down the mast and wet things below. A strip of lead was tacked over the canvas ends and tamped snug to the wood. The coat was then tacked down to the deck and also made watertight by a ring of strip lead over the edge.

The ship's bell hung in a small belfry at the after edge or break of the forecastle. It was a modest little affair when compared with the belfry on some of the larger European ships where much art was displayed in carved decorations so that the belfry became a striking feature of the deck furniture. The bell was the ship's town clock, and on it was struck the time every half-hour throughout the day and night. The bell was also used in the din and uproar of battle for certain important signals to be sounded throughout the ship. The rapid ringing of this bell at all times was an alarm of fire.

The drum was the call to quarters, each man in the ship being assigned to a certain duty and to be at a certain place or station, as it was termed. The ordinary beat of the drum, preceded by one roll, meant exercise at general quarters at the guns, without powder. A quick beat of the drum meant action, with powder, whether only in drill or actual engagement; and when all were at their stations, a roll of the drum was the signal for silence and attention, fore and aft, whereupon all firing or other noise must immediately cease and the word of the next command listened to. After the captain had given his orders, two taps beaten on the drum, was the signal to execute them.

The men of the crew were divided into gun's crews, each, according to his position, being assigned a certain number and certain duties. Some were first-boarders; others, second-boarders; others, pikemen, sail-trimmers, etc. The signal for first-boarders to hurry to leave their guns and assemble on the spar deck, was given by a rattle and also by verbal order. A repetition of this signal would call away the second-boarders from their guns, to be ready to board the enemy's ship. The sounding of a gong was the call for pikemen to assemble on the spar deck to repel boarders. All hands to repel boarders was signaled by the springing of the rattle and sounding of the gong together and also by verbal order.

OLD TIME FRIGATE RATTLE
"Spring the rattle and
Every man to his station."

FIG. 33

Besides the small hand rattles there was, on each deck, a large, hollowed-out, hardwood rattle, built like a coffee grinding mill, attached to the side of a bulkhead, which made a most unearthly noise audible above the roar of battle.

The various ladders about a ship's decks on models are one of the most picturesque features and great care should be taken to make them proportionate in size and not get them too heavy. There is a ladder on each side, from the maindeck up to the forecastle head, and others leading to the quarterdeck, stand fore and aft. Those in hatchways, on large ships, always form an X, crossing each other, so that they straddle the hatch below, if one be there. These are so arranged to prevent confusion in time of battle. All men going up use one ladder and those going down the other, so there can be no interference or delay. On a small ship, like the *Raleigh*, the hatches were too narrow for double ladders and single ladders were used, the ammunition being hauled up from one deck to another.

To make these small ladders is tedious work. I do it now by lightly sawing grooves, spaced and at the proper angle, across the side-pieces of my ladders. I then cut out of paper-thin strips of wood as many steps as are needed. After dipping the edge of a tread or step in glue, I set it up in one of the saw-cuts with a pair of tweezers. All are set up in the same way. After touching the upper edges of all the steps with thin glue, I lay the other side of the ladder on them and gently work each step into its saw-cut and when all are engaged, squeeze gently in a little iron vise and let the glue set.

There was always a set of cleat-like steps fastened to the planking on the outside of old men-of-war, that, with the tumble-home of the topsides, gave a good foothold, and with the aid of a pair of handropes hanging down for one to grasp, a man could mount the sides of a frigate, like the *Raleigh*, quite easily. These steps were always just forward of the break of the poop-deck and on the rail were either a pair of stout stanchions, from the heads of which the handropes hung, or there were billboards, forming at the forward end, a stopping point for the stowage of the hammocks in their hammock nettings atop of the main rail. A short ladder led down from the rail, from these outside steps, to the main gundeck. On large ships of the line there was an elaborate entry-port built on the lower gundeck, where one could enter and mount to the quarterdeck or poop, by ladders within the ship.

FIG. 34. GANGWAY STEPS

Just forward of these gangway steps there was a pair of skid frames reaching from just above the water to the top of the main rail. Their function was to protect the ship's planking and facilitate the hoisting in of water casks and other supplies and for that reason they were located in line with the middle of the main hatchway, so that a water cask hoisted up along the side, on these skids, could be swung inboard directly over the hatchway and lowered into the ship's hold.

Forward, just aft of the fore channels, a somewhat similar piece was fastened vertically from the rail down to receive the main tack. This was called the main chess-tree. A vertical sheave in it received the hauling end of the tack which then passed through the bulwarks over a horizontally set sheave and belayed inboard, the standing end of the main tack being hooked to an eyebolt in the ship's outside planking.

There are other items, such as the hammock nettings, channels, chain-plates, etc., but we have not yet finished with the fittings on the deck, the most important of which is the capstan. This consisted really of two capstans, one on the quarterdeck and another on the gundeck below, both operating on the same shaft or spindle, but the lower end could be disconnected when not needed.

The deck was built up square to the spindle of the capstan with heavy planking, as at the mast partners, forming a platform on which it worked. On the lower barrel, pawls were fitted, like ratchets on a clock wheel, so that when it was turned these pawls, dropping into a ring of notches around the base, securely bolted to the deck, prevented the barrel from unwinding. A metal plate on top of the lower capstan was bolted securely to it and in close contact with it was another plate of similar size, that was fastened to the iron spindle. By dropping several stout pins into concentric holes in these two plates, both capstans turned alike on the same spindle. This was done when heaving anchor or on a heavy job where many hands are required at the capstan bars. By removing the pins one capstan could be used to hoist the fore jeer tackles and the other similarly used to hoist the main-yard.

The spindle in the capstan of the *Raleigh* was a huge spar of the tough-est wood obtainable, such as a piece of live oak. This was cut five-sided and on each face a heavy face-piece, called a "whelp," was bolted which increased the diameter from fif-teen or sixteen inches to about three feet at the point where the cables wound around the middle of it. These whelps were then braced by connect-ing chocks, around the base, with a lighter set around the top just below the head. The head was about four feet in diameter, and a little less than a foot deep, with ten square mortices, called "pigeon holes," into which the capstan bars fitted. A pin, dropped through a hole bored down through the capstan head and then through the end of bar, kept the latter from pulling out. Further precautions were always taken by swiftering the ends of the capstan bars together with a light rope. A shallow score, cut in the end of the capstan bars, received this line which was then looped back over the end, making a very simple yet effective hitch to hold the rope in its place. This prevented the bars from being catapulted out, when too heavy a strain was put upon the capstan, and it should spin around like a buzz saw, sometimes with severe injury to those who were unable to get out of the way in time.

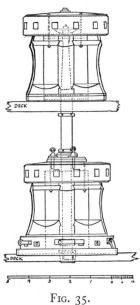

Fig. 35.
CAPSTANS USED ON
OLD SAILING MEN-OF-WAR

The large three-deckers carried large capstans and from an old rule we learn the number of capstan bars in vogue in the days of sailing ships, as follows:

Rate of ship by the number of guns	Number of Capstan Bars	Length of Feet	Bar Inches
Ship of 120 guns	14	14	0
Ship of 100 to 110 guns	14	13	6
Ship of 80 guns	14	13	0
Ship of 74 guns	14	12	6
Ship of 36 to 52 guns	12	11	6
Ship of 28 guns	10	10	0
Corvette of 800 tons	10	9	6
Ship of 16 to 18 guns	10	9	0
Ship of 10 to 14 guns	8	8	6

By the length of these bars one can readily understand how several men were able to line up abreast on each bar. For example, on the corvette size, three or four men could find room to push on each bar which would indicate a gang of thirty to forty men, and in the large ships this amounted to eighty or ninety men.

It was to enthuse this gang and put more push and vim into their efforts, that the ship's fiddler or fifer used to mount to the top of the capstan and strike up a lively air to give unity of action. All hands would then heave together, in time to the tune, and a strain would be put upon the big hauser sufficient to break the anchor's grip in its muddy berth on the bottom.

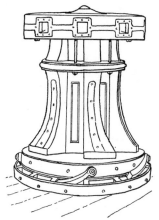

It is a good plan when fitting capstans and many other fittings, for that matter, to see that they are workable and that something does not come in the way of the messenger. Sometimes everything will be all clear, fore and aft, except the forecastle ladder put right directly in the way. By having the run of this messenger in mind, at the time the ladder is placed, it can just as well be shifted to one side a little. Consider the utility of each part of the ship, as you reproduce her in miniature, and make her "workable" in every detail. Don't put in a gun port with gun carriage and gun behind it mounted in great detail and then make a caricature out of it by placing a network of chain plates across the port so the gun could not be used. One of the worst cases I ever saw of unworkable detail was on an elaborately carved and beautifully decorated model. As a sample of wood carving the decorations were a masterpiece; as a workable ship she was a joke. Men didn't build men-of-war and mount their cannon so that many of them could not be fired when they were fighting for their very lives in battle.

FIG. 36. CAPSTAN

From a drawing by John Callow

The same is true with such parts as the ship's chess-trees. Some men consider them mere ornaments to make the outside of the hull look picturesque, so they put them wherever they found most convenient, where, in fact, they could be of no practical use. They should be under the tack of the mainsail when the sail is braced sharp up on a wind.

Another small item that is often overlooked but which goes a long way towards making a model a real little ship, is the proper placing, about her decks, of eyebolts and ringbolts. There are a lot of them, particularly on a man-of-war; but keep them to the proper scale if you want them to look well. The diameter of an eyebolt should be two and a half times, in the clear, the diameter of the iron it is made of, and if a ring be put in this eye, its inside diameter should be five times the iron's diameter. This makes the eyes small, but if made too large they look badly. At each gun-port, on the upper gun deck, there should be five eyebolts and four ringbolts. The latter

Nº.0 Nº.1 Nº.2.
DIA.of BARREL - 7¾ 8¾ 9½.
DIA. of BASE - 18¾ 22½ 24.-
Height - - - 24 27½ 30½

FIG. 37.

IRON CAPSTAN
USED SINCE 1850

are placed two on each side of the port, on a level with the port sill. These are for the heavy breeching rope that stops the recoil of the gun after it has jumped back on the firing. As they are sometimes pulled out, a second eyebolt is provided as a substitute. A little above these ringbolts is an eyebolt, a foot or so away from the port, into which the sill tackles used to run the guns out, when ready to fire, are riveted through the bulwarks. As far forward and aft as the distance between ports will permit is another eyebolt on each side, for the training tackles used to slew the guns, to shoot as far forward and aft as they will point. Directly back of each gun and just clear of the hatch coaming, is an eyebolt in the deck, for the train tackle used to run the guns in for loading. Over the lowerdeck ports, on the lower gun decks of two-decked ships, are two eyebolts used when the gun is run in and stowed in heavy weather. The muzzle is raised and securely lashed to these eyebolts.

The hatch covers are not made in one big cover as it would be too unwieldly and besides, there is no place to stow so big an affair, so they are made in sections and each section should have at least two ringbolts, one at each end on diagonally opposite corners, so that it will balance when picked up by these rings. A score is gouged out so that the rings will be almost flush in the wood, so that when the tarred canvas, tarpaulines are stretched over to keep out the water, these ringbolts will not chafe holes through the tarpaulines.

Hatch coamings on weather decks, have staples, driven in at intervals, over which flat iron bars with slots to engage the staples are pushed compressing the three tarpaulines until the point of a peg can be inserted and then driven in bringing a strong pressure to hold the canvas covers tightly against the coamings.

There are many other places, more on a merchant ship than on a man-of-war, where ringbolts or deck eyebolts are fitted. Eyebolts for the spanker vangs, the mizzen staysail sheets, and some are placed around the mast for if all the gear was made fast to the fife-rails it would pull them off the deck. By taking this strain down under a deck-hook or through an eye or leader block and then up to the fife-rail, the strain upon the latter is down and not up. The jib sheets have lignum-vitae fairheads stapled down on the

forecastle head. All these fittings if put in their proper places add materially to the shippy look of a small model.

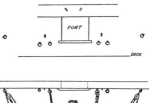

Another item is the deck scuppers, the lead pipes to carry off the water that drains from the crown of the deck, to the trough-like groove at the waterways. Here, lead pipe scuppers are fitted into holes, cut on a downward slant to the outside of the ship, along amidships, where the deck is the lowest and towards which the water would drain.

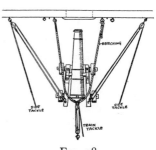

The *Raleigh* had a double steering wheel, one at each end of a sixteen-inch diameter drum, over which the wheel-ropes wound. These wheels were five feet in diameter, with probably

FIG. 38

eight spokes, similar to an old wheel used on the frigate *Constitution* which I had the pleasure of measuring and sketching. However, she had ten spokes in her wheel when hauled out at Boston recently. But she was a larger ship than the *Raleigh* and it is more likely the latter had an eight-spoke wheel and the diameter, as measured from her plans, would be five feet.

The character of the ornamentation on the old wheel is in keeping with that in vogue in the days of the *Raleigh*; Capt. Dan Stannard of Cow Bay, Long Island, N. Y., was a shipwrecker in the 1880's, who burned several

of the old navy sailing ships to get the metal of their hulls. He had purchased an old ship at the Norfolk Navy Yard and when they went to tow her around to New York it was found she had no wheel. Captain Dan went ashore and demanded a wheel as the ship he had purchased was supposed to have one. The Navy Yard people could find no wheel until away back in a corner of an old storage shed they found a wheel covered with cobwebs, and it was put on the ship and she was brought around and beached where

LOWER DECK GUN STOWED.

FIG. 39

the present Manhasset Bay Yacht Club now stands and after being stripped of everything of any value, the bare hulk was burned. An old gentleman to whom Captain Stannard had shown this wheel positively identified it as one that he had often polished the brass of when a boy on the *Constitution*.

That is the wheel I sketched and measured and which is figured here. As any sailor knows, the historic old ship might have had a dozen wheels in the course of her long career. History records the fact that her first wheel was shattered by a cannon ball from the *Java*, during her engagement with that vessel and the wheel of the *Java* was fitted as a makeshift.

A double steering wheel on so small a ship as the *Raleigh*, may seem queer to one who handles a modern wheel with its diamond-screw gear and powerful yet quick-acting leverages; but when we consider that the *Raleigh* had a huge timber, twenty-one feet long, for a tiller, and that the rope side-tackles, after reeving through the blocks had to go over rollers amidships and up to the drum of the wheel, we can realize how hard a sailor had to pull to turn this wheel. In action, when the quick manoeuvring of a ship to bring her guns to bear upon the enemy at a critical moment means victory or defeat, the reason for the double wheel is apparent and sometimes it was all four men could handle. Rawhide was used for the wheelropes, instead of hemp or manila as the latter wore out too quickly. In going into action a tackle was hooked to eyebolts on each side of the ship and then to the tiller for use in case a shot should wreck the steering wheel or cut the wheel ropes. It was called a "relieving tackle," by which the ship could be controlled by men hauling on these tackles, down on the deck where the tiller was being "conned" by an officer on the deck above.

The "channels" are the narrow platforms on the outside of the ship, abreast of each mast, that spread the shrouds so they clear the hammock nettings on men-of-war. These are necessarily very stout timbers but they are tapered at the edge so they do not look clumsy and are doweled together and braced with knees above and below. An old-time, five hundred-ton ship had channels at her main that were twenty-four feet long, two feet wide and five inches thick. At the foremast the fore channels were nineteen feet long and about four and a quarter inches thick. Her mizzen channels were of three-inch stock.

The chain plates that carry the strain of the shrouds over the channels and down to the ship's side, are notched into the outer edge of the channel and a batten covers them over when completed.

The *Raleigh* had old-fashioned, long-link chains such as the *Constitution* carried, made of round iron rod, welded into the proper lengths, according to the increasing rake of the shrouds and for the sake of the ship be very careful to get these chain-plates so the nails holding them to the hull all line up true, on the same strake of planking, and don't let one deadeye stand up above the channel any higher than the others. Keep all snug down on to it.

There are eight shrouds on the foremast and nine on the mainmast, the mizzen having but four, and the after two of the fore are on a stool as the short part of a channel is termed. The reason this fore-channel is so divided will become apparent when you come to stow the waist or sheet anchor. This opening permits the huge, wooden stock that was fitted to the old anchors to be brought in close against the hull and stowed or lashed securely.

The deadeyes for the fore and main were twelve inches in diameter while those of the mizzen were nine inches.

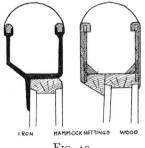

IRON   HAMMOCK NETTINGS   WOOD

FIG. 40

The breast backstay is set up by tackles to the small chain plate set well forward among the deadeye of the lower rigging and the standing or after backstay is set up to the after small deadeye. The top-gallant and royal backstays are set up to eyebolts set up on their own ends, as it is termed when a rope is rove through an eye and doubled back upon itself and lashed.

Merchant ships generally had narrower channels than men-of-war, whose wide, spreading lower rigging and wide or square yards, were distinctly noticeable after looking at the modest rig on the traders.

A distinguishing feature of a man-of-war was the hammock nettings fitted on top of her rails for the stowage of hammocks. Except for the officers, nearly every one slept in hammocks, which, on a craft of the *Raleigh's* size, meant about two hundred hammocks to stow. They made a good breastwork to stop the enemy's small shot and as they had to be removed from the gundeck, to permit the working of the guns, this was found to be the best disposition that could be made of them.

Iron brackets were secured to the top of the rail and formed a U-shaped arm supporting a light rail about three inches square that butted forward and at the gangways against billboards and on these rails a trough of netting was lashed that made a stowage space about a foot square and fifteen to sixteen inches deep. The first hammock was doubled over to fill in the corner space and then each succeeding hammock was laid at an angle of about forty-five degrees and packed down by a man stowing them into a snug mass that was exactly parallel, along their tops, with the rail. An officer standing across the ship sighted the top line to insure a perfect stowage, and when all were in, and the painted canvas cover folded inboard and lashed down the top of the hammocks followed the perfect curve, made by her rail. Each sailor took pride in this and strove to outdo a rival ship.

Some ships had wooden boxes built atop of their rails in which to stow the hammocks, but small wood was dangerous, causing many minor injuries by splinters sent flying when struck by a cannon ball.

Hammock nettings usually ended at the after end of the fore-rigging and the forward end of the mizzen rigging. An opening was left at the gangways and on some ships they were omitted where they interfered with such gear as the main tack.

It was these hammock nettings and high bulwarks that made it necessary for men-of-war to have such wide channels in order to spread the lower rigging so it would clear them.

By experience in handling the cannon aboard ship, certain minimum sizes of gunports had been arrived at and accepted by shipbuilders of and prior to 1755, as a rule to be followed in framing a ship's topsides.

Size of Gun	Height of Port	Breadth of Port	Height of Sill above Deck
A 42 pound gun (shot weight)	2′ 10″	3′ 2″	2′ 4″
A 32 pound gun (shot weight)	2′ 8″	3′ 0″	2′ 3″
A 24 pound gun (shot weight)	2′ 6″	2′ 10″	2′ 1″
A 18 pound gun (shot weight)	2′ 5″	2′ 8″	2′ 0″
A 12 pound gun (shot weight)	2′ 3″	2′ 5″	1′ 11″
A 9 pound gun (shot weight)	1′ 10″	2′ 0″	1′ 9″
A 6 pound gun (shot weight)	1′ 4″	1′ 6″	1′ 6″

The distance between gunports varied between seven and fourteen feet, center to center.

Another rule of about the same date that also includes data on gun carriages is based on the diameter of the shot fired by each gun. Therefore we must first know these diameters, which are as follows:

	Diameter			Diameter
1 lb. shot	1.923″		12 lb. shot	4.403″
2 lb. shot	2.423″		18 lb. shot	5.040″
3 lb. shot	2.793″		24 lb. shot	5.546″
4 lb. shot	3.053″		32 lb. shot	6.106″
6 lb. shot	3.494″		36 lb. shot	6.350″
9 lb. shot	4.000″		42 lb. shot	6.684″

By these rules gunports are spaced apart, center to center, twenty-five times the diameter of the shot. The gunport's length, fore and aft, should be six and one-half diameters; the height, six diameters; and the sill or lower edge of the port should be three and one-half diameters above the deck.

The thickness of the sides or brackets of the gun carriages, should be the same as the diameter of the shot and the axletrees, the same size but square. The bolts holding this carriage together should be one-fifth the diameter of the shot.

The *Raleigh's* plans agree with these rules. Her ports, as scaled off from the draught drawn in 1779, measure, in length, fore and aft, two feet seven inches; in height, two feet five inches; and above deck, to sill, two feet. The distance between her ports in the clear measure is seven feet and adding the half breadth of each port, to get the distance, center to center, gives a distance of nine feet seven inches; a trifle more room than the rule by shots' diameter, which gives nine feet two inches from center to center of ports.

Two-decked ships usually had one solid shutter for the lower deck ports

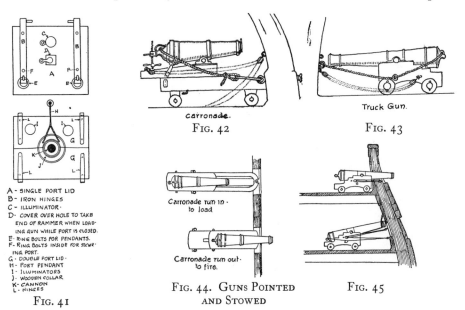

A - SINGLE PORT LID
B - IRON HINGES
C - ILLUMINATOR ·
D - COVER OVER HOLE TO TAKE
END OF RAMMER WHEN LOAD-
ING GUN WHILE PORT IS CLOSED.
E - RING BOLTS FOR PENDANTS.
F - RING BOLTS INSIDE FOR SECUR-
ING PORT.
G - DOUBLE PORT LID ·
H - PORT PENDANT
I - ILLUMINATORS
J - WOODEN COLLAR
K - CANNON
L - HINGES

FIG. 41

carronade.
FIG. 42

Truck Gun.
FIG. 43

Carronade run in
to load

Carronade run out
to fire.

FIG. 44. GUNS POINTED
AND STOWED

FIG. 45

and half shutters for the upper deck. To close the lower ports the guns had to be run in. The port lid was raised by a tackle hooked to an eyebolt in the deck beam above and to a rope pendant that went out through a bee-hole in the ship's side, ending in a span that was fastened to the two ringbolts riveted through the shutter at the lower end of the hinge strap. A small, hinged flap, in the middle of the shutter, could be lowered leaving an open hole through which the handle of the rammer could be passed for loading the gun in bad weather when the shutter was kept closed. At the top of the shutter, in line with the gun sights, was another small, circular shutter that could be turned to open it and give light as well as afford a sight at the enemy.

The *Raleigh* had her guns on an upper deck, well above the water, and had half-ports. The lower half, hinged to drop outward where chains held it horizontally, was called the "buckler." The upper half was put in place and removed by hand, being buckled or clamped tightly into place when the lower lid was pulled up to close the port. These shutters each had a half-circle cut out of their adjoining edges to close up around the gun while it remained run out, its muzzle being kept dry by the insertion of a plug called a "tompion." Some vessels also had the upper lid of the shutter hinged and raised with a pendant and tackle, as on a solid shutter.

FIG. 46.

12-POUND CARRONADE

The guns on the *Raleigh* were old-style, smooth-bore, 9 and 12 pounders on the main gundeck and 6 pounders on her quarterdeck. Guns were not so plentiful in those days and they often had to take what were available. The 12-pound guns would be amidships where there was the most room and the 9 pounders, forward and aft of these, under the decks above the quarterdeck and forecastle-head.

The gun carriages, or naval trucks, were the conventional type of the day

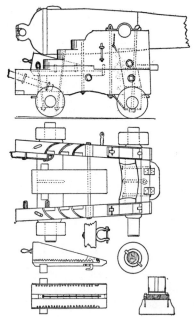

FIG. 47. GUN CARRIAGE

and the accompanying drawing gives the details of their construction. It is taken from *Ordnance Instruction in the United States Navy*, published by the Navy Department in 1866.

There was one difficulty that caused considerable trouble with the guns in the days of the *Raleigh* and that was the fact that some cannon were cast with the trunion exactly in line with the center of the bore while others were cast with it below the center or, as it was then expressed, they were hung by the middle or hung by the thirds.

This is what probably happened when Deacon Gould made the gun carriages at Salem, Mass., in 1799, for the frigate *Essex*. Capt. Edward Preble recorded in his diary, under date of Nov. 17, 1799, the following: "26 twelve pound cannon were taken on board for the main battery; mounted them and found the carriages all too high; dismounted the cannon and sent the carriages on shore to be altered." If his guns were hung by the thirds they would stand up a few inches too high, which quite likely was what happened.

To better understand the handling of guns, the men employed and the instruments used, let me quote the manual exercise:

1. "Silence! Man the starboard (or port) guns!"

At this preparatory order the strictest silence is to be observed. The Captain faces the fort; the men, on the right and left, stand facing the gun; all fix their eyes on the Captain and attentively wait for orders.

2. "Cast loose and provide!"

The Gun Captain commands, sees his gun cleared and cast loose, portlid unbarred ready for tricing up, or half ports taken out; side and train tackles hooked to the side training bolts, and the train-tackle to the eyebolt in the rear of the gun; casts loose and middles breeching and places selvage straps and toggles amidships; takes off lock cover, hands it to the train tackleman, who places it amidships; buckles on his waist belt (with a frog for a pistol, and with it cartridges and percussion caps and a box containing fifty primers fitted to slip on the waist belt); provides himself with a priming wire, puts on and

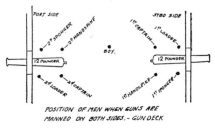

POSITION OF MEN WHEN GUNS ARE MANNED ON BOTH SIDES. – GUN DECK

Fig. 48

secures his thumb-stall; and sees that the gear and implements for the service of the gun are all in place and ready for use, and that the men are properly equipped (several have a frog to hold a battle axe).

Second Captain assists in casting loose and middling breeching; takes off and places amidships sight covers, selvage straps, and toggles; handles quoin; provides thumb-stalls, priming wires, and boring bitt, and equips himself with the first two; clears lock string and lays it in a loose coil round the lock, convenient for use, and buckles on his waist belt, furnished the same as the first captain's. If the gun is furnished with an elevating screw, elevates the gun that the lower half port may be let down.

First Loader, aided by first sponger, casts loose port-lanyard; removes upper half port and passes it to the men on the left side of the gun, who lay it amidships, lets down the half port. On lower deck he casts off port lanyards and mizzen lashings; removes port bar and passes it to the men at the left side of the gun, who lay it amidships; bears outport. On all deck places handswab and chocking-quoin near the ship's side on the left side of the gun; aids first sponger in taking tompion out of muzzle of gun.

Second Loader assists in casting loose; sees the wads in place, and for rifled cannon a pot of grease at hand; hooks outer block of side tackle to side training bolt, on the left side of gun.

113

First Sponger casts loose port-lanyards and aids first loader in removing upper half ports and letting down lower ones, and on lower decks in removing the port-bar, bearing out the port and taking off the muzzle lashings; takes out tompion and passes it to second sponger, who hangs it amidships; places chocking-quoin on the right side of gun, near the ship's side.

Second Sponger assists in casting loose, hooks outer blocks of side tackle to side training bolt on the right side of the gun.

The Spongers take down the sponges and rammers, take off the sponge cap and hang it out of the way; place sponges and rammers together on the right side of the gun; heads towards the breech in the brackets overhead on covered decks, otherwise on deck.

The Side Tacklemen assist in casting loose; on lower decks, aid port-tacklemen, moisten the sponge, being certain that the end of the sponge which touches the bottom of the bore is thoroughly wet.

Shellmen assist in casting loose, provide shot and wads, and proceed to hatchway, ready to pass loaded shell; if ordered.

Train tacklemen lead out and hook train-tackle.

Handspikemen take out the handspikes on their respective sides, and with carriages using a quoin, each standing between his handspikes and the side of the ship, place the heel of their handspikes on the steps of the carriage and under the breech of the gun, and raise it so that the quoin may be eased and the lower half port let down; or when housed, the bed and quoin adjusted. Then each handspikeman will lay his handspike on deck, on his own side of the gun, parallel with its axis, clear of the trucks and butt to rear.

Powder-boy repairs to his proper scuttle for his passing box, which having received he returns and stands a little to the left and in rear of gun; keeping the passing box under his left arm and the cover closely pressed down with his right hand.

When there are fourteen or more men at a gun, the port tacklemen and side tacklemen, on lower decks, lead out port tackle falls and assist in tricing up port, and when high enough, belay the fall.

Of course, a 12-pound gun would not have this number of men but the foregoing will illustrate the work that had to be done. A long 12 pounder's crew consisted of eight men and a boy and a long 6 pounder, of six men and a boy.

When the guns on both sides of the ship were manned simultaneously, the first captain, loader, sponger and handspikemen man the starboard guns and the second captain, leader, sponger and handspikemen the port guns, four men to a gun. When only one side is in use all eight man the gun.

In loading the gun, when it is run in as far as the breeching will permit,

THE FRIGATE "RALEIGH"

WHEN CALLED AWAY	POSITION ~ DUTY AT GUN	LONG 24 POUND GUN	POSITION ~ DUTY AT GUN	WHEN CALLED AWAY
			SHIPS BULWARK	
2º BOARDER	1ST LOADER ~ SIDE TACKLE •		• 1ST SPONGER ~ RAMMER ~ S-T	2º BOARDER
1ST BOARDER	2º " " " •		• 2º " " "	1ST BOARDER
1ST BOARDER	2º SHOT ~ WAD •		• 1ST SHOT & WAD	2º BOARDER
PIKEMAN ~ WINCH-	2º TRAIN - TACKLE ~ CROWBAR •		• 1ST TRAIN-TACKLE ~ CROWBAR	PIKEMAN ~ PIKEMAN
PIKEMAN	2º HANDSPIKE & T-T. •		• 1ST HANDSPIKE ~ T-T	
3º BOARDER	1ST CAPTAIN •		• 2º CAPTAIN	

• POWDER BOY

CREW STATIONS AT 24 LB. GUN.

WHEN CALLED AWAY	POSITION ~ DUTY AT GUN	32 LB. CARRONADE	POSITION ~ DUTY AT GUN	WHEN CALLED AWAY
			SHIP'S BULWARK	
2º BOARDER ~ SAIL TRIMMER	1ST LOADER ~ SIDE TACKLE •		• 1ST SPONGER ~ RAMMER ~ S-T	2º BOARDER ~ SAIL TRIMMER
1ST " " "	2º " " " •		• 2º " " "	PIKEMAN ~ " "
PIKEMAN ~ " "	1ST TRAIN ROPE •		• 2º TRAIN ROPE	" " "
3º BOARDER	1ST CAPTAIN •		• 2º CAPTAIN	1ST BOARDER

• POWDER BOY.

CREW STATIONS AT 32 LB. CARRONADE

its muzzle is only eighteen inches inboard so the sponger has to lean out of the port to insert and manipulate the long handle of the sponge, and then the rammer, to push the cannon ball well down into the muzzle against the cartridge. The loader inserts the charge and shot and assists the sponger in ramming them home.

The small boats carried by the old frigates were a launch, two cutters, a commodore's barge, a pinnace and a jolly boat. In sailing foreign these were sometimes reduced in number, as shown in a letter written at Gibraltar by Capt. Edward Preble of the frigate *Essex* to the Secretary of the Navy, on March 25, 1800, in which he writes:

"As I have four boats, I shall leave my launch here. She takes up so much room on the gundeck, as to exclude the fresh air from passing below, and is very

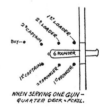

WHEN SERVING ONE GUN—
QUARTER DECK ~ FCKSL.

FIG. 49

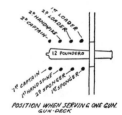

POSITION WHEN SERVING ONE GUN.
GUN-DECK

FIG. 50

much in the way of the guns on the main deck. I have likewise left a spare main yard."

The boats of the *Essex* consisted of a launch, two cutters, a barge and a pinnace, and this was the complement of the *Raleigh* and most frigates of her rating in 1776.

The big line-of-battle ships carried twelve boats, but frigates, being smaller vessels, of course had fewer. These boats were stowed on deck

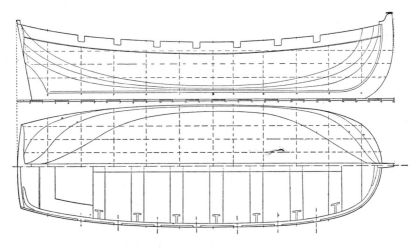

FIG. 51. SHIP'S LONG BOAT IN THE TIME OF THE "RALEIGH"

when going to sea and nested as the fishermen's dories are to date, one inside the other. The seats or thwarts were fitted so they could be removed, for this purpose. The launches, being the largest, were stowed first; the cutters being just a trifle shorter, would stow inside of them. A couple of boats were usually carried on the quarter davits in case a man should fall or be washed overboard.

A small frigate like the *Raleigh*, stowed her launch in chocks amidships and her spare spars were stowed alongside the hatchways, on either side. Some carried their spare main-topsail-yard on the port quarter and the fore-topsail-yard, on the starboard quarter, between the shrouds and bulwarks, on the channels; and their jibboom across the stern davits.

The shape of these old boats has been handed down to us in several ways. Mungo Murray, in Plate 5 of his admirable work, gives us the lines of a ship's long boat, 29 feet 1 inch in length, with plans for the convenience of those unskilled in projecting ships plans which I have drawn out in full (his plate shows the forward and after halves lapped to save space).

THE FRIGATE "RALEIGH"

William Sutherland's book on *Ship Building* (1755), also shows on (Plate 1), the plans of a sixteen-foot ship's boat, in which he gives the outside shape, the lay-out of thwarts, and the position of the thole pins for the oars.

The dimensions of various boats used in the British service, are given in the *Shipwright's Vade-Mecum*, published in 1805, and briefly are as follows:

LAUNCHES

Long	Beam	Depth, Amidships	Depth, Forward	Depth, Aft	Transom	Oars
36′ 0″	10′ 6″	4′ 3″	5′ 0″	5′ 0″	9′ 0″	14
33′ 0″	9′ 9″	4′ 0″	4′ 9″	4′ 9″	8′ 3″	12
30′ 0″	9′ 0″	3′ 10″	4′ 6″	4′ 6″	7′ 6″	12
24′ 0″	7′ 10″	3′ 3″	3′ 9″	3′ 9″	6′ 6″	

LONG BOATS

Long	Beam	Depth, Amidships	Depth, Forward	Depth, Aft	Transom	Oars
32′ 0″	9′ 6″	4′ 3″	5′ 6″	5′ 7″	5′ 11″	14
30′ 0″	9′ 3″	4′ 1″	5′ 4″	5′ 5″	5′ 8″	12
26′ 0″	8′ 9″	3′ 8″	4′ 9″	4′ 10″	5′ 3″	12
22′ 0″	7′ 6″	3′ 6″	4′ 2″	4′ 3″	3′ 9″	
19′ 0″	7′ 1″	2′ 10″	3′ 3″	3′ 4″	3′ 4″	

PINNACES

Long	Beam	Depth, Amidships	Depth, Forward	Depth, Aft	Transom	Oars
32′ 0″	7′ 6″	3′ 3″	4′ 0″	4′ 4″	4′ 7″	14
28′ 0″	6′ 10″	3′ 0″	3′ 8″	4′ 0″	4′ 0″	12
25′ 0″	6′ 10″	2′ 7″	3′ 2″	3′ 5″	3′ 6″	12
17′ 0″	5′ 9″	2′ 5″	2′ 11″	3′ 2″	3′ 0″	

CUTTERS

Long	Beam	Depth, Amidships	Depth, Forward	Depth, Aft	Transom	Oars
30′ 0″	7′ 0″	2′ 10″	3′ 8″	3′ 9″	3′ 3″	12
25′ 0″	6′ 10″	2′ 8″	3′ 3″	3′ 4″	3′ 1″	8
21′ 0″	6′ 7″	2′ 6″	3′ 1″	3′ 1″	2′ 10″	8
16′ 0″	6′ 0″	2′ 3″	2′ 9″	2′ 9″	2′ 4″	6

BARGES

Long	Beam	Depth, Amidships	Depth, Forward	Depth, Aft	Transom	Oars
37′ 0″	7′ 9″	3′ 0″	3′ 10″	4′ 3″	4′ 9″	14

YAWLS

Long	Beam	Depth, Amidships	Depth, Forward	Depth, Aft	Transom	Oars
26′ 0″	6′ 8″	2′ 1″	3′ 6″	3′ 9″	3′ 8″	
16′ 0″	5′ 11″	2′ 4″	3′ ½″	2′ 11½″	2′ 7″	

WHERRIES

Long	Beam	Depth, Amidships	Depth, Forward	Depth, Aft	Transom	Oars
25′ 0″	5′ 11″	2′ 4″	3′ ½″	2′ 11½″	1′ 6″	

Anchors suitable for a ship of the size of the *Raleigh* can be determined, as to their weight, by the rule which says: The weight of the ship's bower anchor, the heaviest one, in pounds, is found by adding the ship's beam and depth of hold and multiplying this sum by 100. The stream anchor should be one-third the weight of the bower anchor. Vessels smaller than frigates had anchors of 500 pounds per hundred tons of their tonnage.

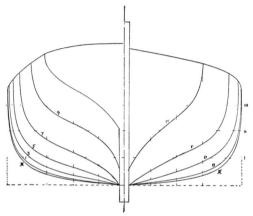

FIG. 52. LINES OF SHIP'S LONG BOAT, 29′ x 9′

The bowers are the anchors stowed on the bows, one on each side of the ship, at the catheads, or just abaft of them, the heavier of the two, if there be any difference, being termed the best bower. The sheet anchors are those stowed just abaft the fore channels and are the same weight as the bowers. The stream anchor is a spare one kept stowed up and down on end in the main hatch, held by lashings to the stanchions. Besides these there are three or four kedge anchors for the small boats. Hemp cables are in size one inch in circumference for every two feet of the ship's breadth of beam.

The correct shape of the anchors has a lot to do with the appearance of a model and it pays to take great care in making them, to get one that has the characteristics of the period the ship represents. The proportions, while they varied somewhat with different makers and different nationalities, were in general as follows: The total length of the arms or flukes was as long as the shank from the crown to the top of the stock. The length of the wooden stock is equal to the length of the shank, plus one-half the diameter of the ring, and its square in size equals one inch for every foot of length of the shank.

The palm is half the length of the arm or fluke, from nib-end to stock, and it is as wide as it is long, its width rounded in to a point at the nib.

The shank tapers from crown to stock being one-third smaller, just below the stock, where the chamfered edges of the stock end in a square. This place is called the small round of the stock.

The stock is made of two pieces of wood that do not quite come together around the square shank of the anchor, which permits their being tightly clamped together by the four iron banks or hoops.

Hoops are so-called, because in the older ships this stock was made round and they were really hoops; but in the time of the *Raleigh*, square stocks and bands were employed.

The stock is parallel for nearly half its length and then the under side is sniped or beveled to half its size at the outer-end. This is tapered so that the hoops may tighten the two halves by being driven on farther.

One noticeable difference in the old anchors was the length of the shank. The *Victory's* old anchor, still preserved on Southsea Promenade, shows a very long shank and rather straight arms, but that this was the common practice at that day is shown by the record of Anchors in the Royal Navy of 1794, for a frigate of 44 guns.

ANCHORS FOR 44-GUN SHIP IN ROYAL NAVY, 1794

Number and weight	L. of Shank	L. of Arm	B. of Palm	T. of Palm	Di. of Ring	Di. of Iron of Ring
4 of 4000 lbs. Bowers	15' 10"	5' 3½"	2' 4"	2⅜"	2' 4"	7¾" to 7"
1 of 1000 lbs. Sheet	10' 4"	3' 5"	1' 7"	1⅛"	1' 7"	4½" to 4"
1 of 500 lbs. Kedge	8' 0"	2' 8"	1' 2"	1"	1' 2"	3½" to 3"

The older anchors were made of square iron and the edges were only slightly chamfered, it being all handwork in those days so no unnecessary labor was expended upon them. With improved forges this chamfering was made more pronounced and finally they were quite rounding on the edges.

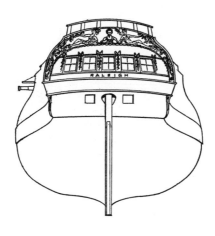

SAIL PLAN of U.S. 44 GUN FRIGATE "CONGRESS". 4

CHAPTER VI

THE FRIGATE "CONGRESS" (4)

HAVING seen what the first American-built frigates were like let us now look at the plans of the 44-gun frigate *Congress* (4), the last sailing frigate built for the United States Navy — destroyed by the Confederate ram *Merrimack*, on Saturday, March 8, 1862, at Hampton Roads, Virginia. Her destruction sounded the death knell not only of the old-time sailing frigates but also those in which steam propelling power had been installed. A new page in history was written in which ironclads were introduced as the naval ships of the future.

The *Merrimack* had been a United States steam-frigate, one of several that were burned and sunk by northern men on April 19, 1861, at the Gosport Navy Yard, just above Norfolk, Virginia, on the Elizabeth River, to prevent them from falling into the hands of the Confederates, who afterwards raised her, cut down her topsides, and on the lower remaining portion of her hull built iron topsides. When she steamed into Hampton Roads on the morning of March 8, 1862, there were anchored between Fortress Monroe and Newport News, the Federal steam frigates *St. Lawrence*, *Roanoke* and *Minnesota*, and the sailing frigate *Congress* (4), while just beyond and to the west of Newport News, was the sailing frigate *Cumberland*. The events of this famous battle are well known. The *Merrimack* rammed and sank the *Cumberland* and with two Confederate gunboats that had accompanied her, she then destroyed the *Congress* (4). Satisfied with their day's work, they put off the destruction of the rest of the Federal fleet till the morrow — but daybreak found the little *Monitor* there which beat off the *Merrimack* and saved the rest of the fleet.

The *Congress* (4) had poured her broadsides against the *Merrimack's* armored side, as she passed on her way to sink the *Cumberland*, and her officers had noted with what little effect. In consequence the *Congress* (4) was got under way in an endeavor to sail close under the protection of the guns of Fortress Monroe. Unfortunately the ship grounded in shoal water and was a helpless target for the three Confederate vessels. She was battered to pieces and many of her crew were mowed down by the raking fire from the enemy. Finally she surrendered, but the fire from shore batteries and the remaining Federal ships became so hot that the Confederate gunboat, with thirty prisoners that had been taken aboard, had to haul off. The rest of the crew of the *Congress* (4) escaped to shore by small boats or by swimming. Set afire by red-hot shot, the *Congress* (4) burned until after midnight when the fire reached her magazine and she blew up with a tremendous explosion.

The first ship in the American Navy to carry the name *Congress* was a 28-gun frigate built in 1776 at Poughkeepsie, N. Y. She was burned by her crew just above West Point to prevent her falling into the hands of the British fleet that was coming up the Hudson River.

The second *Congress* was a galley, mounting eight guns and 18 swivels, that was built and used on Lake Champlain in 1776.

The third *Congress* was a 36-gun ship built at Portsmouth, N. H., in 1799 and broken up at Norfolk, Va., in 1836. She was a frigate of 1268 tons and practically a sister ship to the *Constellation*.

The fourth *Congress* was a 44-gun frigate, 179 feet long, 47 feet 8 inches moulded beam, 22 feet 8 inches depth, and 1867 tons burden. She was the last sailing frigate built for the Navy, her construction not having been commenced until 1839, at Portsmouth, N. H., the same port where the *Raleigh* was built, back in 1776.

The *Congress* (4) was launched in 1841, two years after she was commenced. Other frigates of the same class but slightly smaller, of only 1726 tons burden—the *Cumberland*, *Savannah*, *Raritan* and *St. Lawrence*—had been started in 1825, 1820, 1820 and 1826 respectively, thirteen to nineteen years before, but they were not put afloat until a year or two after the *Congress* (4) was launched, and in the case of the *St. Lawrence*, six years.

Portsmouth, N. H., has always had an enviable reputation for shipbuilding, the navy yard there having a wonderful personnel of very capable mechanics; whereas, the Gosport yard, near Norfolk, Va., where the *St. Lawrence* was built, had much difficulty in obtaining efficient labor. So to Portsmouth belongs the honor of having built the first (or one of the first) and the last sailing frigate for the American Navy.

The little *Raleigh* could be stowed inside the *Congress* (4), her 697 tons being overshadowed more than two and a half times by the 1867 tons of the *Congress* (4), and her armament of 12 pounders and 6 pounders were mere bean shooters compared to the heavy guns on the more modern ship which consisted of a battery of 42 thirty-two pounders and 8 eight-inch guns.

The beautiful frigates of 1797, designed by Joshua Humphreys, have never been equalled by any sailing man-of-war of any other nation, for their combination of beauty and efficiency. Their proportions and heavy con-

Sailors Telling Yarns on an Old-Time Frigate

struction were something entirely new in frigates. They outranked other frigates of their day so completely and were such superior vessels that England tried to imitate them by razeeing some of her line-of-battle ships; cutting down the topsides and so eliminating one of the decks in an effort to get ships whose strength and calibre of guns could cope with the *Constitution*, *President* and *United States*.

These clumsy, reduced English line-of-battle ships did not compare with Humphreys's frigates which were beautifully modelled under water, and could outsail the enemy when it came to a test of speed. The appearance of these American frigates on the water, their graceful poise and balance as outlined in profile gave a most harmonious and pleasing appearance to the nautical eye. The detail of the headrails, brackets and trail-boards, with their vine-like carving, surmounted by the carved figurehead, gave a light and delicate appearance to a bow that behind it all was really massive in its strength.

Aft, the same camouflage so disguised a very plain stern that it, too, by the harmonious relationship between the various rails on the quarter galleries, was handsome in appearance.

The little touches of carving that embellished the vertical pilasters and the exactness of the gradual increase in rake of these vertical members, all pleased the eye; while across the broad stern, its huge arch-board, carved and painted so that, instead of seeing a very plain stern the eye beheld a most graceful series of curves ending above all with a wide, gradually tapered arch, finished off the hull so that it was a delight for any sailor to look upon. Aloft, too, they were finished most completely. Every spar was tapered and stayed to a nicety.

Of all people, sailors are most critical in their examination of a ship. Every spar must slant or rake just so and every stay slant at just a certain angle with reference to other stays or severe criticism will be forthcoming. The length and diameter of every spar, the spacing of the shrouds and deadeyes, in fact, every detail of a ship comes in for a severe scrutiny, even to a ratline that might be ever so slightly out of line with its neighbors. When one of these ships fetched up in a foreign harbor and stowed her canvas, there was nothing but wonder and praise expressed from seafaring men.

In the shape of the hull of these frigates there was a strong resemblance to the shape of the little *Raleigh*, yet it was modified, being not quite so flat in the midship section and the ends were sharper, especially at the bow. This type of ship was so popular in the Navy that many more were constructed from these plans and it was not until the *Congress* (4) was built that this model was changed and her sections were rounded out and the deadrise straightened, discarding entirely the old-style yoke-shaped floor timbers.

Utility was fast stripping the romance from modern men-of-war and discarding much that was dear to the hearts of seamen, but when the quarter galleries and the square stern, decorated like a valentine, with fancy mouldings and relief carved work were wiped away and a bald, round, "kettle" stern appeared, as on the *Congress* (4), sailors took one look, squirted a copious stream of tobacco juice to emphasize their disgust, and turned away.

Engineers had decided, however, that the round stern gave a far more serviceable range in working the stern chase guns, and beauty of appearance no longer was part of the Navy's scheme. Utility alone was demanded and new guns were being invented that could throw a much heavier shot farther than the little twelve pounders of the *Raleigh*. The *Congress* (4) could fire cannon balls from her guns that weighed thirty-two pounds.

It is true that the merchant marine was also doing away with much of the filigree work formerly to be found adorning the ends of shipping—just as the ruffled shirt front was being abolished ashore. Huge, naked, black-hulled ships without a sign of a figurehead and with a narrow, round stern, unlike anything that had heretofore been considered shipshape, began to show up at the wharves in New York. They were the clipper ships, sharpened to a heretofore unheard of degree and they looked their part—the athletes of the marine world.

It was some slight balm to the outraged feelings of the old deepwater men to see these round sterns carried by the clippers, but when a square-sterned clipper warped into her berth beside the pier, the "steamboat," the "kettle," or the "round stern," as it was variously termed, was relegated to the back seat.

We have available all the necessary data to build an accurate model of the *Congress* (4), as the tables of sizes of ropes, blocks, etc., published in that handy book called *The Kedge Anchor*, by Lieutenant Brady, were copied from the official regulations by which the *Congress* (4) and her sister ships were rigged. A study of these tables will give one all the sizes required and in the case of such items as shrouds, will supply information as to how many there were to a side on each mast, where rawhide was used in place of rope as on the sheets of the upper sails, wheel ropes, etc., and in numerous notes where much of the running rigging leads to, points which often confuse the novice. If you are fortunate enough to find a copy of the government "Tables of Allowances," published by the Navy Department, in 1844, from which these were copied, you will have a detailed list of everything put aboard every class of man-of-war of that date, from spars, anchors, cables, boats, etc., to pen and ink, scissors, tacks and even the books to be found in each ship's library. In scanning the lists of rigging in the Boatswain's Department we find patent trusses, iron futtock shrouds, iron bending jack stays, and chain slings, on the lower yards, and as this is a government publication, the fact that these were in use in 1844 may be accepted as authentic.

The boats carried by the *Congress* (4) were nine in number, consisting of a first and second launch, three cutters, a barge, a gig, and a small galvanized iron boat. The sizes of these boats will be appreciated by anyone who makes a model of this ship and are as follows:

Boats Carried by a First Class Frigate

	Length	Breadth	Depth	
1st Launch	34′ 0″	9′ 6″	4′ 2″	Coppered
2d Launch	31′ 0″	8′ 5″	3′ 10″	Coppered
1st Cutter	28′ 0″	7′ 5″	2′ 10″	
2d Cutter	25′ 6″	6′ 8″	2′ 7″	
3d Cutter	27′ 0″	6′ 9″	2′ 6″	
1st Whale Boat	28′ 0″	7′ 2″	2′ 5″	Lap strake built
Barge	28′ 0″	6′ 0″	2′ 4″	
Gig	28′ 0″	5′ 0″	1′ 8″	
Galvanized Iron Boat	18′ 0″	4′ 10″		

The launches had their bottoms coppered and had a roller fitted at both bow and stern and a well, built in amidships, that went through the bottom so that when necessary the ship's anchors could be raised by bringing a cable up through this well and winding it on a horizontal windlass fitted across the boat, worked with heaving bars.

Anchors for a frigate like the *Congress* (4) would be three sheet and and two bower anchors of 3500 pounds each and one stream anchor of 1600 pounds. The regulations, as published in 1844, provided for only four sheet and bower anchors, but this was increased a few years later, to five anchors, the extra one to be carried in the main hatch. Four kedge anchors were provided, one each of the following weights: 1000, 700, 600 and 400 pounds, and the small anchors for the ship's boats were apportioned as follows: first launch, 180 pounds; second launch, 120 pounds; first cutter, 80 pounds; and second cutter, 60 pounds. Two grapnels were provided, one of 100 pounds and one of 50 pounds.

The cables allowed by the regulations were two twenty-two inch (circumference) of 120 fathoms length, hemp cables for the sheet anchors; one, thirteen inch hemp cable of 120 fathoms in length, for the stream anchor; one chain cable of 1 15/16 inch (diameter of iron links) of 165 fathoms and two chain cables of the same size and length for the bowers.

TABLE OF SPARS FOR FIRST CLASS FRIGATE OF THE UNITED STATES NAVY

	Length	Diameter	Masthead
Mainmast	105' 0"	34"	18' 0"
Maintopmast	63' 0"	19.3"	9' 7"
Main-topgallantmast	32' 0"	11"	
Main-royalmast	21' 8"		
Main-flag pole	8' 8"	4"	
Foremast	95' 0"	30.8"	16' 0"
Foretopmast	56' 0"	19.3"	9' 6"
Fore-topgallantmast	29' 0"	11"	
Fore-royalmast	19' 4"		
Fore-flag pole	7' 9"	4"	
Mizenmast	87' 0"	24.8"	12' 4"
Mizentopmast	46' 4"	13.3"	6' 8"
Mizen-topgallantmast	24' 6"	8"	
Mizen-royalmast	16' 4"		
Mizen-flag pole	6' 6"	3.6"	
Bowsprit	66' 0"		
Jib-boom	50' 0"	14.8"	
Flying jib-boom	54' 0"	10.8"	
Pole	8' 8"		

	Length	Diameter	Arm
Main yard	95' 0"	22.6"	4' 9"
Main-topsail yard	71' 6"	17.8"	6' 0"
Main-topgallant yard	44' 0"	10.2"	2 '0"
Main-royal yard	30' 0"	6"	1' 6"
Fore yard	84' 0"	20.2"	4' 6"
Fore-topsail yard	62' 0"	15.5"	5' 3"
Fore-topgallant yard	41' 0"	9.3"	2' 0"
Fore-royal yard	27' 0"	5.4"	1' 3"
Cross-jack yard	66' 0"	13.2"	7' 0"
Mizen-topsail yard	46' 0"	9.5"	4' 0"
Mizen-topgallant yard	30' 0"	.6"	1' 6"
Mizen-royal yard	19' 0"	3.8"	2' 9"
Fore gaff	33' 6"	8.3"	
Main gaff	28' 6"	7.1"	
Mizen gaff	32' 0"	7.8"	
Spanker boom	50' 0"	10.5"	
Ring-tail boom	25' 0"	5"	
Jack gaff	14' 0"	4.2"	
Dolphin striker	18' 0"	7.5"	

THE FRIGATE "CONGRESS" (4)

	Length	Diam.
Main-topmast studding-sail boom	47' 6"	9.9"
Main-topmast studding-sail yard	20' 0"	4.0"
Main-topgallant studding-sail boom	35' 9"	7.4"
Main-topgallant studding-sail yard	20' 0"	4.0"
Fore-lower swinging-boom	51' 3"	10.2"
Lower-studding sail-yard	25' 6"	5.0"
Fore-topmast studding-sail boom	42' 0"	8.8"
Fore-topmast studding-sail yard	25' 9"	5.2"
Fore-topgallant studding-sail boom	31' 0"	6.5"
Fore-topgallant studding-sail yard	18' 6"	3.7"

That one may the better visualize how the crew of the *Congress* (4) were stationed about the ship and at the guns, we give a "watch bill" which shows where each man was located in the ship and who was in the starboard watch and who in the port or larboard watch. A "quarter bill" shows where each man is stationed when the call to quarters sends the men to the guns and otherwise prepares for war, as given in Totten's *Naval Text Book*, published in 1841, by Little & Brown, Boston.

Having shown in diagram how the men were stationed at the 12- and 6-pound guns of the frigate *Raleigh*, we now show how the guns crew of a 32-pound cannon such as the *Congress* (4) carried, was stationed. This diagram shows their duties in connection with the gun and also who were the men to leave the gun when the rattle was sprung and the call of "Boarders repel boarders!" sounded throughout the ship, the first boarders responding to the first call and the second boarders leaving the gun if the call was repeated, and so on.

FORMATION OF WATCH BILL OF A FIRST CLASS FRIGATE OF 54 GUNS
How the Crew is Divided into Two Watches

Rates	Frigate, 1st Class		
Watches	Larboard	Starboard	Total
Officers	1st Lieutenant	Captain	
Idlers	Purser	Master	
	Chaplain	Surgeon	
	Passed Midshipmen	Sig. Lt. Marines	
	Passed Midshipmen	Passed Midshipmen	
	Midshipman Aid	Passed Midshipmen	
	Asst. Surgeon	Asst. Surgeon	
	Prof. of Math.	Clerk	
	Boatswain	Gunner	
	Carpenter	Sailmaker	
	Yeoman	Master's Mate	
	(11)	(11)	22

Watch-Officers	5 Lieutenants		
	15 Passed Midshipmen and Mid.		20
Idlers of the Crew	Ship's Corporal	Master of Arms	
	Orderly Sergeant	Ship Cook	
	Captain of the Hold	Master of Band	
	Signal Quarter Master	Captain of the Hold	
	Surgeon's Steward	Ship's Steward	
	Officer's Steward	Officer's Steward	
	Officer's Cook	Officer's Cook	
	(7)	(7)	14
Petty Officers	2 Boatswain's Mates	2 Boatswain's Mates	
	1 Gunner's Mate	1 Gunner's Mate	
	3 Quartermasters	3 Quartermasters	
	5 Quarter Gunners	5 Quarter Gunners	
	Carpenter's Mate	Carpenter's Mate	
	Armorer	Cooper	
	Sailmaker's Mate		
	Captain of Forecastle	Captain of Forecastle	
	3 Captains of Tops	3 Captains of Tops	
	(18)	(17)	35
Forecastle-head Men	18 Seamen	18 Seamen	
	6 Ordinary Seamen	6 Ordinary Seamen	
	2 Landsmen	2 Landsmen	
	(26)	(26)	52
Fore top Men	16 Seamen	16 Seamen	
	6 Ordinary Seamen	6 Ordinary Seamen	
	2 Boys	2 Boys	
	(24)	(24)	48
Main top Men	16 Seamen	16 Seamen	
	7 Ordinary Seamen	7 Ordinary Seamen	
	3 Boys	3 Boys	
	(26)	(26)	52
Mizzen top Men	8 Seamen	8 Seamen	
	6 Ordinary Seamen	6 Ordinary Seamen	
	4 Boys	4 Boys	
	(18)	(18)	36
Afterguard	9 Seamen	9 Seamen	
	18 Ordinary Seamen	18 Ordinary Seamen	
	13 Landsmen	13 Landsmen	
	(40)	(40)	80

THE FRIGATE "CONGRESS" (4)

Waisters	4 Seamen	4 Seamen	
	7 Ordinary Seamen	7 Ordinary Seamen	
	15 Landsmen	15 Landsmen	
	(26)	(26)	52
Mastmen	4 Seamen	4 Seamen	8
Messengers	3 Boys	3 Boys	6
Musicians	2 1st Class	2 1st Class	
	2 1st Class	1 2d Class	
	(4)	(3)	7
Marines	1 Sergeant	1 Sergeant	
	2 Corporals	1 Corporal	
	1 Drummer	1 Fifer	
	15 Privates	16 Privates	
	(19)	(19)	38
Total War Complement			470

QUARTER BILL OF A FIRST CLASS FRIGATE OF 54 GUNS

Where Each Man in the Crew is Stationed
Quarter Deck

Captain Commanding, 2 Passed Midshipmen or Mid. (Aids)
Clerk to take Minutes
1st Lieutenant, 2 Passed Midshipmen or Mid. (Aids)

Signals

Signal Passed Midshipman
Signal Quartermaster

Gun Deck — 15 long 24 lbrs. — and their opposites.

First Division

The 2d Lieut. commanding, 2 Passed Midshipmen or Midshipmen
1 Quarter Gunner

No. of Gun	Petty Officer	Seamen	Ord. Seamen	Boys	Total at Guns	
1	1 B. M.	5	4	1	13	
2		6	4	1	13	
3	Q. M.	5	4	1	13	
4		6	4	1	13	
5		6	4	1	13	*Total Force of Div.*
	2	28	20	5	65	69

129

Second Division

The 3d Lieut. commanding, 2 Passed Midshipmen or Midshipmen
1 Quarter Gunner

No. of Gun	Petty Officer	Seamen	Ord. Seamen	Landsmen	Boys	Total at Guns	
6		6	4	2	1	13	
7		6	4	2	1	13	
8	1 B. M.	5	4	2	1	13	
9		6	4	2	1	13	
10	Q. M.	5	4	2	1	13	*Total Force of Div.*
	2	28	20	10	1	65	69

Third Division

The 4th Lieut. commanding, 2 Passed Midshipmen or Midshipmen
1 Quarter Gunner

No. of Gun	Petty Officer	Seamen	Ord. Seamen	Landsmen	Boys	Total at Guns	
11		6	4	2	1	13	
12		6	4	2	1	13	
13	Q. M.	5	4	2	1	13	
14		6	4	2	1	13	
15		5	4	2	1	13	*Total Force of Div.*
	1	28	20	10	5	65	69

Spar Deck — 1 long 24, and 11 32 lb. carronades and opposites

Fourth Division — Forecastle

The 5th Lieut. commanding, 2 Passed Midshipmen and Midshipmen
1 Quarter Gunner

No. of Gun	Petty Officer	Seamen	Ord. Seamen	Landsmen	Boys	Total at Guns	
16	Capt. fcksl.	5	4	2	1	13	
17		4	2	2	1	9	
18		3	2	2	1	9	
19	Capt. fr. top	4	2	2	1	9	
20		4	2	2	1	9	*Total Force of Div.*
	2	20	12	10	5	49	53

Fifth Division — Quarter Deck

The 6th Lieut. commanding, 2 Passed Midshipmen, 1 Quarter Gunner

No. of Gun	Petty Officer	Seamen	Ord. Seamen	Landsmen	Boys	Total at Guns
21	Capt. main top	3	2	2	1	9
22		4	2	2	1	9

THE FRIGATE HACK HOAT OF 1750
From an engraving in Chapman's "Architectura Navalis"

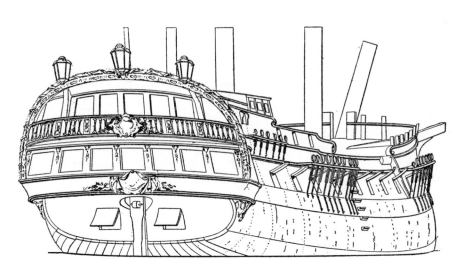

A FRIGATE OF ABOUT 1750
From an engraving in Chapman's "Architectura Navalis"

							Total Force of Div.
23		4	2	2	1	9	
24		4	2	2	1	9	
25	Capt. miz.top	3	2	2	1	9	
26		4	2	2	1	9	
27		4	2	2	1	9	
	2	26	14	14	7	63	67

Total force at the guns   327

Marine Guard

The officers, non-commissioned, and privates of the marine guard are formed forward, aft, or in the gangways, as directed by the Captain commanding.

Force, less those in the tops, Officer, 1; Non-Com. Officers, 6; Music, 2; Privates, 23. Total, 32.

Sixth Division, First Part — Quarter Deck

Sailing Master Commanding, 2 Midshipmen or Passed Midshipmen
1 Master's Mate

Stations	Persons Stationed	Force
Forecastle & gangways	Boatswain, 1 bo'sen's mate, capt. focksl., 4 seamen	7
Foretop	1 midshipman, capt. fore top, 1 foretopman, 3 marines	6
Maintop	1 midshipman, capt. main top, 1 maintopman, 3 marines	6
Mizzentop	1 Midshipman, capt. miz. top, 1 miz. topman, 2 marines	5
Head braces & main rigging	1 Bo'sen's mate, 4 seamen, 4 musicians	9
Main braces & mizzen rigging	2 capt. aft. guard, 2 a. g. ord. seamen, 4 musicians	8
Cross-jack braces	2 2d capts. aft. guard, 2 a. g. ord. seamen	4
Spanker	1 quartermaster, 1 focksl. seaman	2
Ensign	2 aft. guard seamen	2
	Sail maker	1
		50

Sixth Division, Second Part — Lower Deck

		Force
Fore magazine	1 gunner's mate, 1 quarter gunner	2
Fore magazine passage	1 quarter gunner, 1 yeoman, 1 sailing master's mate	3
Fore magazine light room	1 ship's corporal	1
Forward scuttle main deck	Armorer, armorer's mate (ordinary seaman)	2

THE FRIGATE "CONGRESS" (4)

Forward scuttle berth deck	2 officer's cooks	2
Main magazine	Gunner, gunner's mate, 2 quarter gunner's cooper	5
Main magazine passage to pass full boxes	1 quarter gunner, 2 idlers	3
Main magazine passage to pass empty boxes	2 idlers	2
Main magazine light room	Master at Arms	1
To pass empty boxes from hatch to wardroom scuttle	Purser's clerk, 6 idlers (servants)	7
To pass full boxes from scuttle to hatch	Purser, 2 officer's stewards, 4 idlers (landsmen)	7
Shot and wad lockers	2 captains of the hold	2
Galley	Ship's cook	1
Pumps and shot plugs	Carpenter, 2 carpenter's mates, 2 ord. seamen	5
Cockpit	Surgeon, 2 mates, steward, 1 lower hold (ord. seaman), chaplain, prof. of math.	7
Relieving tackles	2 quartermasters	2
		52
	Total force of 6th Division	102
	Total complement	470

NOTE — This table is formed from the war complement allowed by the commissioners. If the maindeck guns are long 32 pounders instead of 24 pounders, requiring 14 men and 1 boy, 1 marine must be stationed at each gun to complete the force.

Students of naval affairs who have read of the various naval engagements between two or more ships can, with such a "quarter bill" to refer to, the better visualize how the battles were fought. It shows how the guns on the maindeck were divided into three divisions of five guns, on each side, each of long 24-pound guns. On the forecastle there was one long 24 pounder for a bow chaser and four 32-pound carronades on each side; while on the quarterdeck the armament consisted of seven 32-pound carronades on each side of the ship. It shows who is down inside the ship passing up the cartridges of powder and the cannon balls to keep the men at the guns supplied with ammunition.

The magazines of the *Congress* (4) were located in the bottom of the ship, one aft, under the heel of the mizzenmast which steps on the orlop or deck forming the roof of the magazine which stowed 212 barrels of powder; and the other, just abaft the foremast, stowing 100 barrels. No lights are ever allowed in these rooms. Lights placed in adjoining rooms shone through glass windows. The powder was passed out of the magazine and the cartridges were filled in an adjoining room known as the "filling room." From there they were passed into the passageway and up through a round hole cut in the berth deck, called a "passing scuttle." Here they were carried forward to where a screen or bulkhead formed of wet blankets was hung up during action and there passed through a couple of holes provided with loose flaps in this "screen." Here, other men took the charge and carried it to a hatchway passing it up to others who handed it to the powder boys or "powder monkeys," as they were nicknamed, who took it to the guns. On the *Congress* (4) eight men were required to supply ammunition for the spardeck and seven men for the maingun deck, besides a few "runner boys" to carry between the passing stations.

The cartridges were nothing but a bag of powder made of white woolen cloth. A 32 pounder used six pounds of powder per charge, so this bag had to hold that quantity. The flat pattern of a cartridge-bag was rectangular for the cylindrical part with a circular piece to form the bottom. These parts were sewed with worsted yarn not less than eight stitches per inch. The "cartridge boxes" or "passing boxes" were not wooden boxes, but cylindrical cases, with caps, made of well-tanned harness or sole leather, usually painted black with the calibre of the gun they served painted on in white letters on the side and top. Where guns on the spardeck required a lighter charge, the lower half of their "passing boxes" was painted white and for the gundeck the lower part was painted red.

For further details on this and similar subjects I would refer the reader to *The Naval Text Book*, written in 1841, by Lieut. B. J. Totten, which is the most complete of any I have yet discovered, and *Ordnance Instructions*, *U.S.N.*, published at Washington in 1866, which goes into minute detail. The first volume describes how the guns were handled and tells, step by step, every phase of the rigging of a ship. It contains a mine of information difficult to find elsewhere. For instance, the spacing of the ratlines is here given definitely as 14 inches apart on the lower rigging and either 12 or 13 inches on the topmast rigging.

While making a comparison between these two American frigates, one of 1776 and one of 1841, it will be interesting to note the appearance of the Swedish frigates, figured by F. H. Chapman in his admirable work — *Architectura Navalis Mercatoria*, published in 1768. These exceptional drawings were executed on copper by a draughtsman named Bogman and give a very clear conception of the detail of these ships whose shape of hull very closely approximates that of our own frigate the *Raleigh*, and seen in perspective will assist the modelmaker in understanding the ship's draughts.

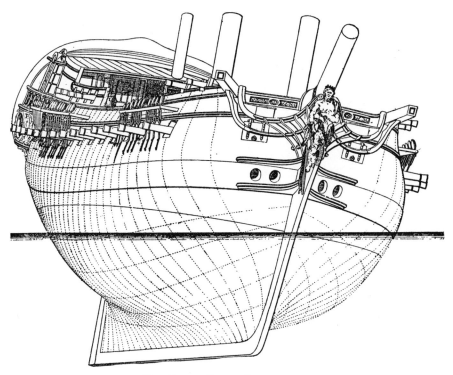

THE ROUND BODIED SHIP OF 1750
From an engraving in Chapman's "Architectura Navalis"

APPENDIX

APPENDIX I

MASTS AND SPARS OF UNITED STATES NAVAL VESSELS

THE following pages are copied from the original manuscript, in three large blank books, written by William Brady, in 1843, while boatswain on board of the line-of-battle ship *North Carolina*. These volumes contain the subject matter published in his book *The Kedge Anchor*, but the tables which are here printed were not included and to-day are of inestimable value to ship model builders and historians. Where the length of the mizzenmast is left blank, one can easily figure how high it came in relation to the mainmast head, the mizzen cap being 3/5ths of the length of the mainmast head below the mainmast cap. This measurement is so given because the mizzenmast step varied; sometimes going to the keel but generally stopping on the orlop deck, some distance above the keel.

For this very valuable contribution to American naval history and permission to print the same, the Marine Research Society is indebted to the generosity of Mr. William Roos of Mamaroneck, N. Y., the present owner of the manuscript.

SHIPS OF THE PAST

DIMENSIONS OF THE SPARS OF A 3 DECKER, A 74, & A FRIGATE OF THE FIRST CLASS — PER NEW ALLOWANCE.

Spars	3 Decker Length ft. ins.	Diameter in. 10ths	Mast-head ft. ins.	74 Length ft. ins.	Diameter in. 10ths	Mast-head ft. ins.	1st Class Frigate Length ft. in.	Diameter in. 10ths	Mast-head ft. in.
Main Mast	132.	42.7	22.	124.6	42.2	20.	105.	34.	18.
Main Topmast	70.	21.5	12.	70.	21.5	12.	63.	19.3	9.7
Main Topgallant Mast	35.	12.		35.	12.		32.	11.	
Main Royal Mast	23.6			23.6			21.8		
Main Flag Pole	9.¾	4.		9.¾	4.		8.8	4.	
Fore Mast	120.	38.8	20.	115.	36.8	8.	95.	30.8	16.
Fore Topmast	63.	21.5	10.6	63.	21.5	10.6	56.	19.3	9.6
Fore Topgallant Mast	32.	12.		32.	12.		29.	11.	
Fore Royal Mast	21.4			21.4			19.4		
Fore Flag Pole	8.6	4.		8.6	4.		7.9	4.	
Mizen Mast	110.	27.5	17.	105.	26.5	16.	87.	24.8	12.4
Mizen Topmast	55.	15.8	9.	55.	15.8	9.	46.4	13.3	6.8
Mizen Topgallant Mast	29.	9.8		29.	9.8		24.6	8.	
Mizen Royal Mast	19.4			19.4			16.4		
Mizen Flag Pole	7.9	3.7		7.9	3.7		6.6	3.6	
			Yd. Arm			*Yd. Arm*			*Yd. Arm*
Main Yard	110.	26.4	5.	107.6	25.7	5.	95.	22.6	4.9
Main Topsail Yard	82.	20.5	7.	78.	19.5	6.6	71.6	17.8	6.
Main Topgallant Yard	52.	11.8	2.	52.	11.8	2.	44.	10.2	2.
Main Royal Yard	36.	7.2	1.6	36.	7.2	1.6	30.	6.	1.6
Fore Yard	100.	24.	5.	96.	23.	5.	84.	20.2	4.6
Fore Topsail Yard	75.	18.8	6.6	71.	17.8	6.	62.	15.5	5.3
Fore Topgallant Yard	48.	10.9	2.	46.	10.7	2.	41.	9.3	2.
Fore Royal Yard	33.	6.6	1.6	33.	6.6	1.6	27.	5.4	1.3
Cross Jack Yard	80.	16.	7.6	80.	16.	7.6	66.	13.2	7.
Mizen Topsail Yard	53.	11.1	4.6	53.	11.1	4.6	46.	9.5	4.
Mizen Topgallant Yard	33.	6.6	1.6	33.	6.6	1.6	30.	6.	1.6
Mizen Royal Yard	23.	4.6	1.	23.	4.6	1.	19.	3.8	.9
Spritsail Yard (old allowance)	73.6	14.4	7.4	71.8	14.	.8	63.4	12.5	6.4
Bowsprit	80.			78.			66.		
Jib-boom	60.	17.8		60.	17.8		50.	14.8	
Flying Jib-boom	61.	12.		61.	12.		54.	10.8	
Pole	9.			9.			8.8		
			Length of pole			*Length of pole*			*Length of pole*
Main Gaff	33.	8.2		33.	8.2		28.6	7.1	
Main Topmast Studding Sail Boom	55.	11.5		53.9	11.		47.6	9.9	
Yard for Main Topmast Studg. Sail	24.	4.8		24.	4.8		20.	4.	
Main Topgallant Stud-sail Boom	41.	8.6		39.	8.2		35.9	7.4	
Yard for Main Topgallant Stud-sail	24.	4.8		24.	4.8		20.	4.	
Fore Gaff	37.	9.2		37.	9.2		33.6	8.3	
Lower Swinging Boom	65.	13.		60.	12.		51.3	10.2	
Yard for lower Studg. Sail	32.6	6.5		30.	6.		25.6	5.	
Fore Topmast Studding Sail Boom	50.	10.5		48.	10.		42.	8.8	
Yard for Fore Topmast Stud-sail	31.	6.2		29.9	6.		25.9	5.2	
Fore Topgallant Studding-sail Boom	37.6	7.8		35.	7.4		31.	6.5	
Yard for Fore Topgallant Stud-sail	22.	4.4		21.	4.2		18.6	3.7	
Spanker Boom	60.	12.5		60.	12.5		50.	10.5	
Ring-tail Boom	30.	6.		30.	6.		25.	5.	
Mizen Gaff	38.	9.4	5.	38.	9.4	5.	32.	7.8	4.6
Jack Gaff	17.	6.		16.	5.5		14.	4.2	
Dolphin Striker	22.	9.	3.	20.	8.5	3.	18.	7.5	2.

DIMENSIONS OF MASTS AND SPARS

	Length Ft.	Head or Arm Inches	Diameter Ft.
Main Mast	124.75	20.44	41.58
Fore Mast	114.75	18.80	38.25
Mizen Mast		15.33	29.10
Main Topmast	70.50	11.28	21.64
Fore Topmast	64.86	10.38	21.64
Mizen Topmast	52.87	8.45	15.33
Main Top Gallant Mast	38.25		11.78
Fore Top Gallant Mast	32.43		10.81
Mizen Top Gallant Mast	26.43		8.8
Main Royal Mast	23.97		
Fore Royal Mast	22.05		
Mizen Royal Mast	17.97		
Main Pole	11.98		
Fore Pole	11.02		
Mizen Pole	8.98		
Main Yard	105.97	4.45	24.9
Main Top Gallant Yard	50.33	2.77	10.56
Fore Yard	97.50	4.09	22.91
Fore Top Gallant Yard	46.50	2.54	9.72
Cross Jack Yard	68.88	3.78	14.46
Mizen Top Gallant Yard	32.22	1.77	6.77
Bowsprit Outboard	48.82		41.58
Jib Boom	39.	2.34	20.67
Flying Jib Boom	31.02	5.93	13.43
Spanker Boom	58.87		13.54
Spanker Gaff	44.14	5.76	8.83

The length of the Topsail Yard Arm to be determined by the Sailmaker's Draft, for the diameter in the slings in inches multiply the length by .25. For the breadth of the Main Top multiply the extreme breadth by .43. And for the length multiply the breadth by .67. For the length and breadth of Fore Top multiply the Main by

.92. For the length and breadth of the Mizen Top multiply the Main by .75. Main & Mizen lower trestle Trees to be equal to the diameter of their respective Topmasts in the Caps. For the depth of Fore lower Trestle Trees multiply the Main by .92. Topmast Trestle Trees in depth to be equal to the diameter of their respective Top Gallant Masts in the Caps. Thickness of trestle trees to be one-half the depth. For the length of after Topmast Crosstrees take one-half of their respective tops. Each Topmast to have three Crosstrees. The length of Fore Mast to be determined by a line parallel to the load line commencing at the top of Keelson under the Main Mast should the Keelson be above the line at the Fore Mast the rise is to be deducted from the length here given. Should the Keelson be below the line the difference between the two is to be added to the length here given. The length of the Mizen Mast to be determined by a line parallel to the load line at two-thirds of the head of Main Mast below the extreme height of that mast. The diameters of lower Masts are intended to include both cheeks, in other words the diameters in the Partners are the extreme diameters. Bowsprits of all vessels to have long bus to set up Fore Stays through as the Topmast Stays are.

Constructors

Saml Humphreys

Francis Grice

Jno Lenthall

Foster Rhodes

June 3^e 1843

DIMENSIONS OF MASTS AND SPARS

DIMENSIONS OF MASTS & SPARS PROPOSED TO THE BUREAU OF CON-
STRUCTION FOR RAZEE INDEPENDENCE AND HER CLASS WHOSE LENGTH
BETWEEN THE PERPENDICULARS IS 188. AND EXTREME BREADTH 51.

	Length	Head or Arm	Diameter
Main Mast	115.	19.14	38.34
Fore Mast	105.08	17.61	35.27
Mizen Mast		14.35	26.84
Main Topmast	66.	10.56	20.26
Fore Topmast	60.72	9.71	20.26
Mizen Topmast	49.05	7.92	14.35
Main Top Gallant Mast	33.05		11.
Fore Top Gallant Mast	30.36		10.12
Mizen Top Gallant Mast	24.75		8.25
Main Royal Mast	22.44		
Fore Royal Mast	20.64		
Mizen Royal Mast	16.83		
Main Pole	11.22		
Fore Pole	10.32		
Mizen Pole	8.42		
Main Yard	101.52	4.26	23.86
Main Top Gallant Yard	48.22	2.65	10.12
Fore Yard	93.40	3.92	21.92
Fore Top Gallant Yard	44.36	2.43	9.31
Cross Jack Yard	66.36	3.63	13.86
Mizen Top Gallant Yard	31.34	1.72	6.58
Spanker Boom	50.04		12.97
Gaff	42.03	Pole 5.5	8.46
Bowsprit Outboard	45.09		38.34
Jib Boom do	36.72	Head 2.20	19.46
Flying Jib Boom	29.37	5.58	12.62

SHIPS OF THE PAST

Dimensions of Masts & Spars proposed to the Bureau of Construction for Frigate United States and her class whose length between the perpendiculars is. 175. and extreme breadth. 54.25.

	Whole Length Ft.	Head & Arms Ft.	Diameter Inches
Main Mast	100.	17.40	33.
Fore Mast	92.	16.	31.67
Mizen Mast		13.05	33.10
Main Topmast	60.	9.60	18.40
Fore Topmast	55.20	8.83	18.40
Mizen Topmast	45.	7.20	13.05
Main Top Gallant Mast	30.		9.60
Fore Top Gallant Mast	27.60		8.83
Mizen Top Gallant Mast	22.50		7.20
Main Royal Mast	20.40		
Fore Royal Mast	18.76		
Mizen Royal Mast	15.30		
Main Pole	10.20		
Fore Pole	9.37		
Mizen Pole	7.63		
Main Yard	90.	3.78	21.15
Main Top Gallant Yard	42.75	2.35	8.98
Fore Yard	82.80	3.48	19.46
Fore Top Gallant Yard	39.35	2.17	8.26
Cross Jack Yard	58.50	3.22	12.28
Mizen Top Gallant Yard	27.78	1.53	5.83
Bowsprit Outboard	40.05		53.
Jib Boom do	32.	1.92	16.96
Flying Jib Boom	25.60	4.86	11.
Spanker Boom	52.50		12.07
Spanker Gaff	39.37	5.01	7.87

DIMENSIONS OF MASTS AND SPARS

DIMENSIONS OF MASTS & SPARS PROPOSED TO THE BUREAU OF CONSTRUCTION FOR FRIGATE CONGRESS AND HER CLASS WHOSE LENGTH BETWEEN THE PERPENDICULARS IS. 179. EXTREME BREADTH. 47.5. OR FIRST CLASS FRIGAT U. S. NAVY.

	Whole Length In feet	Head & Arms In feet	Diameter In inches
Main Mast	109.25	19.	36.42
Fore Mast	100.50	17.48	33.5
Mizen Mast		14.25	25.50
Main Topmast	65.50	10.48	20.10
Fore Topmast	60.26	9.64	20.10
Mizen Topmast	49.12	7.86	14.25
Main Top Gallant Mast	32.75		10.92
Fore Top Gallant Mast	30.13		10.04
Mizen Top Gallant Mast	24.56		8.19
Main Royal Mast	22.27		
Fore Royal Mast	20.40		
Mizen Royal Mast	16.70		
Main Pole	11.13		
Fore Pole	10.20		
Mizen Pole	8.35		
Main Yard	96.66	4.	22.72
Fore Yard	88.92	3.75	20.90
Cross Jack Yard	62.83	2.46	13.20
Main Top Gallant Yard	45.92	2.52	9.64
Fore Top Gallant Yard	42.25	2.33	8.87
Mizen Top Gallant Yard	29.85	1.64	6.27
Spanker Boom	54.		12.42
do Gaff	40.05	2.26	8.10
Bowsprit Outboard	42.75		36.42
Jib Boom	34.02	2.05	18.12
Flying Jib Boom	27.36	5.19	11.76

Comparison of Ships	Pennsyl-vania	Dela-ware	Potomac	U. States	Vandalia
Number of Guns Rated	120.	80.	44.	44.	20.
Actual Number of Guns	126.	90.	52.	52.	24.
Length between perpendiculars including Rabbit of Stem & Stem Post at Cross	210.63	197.16	175.83	174.66	127.29
Length of Keel for Tonnage					
British	173.40	161.30	145.44	144.63	105.80
United States	173.44	161.79	145.67	144.97	106
Breadth of Beam moulded being U. S. Carpenters beam for Tonnage	56.00	53.	45.	43.50	33.91
Beam for Tonnage, British	56.83	53.83	45.58	44.08	34.24
Breadth of Beam, Extreme	57.66	54.50	46.16	44.66	34.58
Height from Timber strake to top of Gun Deck Beam, Midships		21.66	21.16	22.00	15.08
Height from Lower Edge of Rabbit of Keel to top of Gun deck Beam		24.66	23.16	24.00	17.50
Burthen in Tons, British	2978$\frac{51}{94}$	2485$\frac{80}{94}$	1605$\frac{83}{94}$	1494$\frac{77}{94}$	659$\frac{22}{94}$
do U. S. Carpenters	2867$\frac{58}{95}$	2391$\frac{88}{95}$	1552$\frac{50}{95}$	1443$\frac{84}{95}$	641$\frac{70}{95}$
Launching Draught of Water		13.58	1.		
Forward		13.58	12.50		9.66
Aft		18.50	16.50		13.50
Mean		16.04	14.50		11.58
Load Forward		24.33	19.16	21.08	14.25
Aft		26.54	21.83	23.38	16.50
Mean		25.43	20.50	22.23	15.37

DIMENSIONS OF MASTS AND SPARS

York-town	Royal Fredk.	Van-guard	Vernon	Pique	London New class	Truxton Brig	Ship to carry 100 Guns
16	110. *Sup.*	80. *Sup.*	50.	36.	92.	by F. G.	by F. G
16	118.	84.	50.	40.	92.	10 Guns	100
117.62	204.84	190.84	176.00	164.00	205.50	100.00	230.00
96.01	165.41	152.60	144.52	133.24	170.33	82.40	192.30
96.26	167.	153.80	144.92	133.54	170.83	82.60	192.75
32.	58.33	57.00	51.33	48.83	52.67	27.33	57.50
32.41	59.16	57.75	52.	49.33	53.50	27.66	58.25
32.92	60.00	58.50	52.70	49.83	54.33	28.00	59.00
15.00	24.75	24.41	24.08	22.20	23.16	13.00	23.41
16.71	27.50						
$536\frac{33}{94}$	$3079\frac{33}{94}$	$2706\frac{57}{94}$	2082	$1724\frac{46}{94}$	2598	$3151\frac{19}{94}$	$3470\frac{6}{94}$
$518\frac{75}{95}$	$2884\frac{75}{95}$	$2621\frac{58}{95}$	$2009\frac{38}{95}$	$1675\frac{48}{95}$	$2493\frac{7}{95}$	$308\frac{25}{95}$	$3354\frac{9}{95}$
9.20			13.50		15.16	7.00	
12.66			17.50		18.25	10.00	
19.93			15.50		16.70	8.50	
14.79	23.50	23.08	20.75	19.00	23.25	11.50	24.08
15.25	25.50	25.08	21.75	20.41	24.25	13.00	26.75
15.02	24.50	24.08	21.25	19.70	23.75	12.25	25.41

Comparison of Ships	Pennsyl-vania	Dela-ware	Potomac	U. States	Vandalia
Number of Guns Rated	120.	80.	44.	44.	20.
Actual Number of Guns	126.	90.	52.	52.	24.
Depth of Keel & false Keel Clear of Rabbit	2.08	2.50	2.33	2.50	2.00
Height of lower Port Sill Midships above Lead Line	5.	4.75	8.16	7.16	6.37
Length of mean load floating Line including Rabbit of Stem & Stern Ports		195.00	173.50	172.66	126.41
Depth from the mean load floating Line to the Lower Edge of rabbit of keel		23.08	18.25	19.75	13.33
Rake of Fore Mast from a perpendicular to the lead floating line in degrees		1°	2°	3°	3°
Ditto of Main Mast		1°	2°	3°	3°
Ditto of Mizen Mast		$2^\circ\ 30'$	5°	5°	5°
Ditto of Bowsprit		23°	18°	20°	21°
Surface of Sails including Jib, Fore Main & Mizen Coarses, Fore Main & Mizen Top Sails, Fore Main & Mizen Top Gallt. Sails, and Spanker in Square feet	28.211	28.128.47	20.588	205.88	12.711.65
Ditto in proportion to the surface of the load floating Line		3.06	3.01	3.13	3.34

DIMENSIONS OF MASTS AND SPARS

York-town	Royal Fredk.	Van-guard	Vernon	Pique	London New class	Truxton Brig	100 *Guns* *Guns on two Decks*
16	110.	80.	50.	36.	92.		
16	118.	84.	50.	40.	92.	10 Guns	100 Guns
2.00	1.41	1.45	1.25	1.06	2.41	1.83	2.12
5.91	7.00	7.00	9.00	8.50	7.00	5.54	7.25
116.26			176.00	162.75		98.79	229.08
13.50	23.00	22.58	20.50	18.66	21.33	10.41	23.16
5°			2°	1° 30′		12°	2° 30′
5°			2° 30′	2°		12°	3°
6°			4° 30′	5°		12°	5°
22°			25°	24°		20°	20°
10.722			26.77	1.78		28.398	9.78 9.60 34.26 1.63
3.43			3.44			4.59	2.94

COMPARISON OF SHIPS	Pennsyl-vania	Dela-ware	Potomac	U. States	Vandalia
NUMBER OF GUNS RATED	120.	80.	44.	44.	20.
ACTUAL NUMBER OF GUNS	126.	90.	52.	52.	24.
Surface of the Sails to proportion to the Transverse Section		27.78	32.15	30.88	37.13
Ditto in proportion to the weight of the Ship in Tons		6.47	8.95	8.82	13.97
Height of center of Effort above the load floats, line	93.16	88.00	73.39	73.41	53.85
Distance of the center of Effort before the center of Gravity displacement		8.97	11.50	3.50	2.45
Do Do before the load floating Line	16.07	12.25	14.00	8.50	8.00
Height of center of Effort in Proportion to Breadth of Beam	1.66	1.23	1.59	1.68	1.58
Displacement in tons when Launched		2.000	1.222		.547
Do When Loaded		4.348.3	2.300		.909.18½
Weight of Equipment		2.348.3	1.078		.362.18½
In proportion to tonnage		0.98	.069		.056
Weight of Ballast & Tanks In Tons	*T. C.* 335.14	301.05	145.10¼		*T. C.* 46.3
Number of rounds of Shot	97	97	97	97	97
Weight of Shot	174.12	151.14	62.18	56.13	20.9½
Weight of chain Cables	36.03	35.15	25.1	25.1	18.6½

DIMENSIONS OF MASTS AND SPARS

York-town	Royal Fredk.	Van-guard	Vernon	Pique	London New class	Ship to carry 100 Guns	Truxton Brig
16	110.	80.	50.	36.	92.	On two Decks	
16	118.	84.	50.	40.	92.	100.	10 Guns
34.45			39.25			32.42	53.61
15.00			10.44			6.48	27.11
50.25			78.47		87.00	94.99	42.97
3.50			7.59			7.01	1.47
7.16			13.32			8.76	4.13
1.61			1.49		1.65	1.64	
379			1.386		2.212		168.14
749.11			2564.2		4129.9		355.7
370.11			1178.2		1917.9		
071.			.058		.077		
$T.\ C.$ 24.4½	$T.\ C.$ 145.5	110.10	77.15	51.14	28.20	305	9 Tons Ballast
119	74	89	112	97	90	97	95 $T.\ C.$
24.9¼	122.18	107.	93.17	55.8½	118.5¾	138.12	13.11½
17.08	37.3	36.11	30.17	26.2	37.3	36.03	10.12

DIMENSIONS OF MASTS & SPARS PROPOSED TO THE BUREAU OF CONSTRUCTION FOR FIRST CLASS SLOOP SARATOGA WHOSE LENGTH BETWEEN THE PERPENDICULARS IS 147 AND EXTREME BREADTH 36.1.

	Whole Length Ins. Feet	Heads & Arms Ins. Feet	Diam. Ins. Feet
Main Mast	82.80	14.41	27.6
Fore Mast	76.17	13.25	25.39
Mizen Mast		10.80	19.32
Main Top Mast	49.68	7.95	15.25
Fore Top Mast	45.70	7.32	15.25
Mizen Top Mast	37.26	5.96	10.80
Main Top Gallt. Mast	24.84		8.28
Fore Top Gallt. Mast	22.85		7.62
Mizen Top Gallt. Mast	18.63		6.21
Main Royal Mast	16.90		
Fore Royal Mast	15.54		
Mizen Royal Mast	12.67		
Main Pole	8.45		
Fore Pole	7.77		
Mizen Pole	6.33		
Main Yard	79.38	3.34	18.65
Main Top Gallt. Yard	37.70	2.07	7.91
Fore Yard	73.02	3.06	17.16
Fore Top Gallt. Yard	34.68	2.	7.28
Mizen Yard	51.60	2.84	10.83
Mizen Top Gallt. Yard	24.13	1.33	5.06
Bowsprit outboard	32.40		27.6
Jib Boom	25.92	1.56	13.73
Flying Jib Boom	20.73	3.94	8.91
Spanker Boom	44.1		10.14
Spanker Gaff	33.1	4.30	6.61

The length of Top Sail Yards to be determined by the Sail Makers draft. For the diameter in the slings in inches multiply the Length of 25.

For the Breadth of M. Top multiply the extreme breadth by 43, and for the

Length multiply the breadth by 67. For the breadth and Length of Fore Top multiply the main by 92.

For the Breadth and Length of Mizen Top multiply the Main by 75.

Main & Mizen lower Tresselltrees to be equal to the diameter of the diameter of their respective Top Masts, in the Caps.

For the depth of Fore Lower Tresselltrees multiply the Main by 92.

Top M. Tresselltrees in depth to be equal to the diameter of their respective Top Gallt. Masts in the Caps.

Thickness of Tresselltrees to be one-half the depth.

For the length of After Top M. Crosstrees take one-half of their respective tops, back Top Mast to have three crosstrees.

The length of Fore Mast is to be ascertained by a line parallel to the load line commencing at the top of Keelson under the Main Mast. Should the Keelson be above this line at the Fore Mast the rise is to be deducted from the length here given. Should the Keelson be below the line the difference between the two is to be added to the Length here given.

The length of Mizen Mast to be determined by a line drawn parellel to the Load Line at two-thirds of the Head of Main Mast, below the Extreme height of that Mast. The diameters of Lower Masts are intended to include both Cheeks, in other words the diameters in the partners are the Extreme diameters.

Bowsprits of all Vessells to have long Bees to Sett up fore Stays through, as the Top Mast Stays are.

June 3, 1843.

New Plan for masting & Sparing Ships of War by Board of Naval Constructors June, 1843, in the City of Washington.

Length of M. Mast multiply Extreme breadth by 2.3.

Length of Fore Mast Multiply Length of M. Mast by 92.

Diameter of F. & M. Multiply by 333, this Size includes Cheeks.

Length of Mizen Mast, ⅓ Length Main Mast head above under part of Main Tresselltrees.

Diameter of Mizen 7/10 of Main Mast.

For the length of Fore & Main Top Masts Multiply the Length of their Respective Lower Masts by 565 for Ships of the Line, and 6 for Smaller Ships.

For Length of Mizen Top Masts multiply the M. Top Mast by 75.

For Length of Top Gallt. Masts Multiply their Respective Top Masts by 5.

For Length of Royal Masts Multiply their Respective Top. Gallt. Masts by 68.

For length of Poles Multiply their Respective Royal Masts by 5.

For Heads of Lower Masts Multiply their Respective Top Masts by 29.

For Heads of Top Masts Multiply their Respective Gallt. Masts by 32.

For diameter in inches of Main Top Masts in Cap multiply the Length by 307. Fore Top Masts Same as Main.

For diameter of Mizen Top Mast in the Cap multiply the Length by 29.

For diameter of Top Gallt. Masts in the Cap multiply the length by 333.

Bowsprit—for length Outboards Multiply the extreme breadth by 9.

The diameter in bed same as M. M. in Partners.

Jib Boom—for length outside Cap multiply the length of Bow Sprit by 8, which will include the pole which is .06 of whole Length out Board.

Fly Jib Boom—for length outside Jib Boom multiply the Length of the Jib Boom outside by 8, and this Length by 19, will give the length of Pole.

For Diameter of Jib Boom in inches multiply the whole out Board Length by 53.

For Diameter of Fly Jib Boom in inches multiply the whole Length out including Pole by 43.

For the Length of Spanker Boom in Ships multiply the Length between perpendiculars by 3.

For diameter of ditto multiply the length by .23.

For length of Spanker Gaff multiply the length of Spanker Boom by 75, and for the Length of Pole deduct 13, of the whole length.

The diameter in inches is the whole Length multiplied by 32.

The Spanker or Main Boom in Brigs—the Length of Main Yard in the Short Sloops, 10, so called and the Levant & Cyane. For yards multiply by 56, of the Length between perpendiculars. For Main Yards multiply the length between perpendiculars by 54, as in x 062, diameter 235, Fore Yard multiply the length of Main Mast by 92, all in the Jacks or Mizen Yard x 65, of main all yards of Mizen Same M. Top Gallt. Yard x 475 of Main Yard.

Fore Yard Arm of X Jack Yard multiply the length by 055, this to the Top Gallt. Yard.

For M. Top multiply the Breadth extreme by 43 for width, for Length take ⅔ of Breadth. 667.

For F. Top x 92 of the Main—Tresselltrees the Main and Mizen are the depth of the diameter of Top Masts—the depth and thickness of the Fore is 92 of the Main Mizen Top 75 of M. Top.

After Top M. Crosstrees ½ the Breadth of their respective Tops.

MASTS & SPARS OF SLOOP OF WAR PLYMOUTH.

Built at Boston by Saml. Pook

	Length Feet	Inches	Feet	Inches
Length on Spar Deck	154			
Length of Keel	137	6		
Length from Stern to Fore Mast	27	6		
Length from Fore to Main Mast	57	6		
Length from Main to Mizen Mast	42			
Length from Mizen to Topsail	25	6	Mast Head	
Length of Fore Mast from Spar Deck	25	6	14	3
Length of Main Mast from Spar Deck	61	6	14	3
Length of Mizen Mast from Spar Deck	51	3	10	4
			Yard Arm	
Length of Fore Yard (one-half)	38	3	3	3
Length of Main Yard (one-half)	38	3	3	3
Length of Cross Jack Yard	25	3	2	
Length of Spanker Boom	44			
Length of Fore Top Sail Yard (one-half)	29	4	6	
Length of Main Top Sail Yard (one-half)	29	4	6	
Length of Mizen Top Sail Yard(one-half)	21	3	4	9
			Mast Head	
Length of Fore Top Mast	46		7	7
Length of Main Top Mast	46		7	7
Length of Mizen Top Mast	36	3	6	
			Yard Arm	
Length of Fore T. Gallt. Yard (one-half)	17	9	2	
Length of Main T. Gallt. Yard (one-half)	17	9	2	
Length of Mizen T. Gallt. Yard(one-half)	12		1	4
Length of Fore Top Gallt. Mast	23	9		
Length of Main Top Gallt. Mast	23	9		
Length of Mizen Top Gallt. Mast	18	6		
Length of Fore Royal Mast	16	4	with the pole	
Length of Main Royal Mast	16	4	" " "	
Length of Mizen Royal Mast	12	9	" " "	
			Yard Arm	
Length of Fore Royal Yard (one-half)	12	10	1	3
Length of Main Royal Yard (one-half)	12	10	1	3
Length of Mizen Royal Yard(one-half)	8	6	1	
Length of Bowsprit Out Board	34			
Length of Jib Boom	38	9		
Length of Flying Jib Boom	19	9	*From Jib Boom Head*	

NEW PLAN FOR MASTING

Table of Masts & Spars of Vessells of the U. S. Navy, Prepared by F. Grice, N. Constructor, U. S. N. Yard.

	120 Guns	80 Guns	74 Guns	44 Guns	22 Guns	20 Guns	16 Guns	10 Guns Brig
	Pensyla or class	Delaware or class	Franklyn or class	Potomac	Albany	Levant	Yorktown	Truxton
	Feet Ins.	Feet Ins.	Feet Ins.	Feet Ins.	Feet Ins.	Feet Ins.	Feet Ins.	Feet Ins.
Length between Perpendiculars	212.11	199.2	190.10	177.10	150.7	134.7	119.7	102.6
Breadth, Extreme	57.6	54.6	51.7½	46.2	39.6	36.	32.11	28.2
Depth	24.3	21.7	19.9	21.2	18.	15.	15.	13.
U. S. Custom House Tonnage	3104.65.95	2602.34	2243.34	1684.14	1041.90	770.3	569.30	329.89

Masts & Spars	Msts.	Yds.	Msts.	Yds.	Msts.	Yds.	Msts.	Yds.	Msts.	Yds.	Msts.	Yds.	Msts.	Yds.	Msts.	Yds.
Fore	121.	100.	115.	96.	105.	90.	95.	84.	84.1	77.	72.	65.	65.6	60.9	65.6	55.
Top	63.	75.	63.	71.	63.	67.	56.	62.	50.	57.	43.	49.	42.	45.6	37.6	42.
Top Gallant	37.6	48.	32.	46.	37.	45.	29.	41.	25.3	39.	23.	32.	21.	30.6	19.	28.
Royal	22.	23.	22.	33.	22.	30.	20.	27.	16.	28.	15.	22.	13.	20.6	13.	20.
Pole	17.		11.		6.		10.		8.		5.		6.		5.	
Main	132.	110.	124.6	107.6	117.	105.	105.	95.	89.7	77.	80.	75.	72.	67.6	68.3	55.
Top	70.	82.	70.	78.	70.	77.	63.	71.	50.	57.	47.	56.	45.	50.6	37.6	42.
Top Gallant	41.	52.	41.	52.	41.	51.	32.	30.	25.	39.	24.	37.	22.	34.	19.	28.
Royal	24.	36.	24.	36.	24.	35.	22.	20.	16.	28.	16.	25.	14.	22.9	13.	20.
Pole	18.		12.		6.		11.		8.		5.		7.		5.	
Mizen	†99.	80.	†97.	80.	98.	80.	84.	66.	‡70.3	47.	66.	53.	§54.6	52.		
Top	55.	52.	55.	52.	53.	49.	46.	45.	38.	39.	37.	36.6	32.	34.	19.	
Top Gallant	33.	33.	29.	33.	33.	32.	24.	30.	19.	25.	20.	29.6	16.	21.		
Royal	20.	23.	20.	23.	20.	21.9	16.	19.	13.	17.	13.	15.	12.	14.		
Pole	14.		10.		5.		8.		6.		4.		5.			
Bowsprit Out Board	54.		56.		48.		45.9		32.8		33.		30.		22.	
Jib Boom from Cap	43.		40.		36.		32.9		29.		25.6		22.9		21.	
Flying Jib Boom	24.		21.		20.		21.3		19.		14.6		13.3		15.	
Spanker Boom	61.6		60.		60.		50.		41.		35.		34.		50.	
Gaff	38.10		38.		38.		30.		35.		28.		28.		32.	

† Steps on Orlop Deck.

‡ Steps on Birth Deck.

§ Mast Head in a line with Tresselltrees.

Note — It has been decided by the Bureau of Construction and Equipment U. S. N. that the yards, top-masts, top Gallt. Masts, on the fore & Main Masts, should be alike hereafter. The rule is to take the mean of the present spars as the standard, for instance, the F. Yard of the *Potomac* is 84 feet, the Main 95 feet, Total 179 feet.

The Mean is the size of the Fore & Main Yards, 89 feet, 6 inches.

SHIPS OF THE PAST

THE NUMBER AND WEIGHT OF ANCHORS FOR THE DIFFERENT CLASSES OF VESSELLS DECIDED ON BY THE BOARD TO BE AS FOLLOWS EXCLUSIVE OF THE WEIGHT OF THE STOCK.

Classes of Vessells	Bowers & Waists	Stream	Kedges
	Lbs.	Lbs.	Lbs.
3 Deckers	4 of 10500	1 of 3200	6 of 1400, 1200, 1000, 800, 700, 600
2 Deckers first class	4 " 9500	1 " 3000	5 " 1200, 900, 750, 600, 500
2 Deckers second class	4 " 8500	1 " 2800	5 " 1000, 900, 750, 600, 450
Razee	4 " 8000	1 " 2600	5 " 1000, 900, 750, 600, 450
Frigate first class	4 " 7000	1 " 1600	4 " 900, 700, 600, 400
Frigate second class	4 " 5000	1 " 1400	4 " 850, 700, 600, 400
Sloops first class	4 " 3800	1 " 1000	3 " 600, 450, 300
Sloops second class / Sloops third class	1 " 3200 / 2 " 3000 / 1 " 2800	1 " 800	3 " 600, 450, 300
Brigs first class	3 " 2000	1 " 700	2 " 450, 300,

Weight of Anchors Exclusive of Stocks for the different classes of Vessells in the U. S. Navy.

Classes of Vessels	Bowers & Sheet		Stream		Kedges	
	No.	Lbs.	No.	Lbs.	No.	Lbs.
74 of 3 Decks	4 of 10500		1 of 3200		6 of 1400, 1200, 1000, 800, 700, 600	
74 1st class 2 decks	4 " 9500		1 " 3000		5 " 1200, 900, 750, 600, 500	
2nd class 2 decks	4 " 8500		1 " 2800		5 " 1000, 900, 750, 600, 450	
Razee	4 " 8500		1 " 2600		5 " 1000, 900, 750, 600, 450	
Frigate 1st class	4 " 7000		1 " 2600		4 " 900, 700, 600, 400	
Frigate 2nd class	4 " 5000		1 " 1400		4 " 850, 700, 600, 400	
Sloops 1st class	4 " 3800		1 " 1000		3 " 600, 450, 300	
Sloops 2nd class / Sloops 3rd class	1 " 3200 / 2 " 3000 / 1 " 2800		1 " 1000		3 " 600, 450, 300	

APPENDIX II

LIST OF PLANS OF SHIPS

THE following list, showing the existence of plans of various types of ships and where to find them, has been compiled as an aid to the ship model builder. It by no means covers the entire field but is presented as a suggestive list of accurately drawn plans available to anyone proposing to build the model of a ship and have it right. If one is intending to put in the hours of work necessary to produce a model every care should be taken at the outset to secure accurate plans. Most of the plans here listed are from the builder's own drawings. They include William H. Webb's plans, privately printed in two large volumes, from which we have selected only the sailing ships.

The plans of the United States navy ships are all redrawn from the originals in the archives of the Bureau of Construction and Repair at the Washington Navy Yard, with the kind permission of Admiral Taylor who permitted the author to do so in order to perpetuate to posterity what the old sailing ships of the American Navy were like. The plans of the *Raleigh*, reproduced in this volume, were kindly furnished by the British Admiralty for the same purpose. It is proposed to publish a selection from these plans in succeeding volumes together with many others possible that it is to resurrect from contemporary figures which a naval architect can easily translate into plans. It was by this process that the author was able to produce the plans of the clipper ships *Rainbow* and *Red Jacket* and the bark *James A. Wright* and several others.

There are many volumes containing plans of ships not included in this list — those of French, Dutch, Spanish and other countries — but enough are here included to keep the model builder busy for several years.

We have not attempted to list yachts — that subject would require several books in itself. The New York Yacht Club has a collection of models that fills a large model room and in the United States National Museum at the Smithsonian Institute, Washington, D. C., there is an immense collection of all kinds of water craft used in the United States together with original builder's block models of many a famous ship. Those in search of the model of some particular ship, not listed here, would do well to inquire at the Smithsonian Institute first and then at Salem or Boston where are preserved the largest collections of models of the American merchant marine to be found in the country.

L — Lines.   S — Sail Plan

ADDRESSES:

Ship Model Society of Rhode Island, 75 Upton Ave., Providence, R. I.
Charles G. Davis, 52 Park Ave., Port Washington, N. Y.
C. R. Sawyer, 11 Stark St., Manchester, N. H.

Clipper Ship	*Ann McKim* (1833), L. S.	Ship Model Soc. of R. I.; *also,* Hall, *Ship Building Industry in U. S.*
do	*Rainbow* (1845 - Griffiths), L. S.	C. G. Davis.
do	*Sea Witch* (1846 - Griffiths), L. S.	Davis, *Ship Models and How to Build Them.*
do	*Stag Hound* (1850 - McKay), L. S.	*The Rudder,* 1902, p. 202; *also,* Hall, *Ship Building Industry in U. S.*
do	*Celestial* (1850 - Webb), L. S.	*Plans of W. H. Webb Ships,* 2 vols.
do	*Flying Cloud* (1851 - McKay), L. S.	Magoon, *The Frigate Constitution and other Historic Ships;* also, *The Rudder,* 1902, p. 204; *also* Hall, *Ship Building Industry in U. S.*
do	*Nightingale* (1851 - Hanscom), L.	U. S. *Nautical Magazine,* III, p. 9.
do	*Challenge* (1851 - Webb), L. S.	*Plans of W. H. Webb Ships,* 2 vols.
do	*Invincible* (1851 - Webb), L. S.	do
do	*Sword Fish* (1851 - Webb), L. S.	do
do	*Westward Ho* (1851 - Webb), L. S.	do
do	*Flying Dutchman* (1852 - Webb), L. S.	do
do	*Sovereign of the Seas* (1852 - McKay), L. S.	Hall, *Ship Building Industry in U. S.*
do	*Young America* (1853 - Webb), L. S.	*Plans of W. H. Webb Ships,* 2 vols.
do	*Flyaway* (1853 - Webb), L. S.	do
do	*Comet* (1853 - Webb), L. S.	do
do	*Red Jacket* (1853 - Pook des.), L. S.	C. G. Davis; *also* Hall, *Ship Building Industry in U. S.*
do	*Herald of the Morning* (1853 - Pook des.), L. S.	do
do	*Dreadnaught* (1853 - Currier), L. S.	C. G. Davis.
do	*Great Republic* (1853 - McKay), L. S.	*Marine Engineering,* Aug. - Sept., 1901; *also* Hall, *Ship Building Industry in U. S.*
do	*James Baines* (1854 - McKay), L. S.	do
do	*Lightning* (1854 - McKay), L. S.	*The Rudder,* 1902, p. 225; *also* Hall, *Ship Building Industry in U. S.,* and U. S. *Nautical Magazine,* III, p. 188.
do	*Champion of the Seas* (1854 - McKay), L. S.	*The Rudder,* 1902, p. 226.
do	*Intrepid* (1856 - Webb), L. S.	*Plans of W. H. Webb Ships,* 2 vols.
do	*Black Hawk* (1857 - Webb), L. S.	do

LIST OF PLANS OF SHIPS

Ship *Mayflower* (1620), L. S.

do *East Indiaman* (1790?), L.

do Merchant Ship (1800), L.

do (60 Ton Ship) (1800), L. S.
do *Philadelphia* Packet (1824), L.
do *Helena* (1841 - Webb), L. S.
do *James D. Farwell* (1841 - Currier), L.
do *Pacific* (1843 - Currier), L.
do *Fredonia* (1845 - Currier), L.
do *John Currier* (1846 - Currier), L.
do *Fanchon* (1847 - Currier), L.
do *Castilian* (1848 - Currier), L.
do *Flying Scud* (1853 - Metcalf), S.
do *Tricolor* (1855 - Jones), L. S.
do *Edward Sewall* (1899 - Sewall), S.

do *Arthur Sewall* (1899 - Sewall), S.
do *Lord of the Isles* (1899), L.

Packet Ship *Montezuma* (1843 - Webb), L. S.
  do   *Yorktown* (1843 - Webb), L. S.
  do   *Fidelia* (1843 - Webb), L. S.
  do   *Havre* (1845 - Webb), L. S.
  do   *Washington Irving* (1845 - McKay), S.

  do   *Albert Gallatin* (1849 - Webb), L. S.
  do   *Guy Mannering* (1849 - Webb), L. S.
  do   *Oriental* (1849 - Brown & Bell), L.
  do   *Joseph Walker* (1850 - Webb), L. S.
  do   *Isaac Webb* (1850 - Webb), L. S.
  do   *Isaac Wright* (1850 - Webb), L. S.
Bark *Allioth* (1836 - Currier), L.
  do *Snapdragon* (1853 - Webb), L. S.
  do *James A. Wright* (1877 - Jackson &
      Sharpe), L. S.
Brig 96 ton vessel (1820 - L. McKay), L.

  do *Malek-Adhel* (1840 - Webb), L. S.
  do *Ramon de Zaldo* (1844 - Webb), L. S.
  do *Volante* (1850 - Webb), L. S.
Clipper Brig *Newsboy* (1854 - Lawlor), L. S.
Pilot Schooner *Mary* (1800), L.
  do   59 tons (1820 - L. McKay), L.
  do   *Skiddy* (1820 - Skiddy), L. S.
  do   *John McKeon* (1838 - Webb), L. S.
  do   *Mary Taylor* (1849), L. S.

Magoon, *Frigate Constitution and other Historic Ships.*
Lubbock, *The Blackwall Frigates,* p. 32.
Chatterton, *Ships and Ways of Other Days.*
C. G. Davis.
  do
Plans of W. H. Webb Ships, 2 vols.
C. R. Sawyer.
  do
  do
  do
  do
C. G. Davis.
  do
  do
American Shipbuilder, October 12, 1899.
Marine Engineering, May, 1899.
Chatterton, *Ships and Ways of Other Days.*
Plans of W. H. Webb Ships, 2 vols.
  do
  do
Sailing Ships of New England, Series II.
Plans of W. H. Webb Ships, 2 vols.
  do
Griffiths, *Naval Architecture.*
Plans of W. H. Webb Ships, 2 vols.
  do
  do
C. R. Sawyer.
  do

C. G. Davis.
McKay, *The Practical Shipbuilder; also* C. G. Davis.
Plans of W. H. Webb Ships, 2 vols.
  do
  do
U. S. Nautical Magazine, IV, 277.
Paris, *Souvenirs de Marine.*
McKay, *The Practical Shipbuilder.*
C. G. Davis.
Plans of W. H. Webb Ships, 2 vols.
C. G. Davis.

Schooner	*Baltimore Privateer* (1800), L.	Paris, *Souvenirs de Marine.*
do	Baltimore Clippers (1824), L. S.	Davis, *Ships of the Past.*
do	*Ligera* (1840 - Webb), L. S.	*Plans of W. H. Webb Ships,* 2 vols.
do	*Plendome* (1843 - Webb), L. S.	do
do	*Manhasset* (1843 - Webb), L. S.	do
do (topsail)	*Gladiator,* L. S.	Ship Model Soc. of R. I.
do do	*Fanny* (1853 - Webb), L. S.	*Plans of W. H. Webb Ships,* 2 vols.
do	*Peri* (1858 - Harvey), L. S.	C. G. Davis.
do	*Smuggler* (1877), L. S.	do
do	*Helen B. Thomas* (1902 - McManus), L. S.	*Marine Engineering,* June, 1902.
do	*William L. Douglass* (1903 - Crowinshield), L. S.	*Nautical Gazette,* Aug. 6, 1903.
do	*Bluenose* (1920), L. S.	Magoon, *Frigate Constitution and other Historic Ships.*
Schooner Yacht	*Wave* (1832 - Stevens), L.	C. G. Davis.
do	*Northern Light* (1839 - Winde), L.	*The Rudder,* July, 1904.
Sloop	*Sparrow Hawk* (1626), L.	*Sailing Ships of New England,* Series I.
do	*Hudson River* (1830 - McKay), L.	C. G. Davis.
do	*North River* (N. Y.), L. S.	Ship Model Soc. of R. I.
do	*Victorine* (1848 - Welsie), L.	Griffiths, *Naval Architecture.*
do	*Yosemite* (1868 - Van Cott), L.	C. G. Davis.
do	Staten Island Sloop, L.	do
do	54 Ton Sloop, L.	do
Cutter	English Cutter (1810), L.	*Yachting,* July, 1915.
Long Boat	English Long Boat (1756), L.	Murray, *Treatise on Shipbuilding.*
do	do (1755), L.	Sutherland, *Shipbuilder's Assistant.*
Ship's Small Boats, L.		Paris, *Souvenirs de Marine.*
Whaleboat, L.		*The Rudder,* March, 1900.
Viking Ship	Gokstad Ship (900 A.D.), L. S.	Magoon, *Frigate Constitution and other Historic Ships.*
Carack	*Santa Maria* (1492), L. S.	do
Grand Tartane, L. S.		Ship Model Soc. of R. I.
Line-of-Battle Ship	*Pennsylvania* (1837), L. S.	C. G. Davis.
do	*Ohio* (1820), L. S.	do
do	*North Carolina* (1820), L. S.	do
do	*Franklin* (1841), L. S.	do
Frigate	*Raleigh* (1775), L. S.	Davis, *Ships of the Past.*
do	*Hague* (1777), L. S.	C. G. Davis.
do	*Constitution* (1797), L. S.	Magoon, *Frigate Constitution and other Historic Ships.*
do	*Constitution* (1797), L. S.	C. G. Davis.
do	*United States* (1797), L. S.	do
do	*Constellation* (1797), L. S.	do
do	*Essex* (1799), L. S.	do
do	*Macedonian* (1812), L. S.	do
do	*Guerriere* (1814), L. S.	do
do	*Congress* (1841), L. S.	do
do	*Niagara* (1857), L. S.	*U. S. Naut. Magazine,* VI, 209, 297.

Sloop of War	*Erie* (1812), L. S.		C. G. Davis.
do	*Ontario* (1812), L. S.		do
do	*Argus* (1814), L. S.		do
do	*John Adams* (1830), L. S.		do
do	*Cyane* (1841), L. S.		do
do	*Levant* (1841), L. S.		do
do	*Dale* (1839), L. S.		do
do	*Preble* (1839), L. S.		do
do	*Marion* (1839), L. S.		do
do	*Yorktown* (1839), L. S.		do
do	*Decatur* (1839), L. S.		do
do	*St. Mary's* (1844), L. S.		do
Brig of War	*Lexington* (1775), L. S.		do
do	*Cabot* (1775), L. S.		do
do	*Diligent* (1777), L. S.		do
do	*Boxer* (1815), L. S.		do
do	*Dolphin* (1836), L. S.		do
do	*Porpoise* (1836), L. S.		do
do	*Truxton* (1841), L. S.		do
do	do	L. S.	Ship Model Soc. of R. I.
do	*Perry* (1844), L. S.		C. G. Davis.
Schooner of War	*Porpoise* (1820), L. S.		do
do	*Dolphin* (1821), L. S.		do
do	*Shark* (1821), L. S.		do
do	*Boxer* (1831), L. S.		do
do	*Enterprise* (1831), L. S.		do
Ship	*Royal Sovereign* (1804), L.		Knowles, *Naval Architecture.*
Ships	Several (1812), L. S.		Steel, *Elements and Practice of Naval Architecture.*
do	do	L. S.	Kendall, *Naval Architecture.*
do	do	(1850), L. S.	Griffiths, *Treatise of Marine Architecture.*
do	Various (1775), L. S.		Chapman, *Architectura Navalis.*
do	do	L. S.	Paris, *Musée de la Marine du Louvre.*
do	do	(1839), L. S.	McKay, *Practical Shipbuilder.*
Ships of War	Various,	S.	Edge, *Equipment and Displacement of Ships of War.*

PLANS OF SHIPS

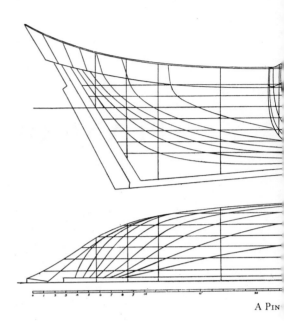

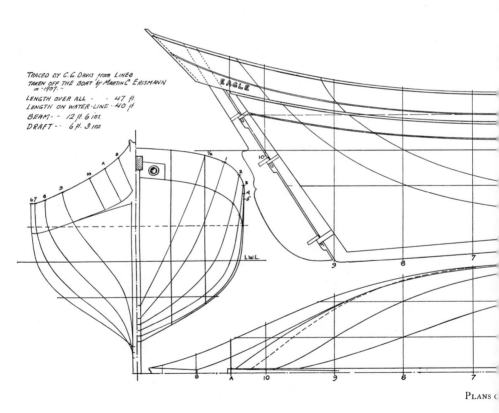

TRACED BY C.G. DAVIS from LINES
TAKEN OFF THE BOAT by MARTIN C. ERISMANN
in -1907.-
LENGTH OVER ALL - · 47 ft.
LENGTH ON WATER-LINE · 40 ft
BEAM- - 12 ft. 6 ins.
DRAFT -- 6 ft. 3 ins.

EAGLE

L.W.L.

PLANS (

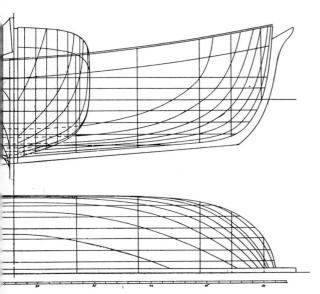

YEAR 1800

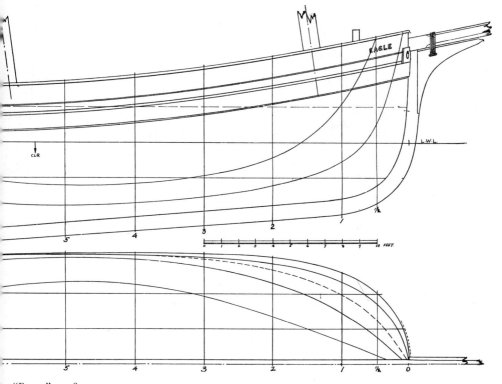

ᴋʏ "EAGLE" OF 1820

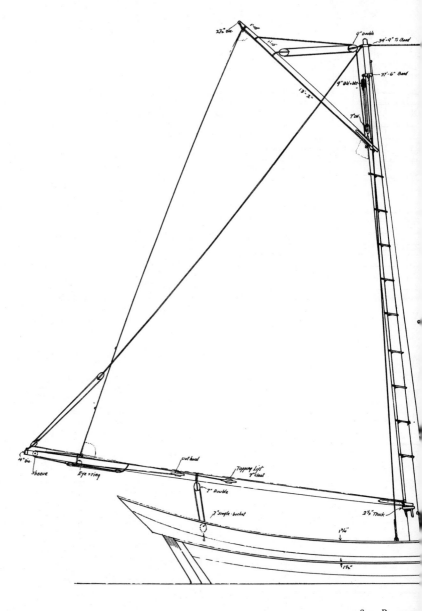

SAIL PLAN OF

From drawing by Martin C. E

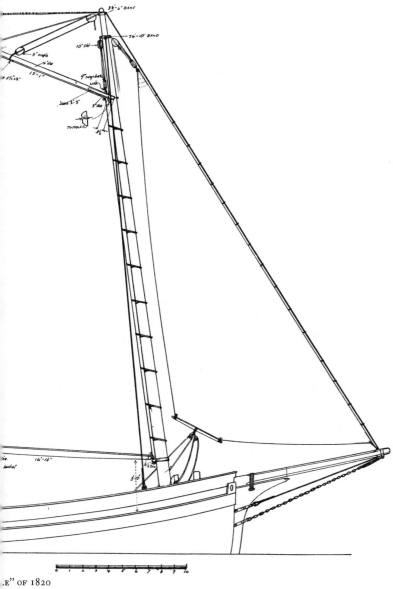

E" OF 1820

y of Montfort Amory, Esq.

169

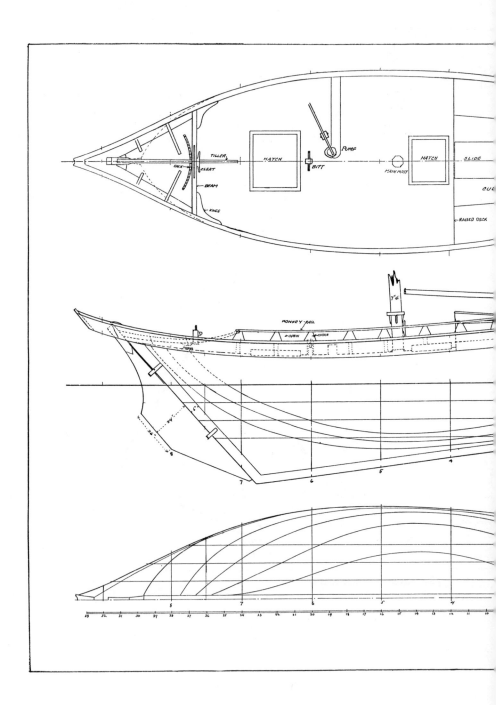

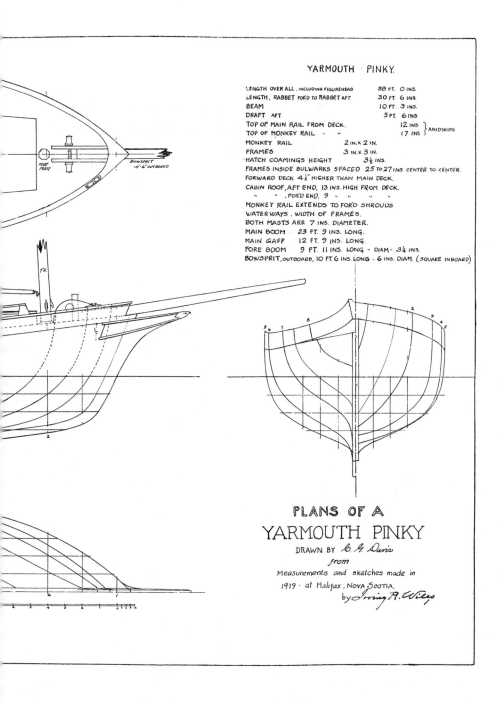

YARMOUTH · PINKY.

LENGTH OVER ALL , INCLUDING FIGUREHEAD	38 FT. 0 INS.
LENGTH , RABBET FOR'D TO RABBET AFT	30 FT. 6 INS.
BEAM	10 FT. 3 INS.
DRAFT AFT	5 FT. 6 INS.
TOP OF MAIN RAIL FROM DECK.	12 INS. } AMIDSHIPS
TOP OF MONKEY RAIL " "	17 INS.
MONKEY RAIL	2 IN. X 2 IN.
FRAMES	3 IN. X 3 IN.
HATCH COAMINGS HEIGHT	3½ INS.

FRAMES INSIDE BULWARKS SPACED 25 TO 27 INS. CENTER TO CENTER.
FORWARD DECK 4½" HIGHER THAN MAIN DECK.
CABIN ROOF, AFT END, 13 INS. HIGH FROM DECK.
" " , FOR'D END. 9 " " " "
MONKEY RAIL EXTENDS TO FOR'D SHROUDS
WATERWAYS , WIDTH OF FRAMES.
BOTH MASTS ARE 7 INS. DIAMETER.
MAIN BOOM 23 FT. 9 INS. LONG.
MAIN GAFF 12 FT. 9 INS. LONG.
FORE BOOM 9 FT. 11 INS. LONG - DIAM- 3¼ INS.
BOWSPRIT, OUTBOARD, 10 FT. 6 INS. LONG - 6 INS. DIAM. (SQUARE INBOARD)

BOWSPRIT
10'-6" OUTBOARD

FORE
MAST

PLANS OF A
YARMOUTH PINKY
DRAWN BY C. G. Davis
from
Measurements and sketches made in
1919 · at Halifax , Nova Scotia.
by Irving R. Wiley

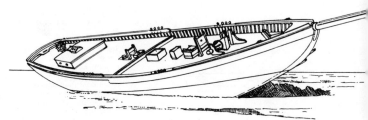

FISHING SCHOONER "HENRY FORD" ASHORE ON CAPE ANN, MASS., IN 1922
Lost June 19, 1928, at Rocky Harbor, Bonny Bay, N. F.

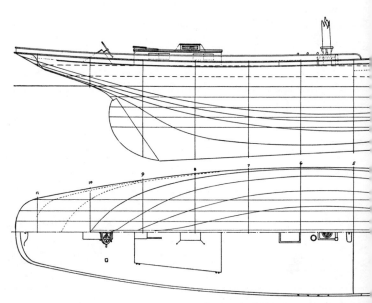

PLANS OF FISHING SCHOONER "COLU

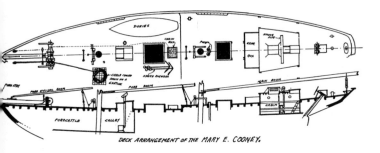

DECK ARRANGEMENT OF THE *MARY E. COONEY.*

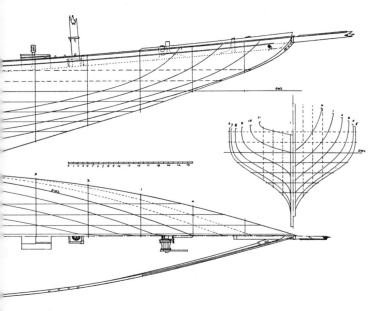

by Burgess & Paine · Boston. Mass.

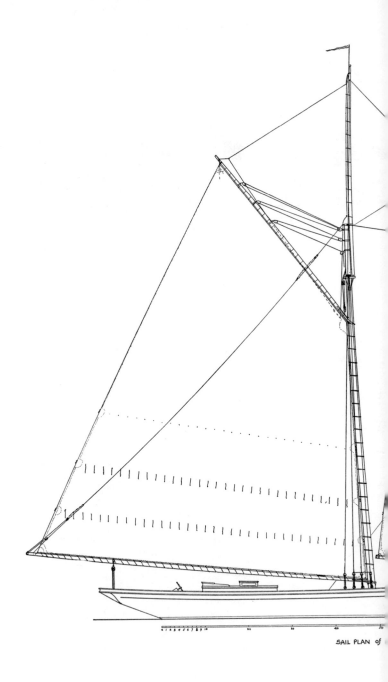

SAIL PLAN of

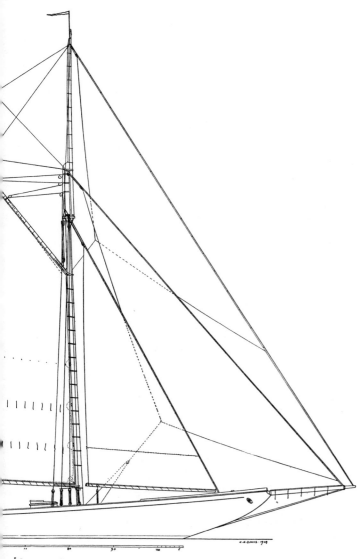

ER "COLUMBIA"

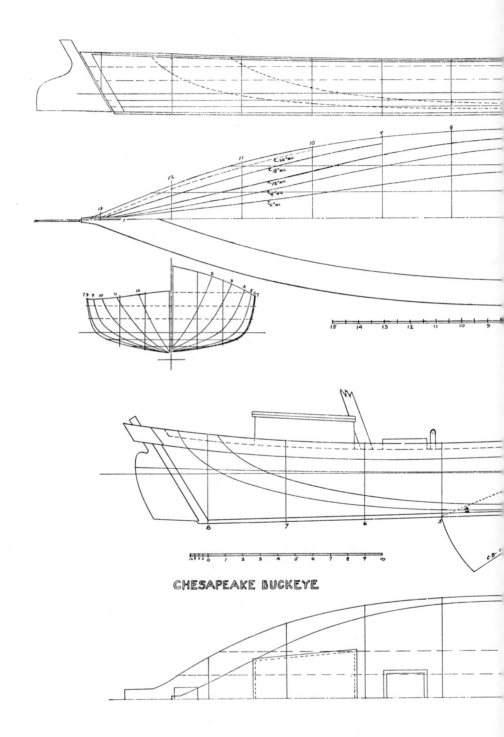

CHESAPEAKE BUCKEYE

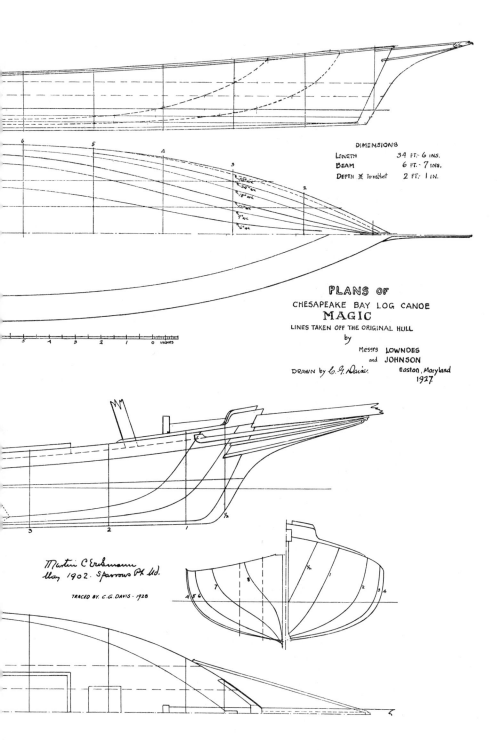

DIMENSIONS

LENGTH	34 FT.- 6 INS.
BEAM	6 FT.- 7 INS.
DEPTH X to rabbet	2 FT.- 1 IN.

PLANS OF
CHESAPEAKE BAY LOG CANOE
MAGIC
LINES TAKEN OFF THE ORIGINAL HULL
by
Messrs LOWNDES
and JOHNSON
DRAWN by C. G. Davis.   Easton, Maryland
1927

Martin C Erdmann
May 1902. Sparrows Pt. Md.

TRACED BY. C. G. DAVIS · 1928

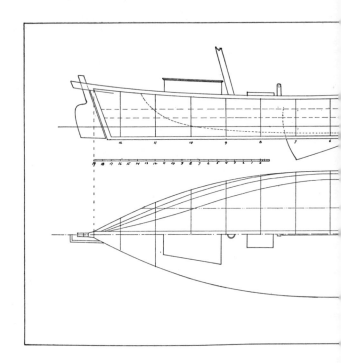

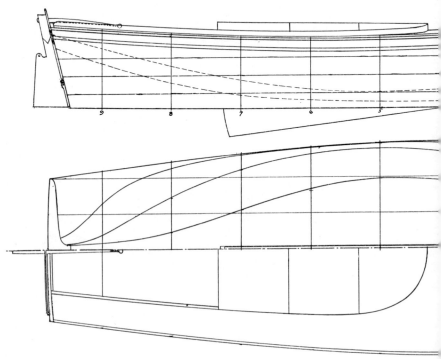

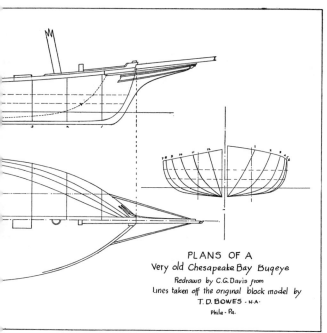

PLANS OF A
Very old Chesapeake Bay Bugeye
Redrawn by C.G. Davis from
Lines taken off the original block model by
T. D. BOWES · N·A·
Phila - Pa.

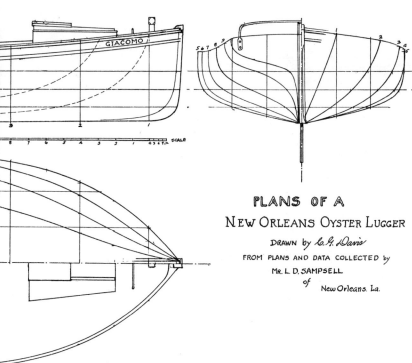

GIACOMO

SCALE

PLANS OF A
NEW ORLEANS OYSTER LUGGER
DRAWN by C. G. Davis
FROM PLANS AND DATA COLLECTED by
MR. L. D. SAMPSELL
of
New Orleans. La.

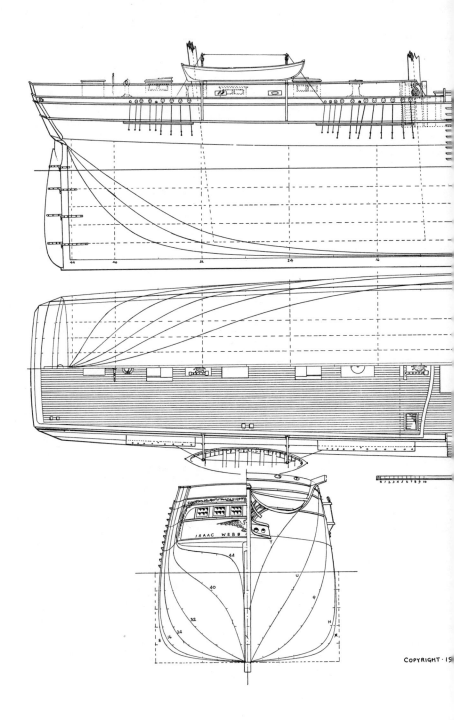

ISAAC WEBB

COPYRIGHT·19

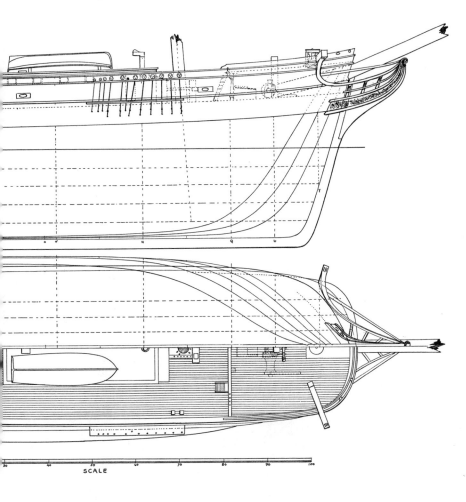

SCALE

PLANS OF THE

W YORK and LIVERPOOL PACKET-SHIP

ISAAC WEBB.

A FAMOUS BLACK BALL LINER

BUILT BY W.H.WEBB AT NEW YORK IN 1850

Length on deck	185'-0"
Beam moulded	38'-10"
Depth of hold	27'-3"
Tonnage C.H	1800 TONS

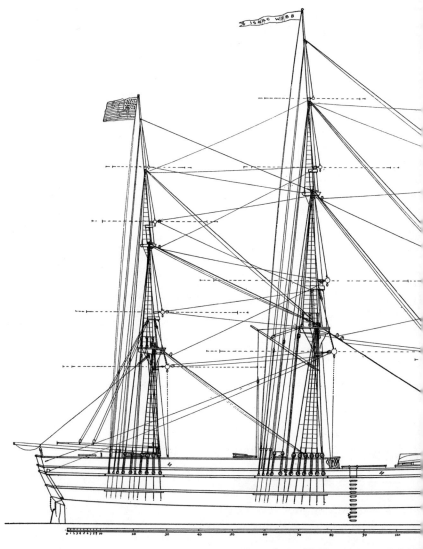

Rigging Plan of the Packet Ship ISAAC
built at N.Y. in

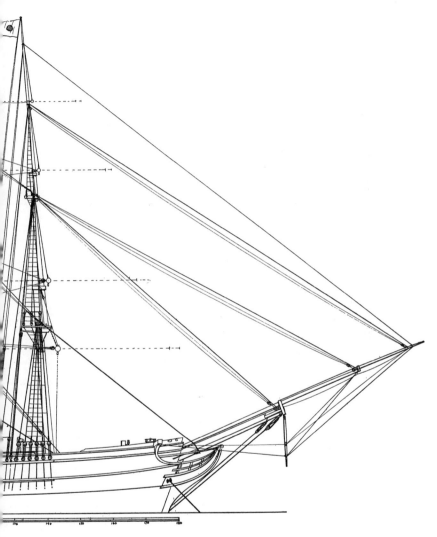

of the Black Ball Line.

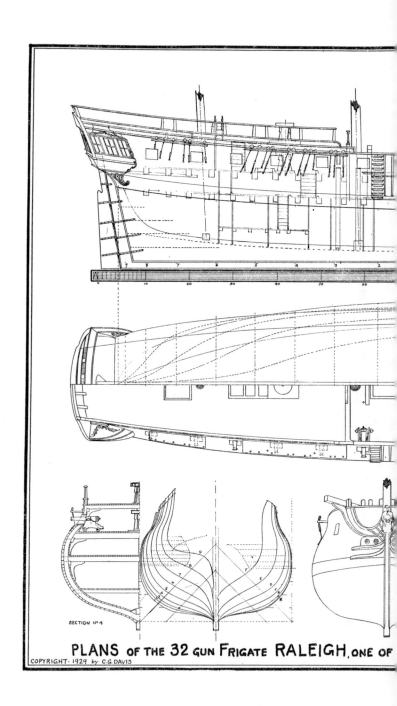

PLANS of the 32 gun Frigate RALEIGH, one of

SECTION Nº 4

184

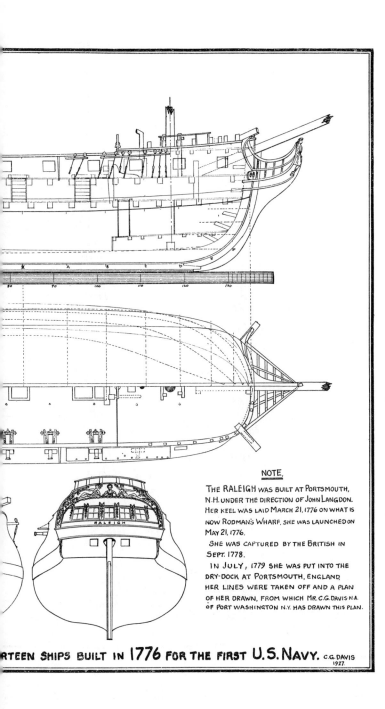

NOTE,

THE RALEIGH WAS BUILT AT PORTSMOUTH,
N.H. UNDER THE DIRECTION OF JOHN LANGDON.
HER KEEL WAS LAID MARCH 21, 1776 ON WHAT IS
NOW RODMAN'S WHARF, SHE WAS LAUNCHED ON
MAY 21, 1776.

SHE WAS CAPTURED BY THE BRITISH IN
SEPT. 1778.

IN JULY, 1779 SHE WAS PUT INTO THE
DRY-DOCK AT PORTSMOUTH, ENGLAND.
HER LINES WERE TAKEN OFF AND A PLAN
OF HER DRAWN, FROM WHICH MR. C.G. DAVIS N.A.
OF PORT WASHINGTON N.Y. HAS DRAWN THIS PLAN.

RTEEN SHIPS BUILT IN 1776 FOR THE FIRST U.S. NAVY. C.G. DAVIS
1927.

Sail Plan of the frigate RALE

186

t at Portsmouth . N.H. - 1776.

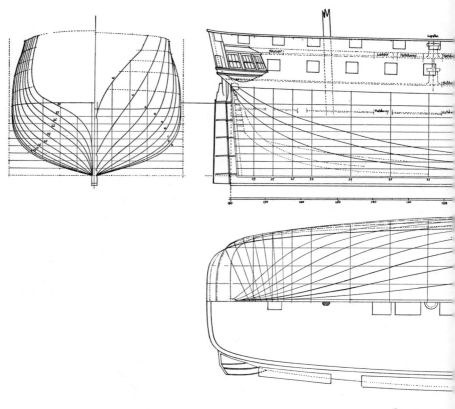

PLANS OF U.

La

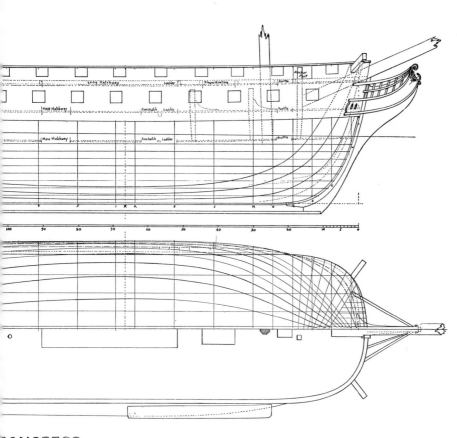

CONGRESS. 44 GUNS.

~~smouth N H · 1841.~~

INDEX

Active (Block Island boat), 5, 6
Akbar (frigate), 82
Albany (ship), 157
Albert Gallatin (packet ship), 161
Albion (packet ship), 58, 75
Alliance (frigate), 78, 89
Allioth (bark), 161
America (ship), 78
Amity (packet ship), 58, 75
Anchors, 118, 125, 158
Ann McKim (clipper ship), 160
Argus (sloop of war), 163
Arthur Sewall (ship), 161

Baltimore Clippers and other Southern
   Craft, 37-55
Barges, 117
Black Ball Line, 56, 57
Black Hawk (clipper ship), 160
Block Island, 3, 8
Block Island boats, 3-13, 17
Bluenose (schooner), 32, 162
Boats, Dimensions of, 117, 125
Boston (frigate), 79.
Boston & Liverpool Packet Line, 58
Bowers, Sylvester, 78
Boxer (brig of war), 163
Boxer (schooner of war), 163
Brady, William, 139
Briggs, Enos, 79, 85
Britannia (packet ship), 76
Buckeye, 48, 49
Bugeye, 46, 47

Bulwarks, 96
Burgess, Edward, 27
Burgess & Paine, 32
Burgundy (packet ship), 75

Cables, 99, 125
Cabot (brig of war), 163
Cambridge (packet ship), 75
Canada (packet ship), 58, 75
Cannon, 112
Cannon shot, 110
Capstan, 104
Cartridges, 134
Carysfort (frigate), 79
Castilian (ship), 161
Caswell, Benjamin, 6
Catboats, 3
Celestial (clipper ship), 160
Chain plates, 108
Challenge (clipper ship), 64, 160
Champion of the Seas (clipper ship), 160
Channels, 108
Chanties, 72
Chapman, F. H., 134
Chebacco boats, 14-16, 24, 25
Chesapeake (frigate), 89
Chesapeake Bay, 37-50
Chesapeake Bay canoe, 46
Cleopatra (frigate), 80
Colleen Bawn (lugger), 40
Collins, Joseph W., 24, 27
Columbia (packet ship), 75
Columbia (schooner), 32

INDEX

Comet (clipper ship), 160
Congress (frigate), 79, 89, 94, 120-134, 162
Connelly, C. M., 5
Connolly, James B., 28
Constellation (frigate), 89, 162
Constitution (frigate), 80, 82, 83, 89, 107, 162
Contest (clipper ship), 88
Cope, Thomas P., 56
Cope Line, 60
Cornelius Grinnell (packet ship), 74
Cornwallis (frigate), 82
Courier (packet ship), 58, 75
Crescent (frigate), 79
Crew, 127-133
Cross, Stephen and Ralph, 78
Crowninshield, B. B., 34
Cruti Bros., 50
Cumberland (frigate), 121, 122
Cutters, 117
Cyane (sloop of war), 163
Cynthia (buckeye), 49

Dale (sloop of war), 163
Dauntless (Block Island boat), 6, 12
Davis, Theodore W., 94
Decatur (sloop of war), 163
Deep ship, 81
Delaware (frigate), 78, 142, 148, 150, 157
Delaware (ship), 141
Dennis, H. W., 32
Desdemona (packet ship), 60
Diligent (brig of war), 163
"Dogbody," 24
Dolphin (brig of war), 79, 163
Dolphin (schooner of war), 163
Dory, Lines of a, 30
Dover (ship), 58, 59

Dreadnaught (clipper ship), 64, 74, 160

East Indiaman (ship), 161
Edward Sewall (ship), 161
Effingham (frigate), 78
Elsie (schooner), 32
Enchantress (schooner), 28
Enterprise (schooner), 42
Enterprise (schooner of war), 163
Erie (sloop of war), 83, 163
Erismann, Martin C., 6, 10, 12, 49
Esperanto (schooner), 32
Essex (frigate), 79, 85, 115, 116, 162
Express (schooner), 27

Fame (Chebacco boat), 15
Fanchon (ship), 161
Fanny (schooner), 162
Farragut, Admiral, 94
Fidelia (packet ship), 161
Fisherman's races, 30
Fishing schooners, 24-35
Flora (frigate), 80
Flyaway (clipper ship), 160
Flying Cloud (clipper ship), 64, 160
Flying Dutchman (clipper ship), 64, 160
Flying Scud (ship), 161
Follansbee, Capt. Alonzo, 70
Francis P. Mesquita (schooner), 30
Frank Atwood (schooner), 27
Franklin (ship), 157, 162
Fredonia (schooner), 27
Fredonia (ship), 161
Freeman, Capt. Chas. H., 95
Frigates, 77-135
Full-built ship, 81

Gangway steps, 103
Gazelle (ship), 64
George (brig), 88

INDEX

Giacomo (lugger), 50
Gladiator (schooner), 162
Glasgow (frigate), 80
Gloucester fishing schooners, 4
Gracie (schooner), 27
Grampus (schooner), 27
Great Republic (clipper ship), 160
Grice, Francis, 142, 157
Griffiths, J. W., 64
Gun crew, 113
Gunports, 110
Guerriere (frigate), 162
Guy Mannering (packet ship), 64, 161

Hackett, James H., 78, 80, 85, 89
Hague (frigate), 80, 89, 162
Hall, Samuel, 27
Hammock nettings, 109
Hancock (frigate), 78
Hancock (frigate), 89
Harrison, Capt. Jas. L., 49
Harry Belden (schooner), 30
Havre (packet ship), 161
"Heel tappers," 15, 24, 25
Helen B. Thomas (schooner), *frontispiece*, 27, 30, 31, 162
Helena (ship), 161
Henry Ford (schooner), 32
Herald of the Morning (clipper ship), 160
Humphreys, Joshua, 78, 80, 82, 89, 122
    Samuel, 142
Hyslop, John, 6, 8

Independence (frigate), 142
Intrepid (clipper ship), 160
Invincible (clipper ship), 160
Iris (frigate), 89
Irish emigrants, 66-69
Isaac Webb (packet ship), 56-76, 161

Isaac Wright (packet ship), 76, 161
Island Belle (Block Island boat), 4, 6, 8, 12

James D. Farwell (ship), 161
James A. Wright, 95
James A. Wright (bark), 161
James Baines (clipper ship), 160
James Cropper (packet ship), 58, 62, 75
James Munroe (packet ship), 58, 75
James W. Parker (schooner), 30
Jamestown (sloop of war), 84
Java (frigate), 108
Jessie Costa (schooner), 30
John Adams (sloop of war), 163
John Currier (ship), 161
John McKeon (pilot schooner), 161
Jones, Capt. John Paul, 84
Joseph Walker (packet ship), 64, 161
July (pink), 23

Kearsarge (Gloucester schooner), 5
Kearney, Denis, 66

Lady of the Lake (lugger), 50
Launches, 117, 125
Lawlor, D. J., 27
Laurence & Tudor, 94
Lena M. (Block Island boat), 6
Lenthall, John, 142
Levant (ship), 157
Levant (sloop of war), 163
Lexington (brig of war), 163
Liberty (sloop), 28
Ligera (schooner), 162
Lightning (clipper ship), 64, 160
Lion (Chebacco boat), 16
Lipton, Sir Thomas, 30
London (ship), 147, 148, 151
Long boat, 116-118

INDEX

Lord of the Isles (ship), 161
Lowell, Capt. ——, 70
Lucas, Capt. ——, 88
Lugger, New Orleans, 50, 51
Lugger, Penzance, 40

Macedonian (frigate), 162
McKay, Donald, 27, 63, 64
Magazine, 133
Magic (bugeye), 48
Magnifique (ship), 79
Magoun, Thacher, 58
Maine (pink), 18, 22, 23
Malek-Adhel (brig), 161
Manhasset (schooner), 162
Mansfield, C. H., 18
Marion (sloop of war), 163
Marshall, Capt. Benjamin, 57
Mary (pilot schooner), 161
Mary (pink), 18
Mary E. Clooney (schooner), 34
Mary Taylor (pilot schooner), 161
Massasoit (schooner), 27
Masts, 85-87, 126, 139-157
Mayflower (schooner), 32
Mayflower (ship), 161
Meneola (schooner), 34
Merrimack (ram), 121
Mildred Addison (schooner), 40, 42
Minnesota (frigate), 121
Mitchell, Sylvester D., 6
Montgomery (frigate), 94
Montezuma (packet ship), 62, 64, 65, 76, 95, 161
Morris, Robert, 80
Murray, Mungo, 81, 116

Naples (ship), 70
Nestor (packet ship), 58, 75
New York (packet ship), 76

Newport (R. I.), 3, 4, 12
Newsboy (clipper brig), 161
Niagara (frigate), 162
Nightingale (clipper ship), 160
North Carolina (ship), 141, 162
Northern Light (yacht), 162

Ocean (pink), 17
Ohio (ship), 88, 162
Ontario (sloop of war), 163
Orbit (packet ship), 58, 75
Oriental (packet ship), 161
Osceola (schooner), 34
Oxford (packet ship), 75

Pacific (packet ship), 58, 75
Pacific (ship), 161
Packet ship, Life on a, 66
Packet ships, 56-76
Paint, 21, 52
Patillo, Capt. James, 22
Patton, ——, 66
Paulding, Capt. ——, 84
Peggy (brigantine), 88
Pennsylvania (frigate), 146, 148, 150, 157
Pennsylvania (ship), 162
Pensacola, Fla., 34
Penzance lugger, 40
Peri (schooner), 162
Perry (brig of war), 163
Philadelphia (packet), 161
Phoenix (frigate), 79
Pink (pink), 17
Pinkys, 3, 14-23
Pinnaces, 117
Pique (ship), 147, 148, 151
Plans of ships, 159-163
Plendome (schooner), 162
Plymouth (sloop of war), 156

INDEX

Polly (schooner), 18, 25
Pook, Samuel H., 64
Porpoise (brig of war), 163
Porpoise (schooner of war), 163
Potomac (frigate), 142, 148, 150, 157
Potomac (ship), 89
Preble, Capt. Edward, 112, 115
Preble (sloop of war), 163
President (frigate), 80, 89
Providence (frigate), 78
Pumps, 100

Quoddy boats, 14, 16

Racer (clipper ship), 74
Races, Fisherman's, 30
Rainbow (clipper ship), 64, 160
Raleigh (frigate), 77-119, 162
Ramon de Zaldo (brig), 161
Randolph (frigate), 78
Ranger (ship), 78, 84
Raritan (frigate), 122
Rattle, 102
Red Jacket (clipper ship), 64, 160
Rhode Island (Block Island boat), 4
Rhodes, Foster, 142
Rigging details of fisherman, 33
Roanoke (frigate), 121
Roaring Bessie (Block Island boat), 6
Robinson, Capt. Andrew, 25, 87
Romp model, 26
Roos, William, 139
Rose, John, 6
  Lemuel B., 6
Rose Dorothea (schooner), 30
Roue, W. J., 32
Round Bodied Ship, 135
Rousseau (packet ship), 60
Royal Frederick (ship), 147, 148, 151
Royal Sovereign (ship), 163

St. Denis, 58, 70
St. Lawrence (frigate), 84, 121, 122
St. Mary's (sloop of war), 163
Sampsell, L. D., 50
Samuels, Capt. Samuel, 74
Santa Maria (carack), 162
Sappho (Block Island boat), 6
Saratoga (sloop of war), 152
Savannah (frigate), 122
Schooner, Clipper, 36-45
Schooners, Fishing, 24-35
Sea Witch (clipper ship), 64, 160
Shark (schooner of war), 163
Skiddy (pilot schooner), 161
Smith, Capt. John, 37
Smuggler (schooner), 162
Snapdragon (bark), 161
Solebay (frigate), 80
Sovereign of the Seas (clipper ship), 160
Sparrow Hawk (sloop), 162
Spars, 84-87
Sponge boats, 52-54
Stag Hound (clipper ship), 160
Stannard, Capt. Dan, 107
Stevens, Merrill, 52
Stoddart, Benjamin, 89
Story, Arthur Dana, 32
Stowell, Capt. ——, 67
Sutherland, William, 117
Swedish frigates, 134
Sword Fish (clipper ship), 160

T. S. Negus (pilot boat), 28
Telegraph (schooner), 27
Thisbe (frigate), 80
Thomas Lynch (Block Island boat), 6
Thomas W. Lawson (schooner), 54
Thompson, Jeremiah, 57
Thompson, William Francis, 57
Tiger (pinky), 22, 23

Tom (ship), 88
Totten, Lieut. B. J., 134
Trenton (pink), 23
Tricolor (ship), 161
Trumbull (frigate), 89
Truxton (brig), 147, 148, 151, 157, 163

United States (frigate), 80, 89, 144, 146, 148, 150, 162

Vandalia (ship), 146, 148, 150
Vanguard (ship), 147, 148, 151
Venus (ship), 79
Vermont (ship), 83
Vernon (ship), 147, 148, 151
Victorine (sloop), 28, 30, 162
Viking ship, 162
Vincennes (sloop of war), 83
Virginia (frigate), 78
Volante (brig), 161

W. H. Van Name (schooner), 28
Wallace Blackford (schooner), 28
Warren (frigate), 78
Washington (frigate), 78
Washington Irving (packet ship), 161

Watch bill, 127
Wave (yacht), 162
Webb, William, 15
    William H., 56, 63
Webber, Capt. T. R., 88
Westervelt, A. T., 58
Westward Ho (clipper ship), 160
Whale ships, 6
Wheels, 107
Wherries, 117
William L. Douglass (schooner), 162
William Thompson (packet ship), 58, 75
Wiles, Irving R., v, 18
Wills, J. R., 40
Wright, Isaac, 57

Yankee Hero (Quoddy boat), 16
Yawls, 117
Young America (clipper ship), 160
Yorkshire (packet ship), 76
Yorktown (packet ship), 64, 147, 148, 151, 157, 161
Yorktown (sloop of war), 163
Yosemite (sloop), 162

A CATALOGUE OF SELECTED DOVER BOOKS
IN ALL FIELDS OF INTEREST

A CATALOG OF SELECTED DOVER
BOOKS IN ALL FIELDS OF INTEREST

LASERS AND HOLOGRAPHY, Winston E. Kock. Sound introduction to burgeoning field, expanded (1981) for second edition. 84 illustrations. 160pp. 5⅜ × 8¼. (EUK)   24041-X Pa. $3.50

FLORAL STAINED GLASS PATTERN BOOK, Ed Sibbett, Jr. 96 exquisite floral patterns—irises, poppie, lilies, tulips, geometrics, abstracts, etc.—adaptable to innumerable stained glass projects. 64pp. 8¼ × 11.   24259-5 Pa. $3.50

THE HISTORY OF THE LEWIS AND CLARK EXPEDITION, Meriwether Lewis and William Clark. Edited by Eliott Coues. Great classic edition of Lewis and Clark's day-by-day journals. Complete 1893 edition, edited by Eliott Coues from Biddle's authorized 1814 history. 1508pp. 5⅜ × 8½.
21268-8, 21269-6, 21270-X Pa. Three-vol. set $22.50

ORLEY FARM, Anthony Trollope. Three-dimensional tale of great criminal case. Original Millais illustrations illuminate marvelous panorama of Victorian society. Plot was author's favorite. 736pp. 5⅜ × 8½.   24181-5 Pa. $8.95

THE CLAVERINGS, Anthony Trollope. Major novel, chronicling aspects of British Victorian society, personalities. 16 plates by M. Edwards; first reprint of full text. 412pp. 5⅜ × 8½.   23464-9 Pa. $6.00

EINSTEIN'S THEORY OF RELATIVITY, Max Born. Finest semi-technical account; much explanation of ideas and math not readily available elsewhere on this level. 376pp. 5⅜ × 8½.   60769-0 Pa. $5.00

COMPUTABILITY AND UNSOLVABILITY, Martin Davis. Classic graduate-level introduction th theory of computability, usually referred to as theory of recurrent functions. New preface and appendix. 288pp. 5⅜ × 8½. 61471-9 Pa. $6.50

THE GODS OF THE EGYPTIANS, E.A. Wallis Budge. Never excelled for richness, fullness: all gods, goddesses, demons, mythical figures of Ancient Egypt; their legends, rites, incarnations, etc. Over 225 illustrations, plus 6 color plates. 988pp. 6⅛ × 9¼. (EBE)   22055-9, 22056-7 Pa., Two-vol. set $20.00

THE I CHING (THE BOOK OF CHANGES), translated by James Legge. Most penetrating divination manual ever prepared. Indispensable to study of early Oriental civilizations, to modern inquiring reader. 448pp. 5⅜ × 8½.
21062-6 Pa. $6.50

THE CRAFTSMAN'S HANDBOOK, Cennino Cennini. 15th-century handbook, school of Giotto, explains applying gold, silver leaf; gesso; fresco painting, grinding pigments, etc. 142pp. 6⅛ × 9¼.   20054-X Pa. $3.50

AN ATLAS OF ANATOMY FOR ARTISTS, Fritz Schider. Finest text, working book. Full text, plus anatomical illustrations; plates by great artists showing anatomy. 593 illustrations. 192pp. 7⅛ × 10¼.   20241-0 Pa. $6.00

EASY-TO-MAKE STAINED GLASS LIGHTCATCHERS, Ed Sibbett, Jr. 67 designs for most enjoyable ornaments: fruits, birds, teddy bears, trumpet, etc. Full size templates. 64pp. 8¼ × 11.   24081-9 Pa. $3.95

TRIAD OPTICAL ILLUSIONS AND HOW TO DESIGN THEM, Harry Turner. Triad explained in 32 pages of text, with 32 pages of Escher-like patterns on coloring stock. 92 figures. 32 plates. 64pp. 8¼ × 11.   23549-1 Pa. $2.50

TOLL HOUSE TRIED AND TRUE RECIPES, Ruth Graves Wakefield. Popovers, veal and ham loaf, baked beans, much more from the famous Mass. restaurant. Nearly 700 recipes. 376pp. 5⅜ × 8½. 23560-2 Pa. $4.95

FAVORITE CHRISTMAS CAROLS, selected and arranged by Charles J.F. Cofone. Title, music, first verse and refrain of 34 traditional carols in handsome calligraphy; also subsequent verses and other information in type. 79pp. 8⅜ × 11. 20445-6 Pa. $3.00

CAMERA WORK: A PICTORIAL GUIDE, Alfred Stieglitz. All 559 illustrations from most important periodical in history of art photography. Reduced in size but still clear, in strict chronological order, with complete captions. 176pp. 8⅜ × 11¼. 23591-2 Pa. $6.95

FAVORITE SONGS OF THE NINETIES, edited by Robert Fremont. 88 favorites: "Ta-Ra-Ra-Boom-De-Aye," "The Band Played On," "Bird in a Gilded Cage," etc. 401pp. 9 × 12. 21536-9 Pa. $10.95

STRING FIGURES AND HOW TO MAKE THEM, Caroline F. Jayne. Fullest, clearest instructions on string figures from around world: Eskimo, Navajo, Lapp, Europe, more. Cat's cradle, moving spear, lightning, stars. 950 illustrations. 407pp. 5⅜ × 8½. 20152-X Pa. $4.95

LIFE IN ANCIENT EGYPT, Adolf Erman. Detailed older account, with much not in more recent books: domestic life, religion, magic, medicine, commerce, and whatever else needed for complete picture. Many illustrations. 597pp. 5⅜ × 8½. 22632-8 Pa. $7.95

ANCIENT EGYPT: ITS CULTURE AND HISTORY, J.E. Manchip White. From pre-dynastics through Ptolemies: scoiety, history, political structure, religion, daily life, literature, cultural heritage. 48 plates. 217pp. 5⅜ × 8½. (EBE) 22548-8 Pa. $4.95

KEPT IN THE DARK, Anthony Trollope. Unusual short novel about Victorian morality and abnormal psychology by the great English author. Probably the first American publication. Frontispiece by Sir John Millais. 92pp. 6½ × 9¼. 23609-9 Pa. $2.95

MAN AND WIFE, Wilkie Collins. Nineteenth-century master launches an attack on out-moded Scottish marital laws and Victorian cult of athleticism. Artfully plotted. 35 illustrations. 239pp. 6⅛ × 9¼. 24451-2 Pa. $5.95

RELATIVITY AND COMMON SENSE, Herman Bondi. Radically reoriented presentation of Einstein's Special Theory and one of most valuable popular accounts available. 60 illustrations. 177pp. 5⅜ × 8. (EUK) 24021-5 Pa. $3.50

THE EGYPTIAN BOOK OF THE DEAD, E.A. Wallis Budge. Complete reproduction of Ani's papyrus, finest ever found. Full hieroglyphic text, interlinear transliteration, word-for-word translation, smooth translation. 533pp. 6½ × 9¼. (USO) 21866-X Pa. $8.50

COUNTRY AND SUBURBAN HOMES OF THE PRAIRIE SCHOOL PERIOD, H.V. von Holst. Over 400 photographs floor plans, elevations, detailed drawings (exteriors and interiors) for over 100 structures. Text. Important primary source. 128pp. 8⅜ × 11¼. 24373-7 Pa. $5.95

REASON IN ART, George Santayana. Renowned philosopher's provocative, seminal treatment of basis of art in instinct and experience. Volume Four of *The Life of Reason.* 230pp. 5⅜ × 8. 24358-3 Pa. $4.50

LANGUAGE, TRUTH AND LOGIC, Alfred J. Ayer. Famous, clear introduction to Vienna, Cambridge schools of Logical Positivism. Role of philosophy, elimination of metaphysics, nature of analysis, etc. 160pp. 5⅜ × 8½. (USCO) 20010-8 Pa. $2.75

BASIC ELECTRONICS, U.S. Bureau of Naval Personnel. Electron tubes, circuits, antennas, AM, FM, and CW transmission and receiving, etc. 560 illustrations. 567pp. 6½ × 9¼. 21076-6 Pa. $8.95

THE ART DECO STYLE, edited by Theodore Menten. Furniture, jewelry, metalwork, ceramics, fabrics, lighting fixtures, interior decors, exteriors, graphics from pure French sources. Over 400 photographs. 183pp. 8⅜ × 11¼. 22824-X Pa. $6.95

THE FOUR BOOKS OF ARCHITECTURE, Andrea Palladio. 16th-century classic covers classical architectural remains, Renaissance revivals, classical orders, etc. 1738 Ware English edition. 216 plates. 110pp. of text. 9½ × 12¾. 21308-0 Pa. $10.00

THE WIT AND HUMOR OF OSCAR WILDE, edited by Alvin Redman. More than 1000 ripostes, paradoxes, wisecracks: Work is the curse of the drinking classes, I can resist everything except temptations, etc. 258pp. 5⅜ × 8½. (USCO) 20602-5 Pa. $3.50

THE DEVIL'S DICTIONARY, Ambrose Bierce. Barbed, bitter, brilliant witticisms in the form of a dictionary. Best, most ferocious satire America has produced. 145pp. 5⅜ × 8½. 20487-1 Pa. $2.50

ERTÉ'S FASHION DESIGNS, Erté. 210 black-and-white inventions from *Harper's Bazar,* 1918-32, plus 8pp. full-color covers. Captions. 88pp. 9 × 12. 24203-X Pa. $6.50

ERTÉ GRAPHICS, Erté. Collection of striking color graphics: *Seasons, Alphabet, Numerals, Aces* and *Precious Stones.* 50 plates, including 4 on covers. 48pp. 9⅜ × 12¼. 23580-7 Pa. $6.95

PAPER FOLDING FOR BEGINNERS, William D. Murray and Francis J. Rigney. Clearest book for making origami sail boats, roosters, frogs that move legs, etc. 40 projects. More than 275 illustrations. 94pp. 5⅜ × 8½. 20713-7 Pa. $1.95

ORIGAMI FOR THE ENTHUSIAST, John Montroll. Fish, ostrich, peacock, squirrel, rhinoceros, Pegasus, 19 other intricate subjects. Instructions. Diagrams. 128pp. 9 × 12. 23799-0 Pa. $4.95

CROCHETING NOVELTY POT HOLDERS, edited by Linda Macho. 64 useful, whimsical pot holders feature kitchen themes, animals, flowers, other novelties. Surprisingly easy to crochet. Complete instructions. 48pp. 8¼ × 11. 24296-X Pa. $1.95

CROCHETING DOILIES, edited by Rita Weiss. Irish Crochet, Jewel, Star Wheel, Vanity Fair and more. Also luncheon and console sets, runners and centerpieces. 51 illustrations. 48pp. 8¼ × 11. 23424-X Pa. $2.00

DECORATIVE NAPKIN FOLDING FOR BEGINNERS, Lillian Oppenheimer and Natalie Epstein. 22 different napkin folds in the shape of a heart, clown's hat, love knot, etc. 63 drawings. 48pp. 8¼ × 11.   23797-4 Pa. $1.95

DECORATIVE LABELS FOR HOME CANNING, PRESERVING, AND OTHER HOUSEHOLD AND GIFT USES, Theodore Menten. 128 gummed, perforated labels, beautifully printed in 2 colors. 12 versions. Adhere to metal, glass, wood, ceramics. 24pp. 8¼ × 11.   23219-0 Pa. $2.95

EARLY AMERICAN STENCILS ON WALLS AND FURNITURE, Janet Waring. Thorough coverage of 19th-century folk art: techniques, artifacts, surviving specimens. 166 illustrations, 7 in color. 147pp. of text. 7⅞ × 10¾. 21906-2 Pa. $8.95

AMERICAN ANTIQUE WEATHERVANES, A.B. & W.T. Westervelt. Extensively illustrated 1883 catalog exhibiting over 550 copper weathervanes and finials. Excellent primary source by one of the principal manufacturers. 104pp. 6⅛ × 9¼.
24396-6 Pa. $3.95

ART STUDENTS' ANATOMY, Edmond J. Farris. Long favorite in art schools. Basic elements, common positions, actions. Full text, 158 illustrations. 159pp. 5⅜ × 8½.   20744-7 Pa. $3.50

BRIDGMAN'S LIFE DRAWING, George B. Bridgman. More than 500 drawings and text teach you to abstract the body into its major masses. Also specific areas of anatomy. 192pp. 6½ × 9¼. (EA)   22710-3 Pa. $4.50

COMPLETE PRELUDES AND ETUDES FOR SOLO PIANO, Frederic Chopin. All 26 Preludes, all 27 Etudes by greatest composer of piano music. Authoritative Paderewski edition. 224pp. 9 × 12. (Available in U.S. only)   24052-5 Pa. $6.95

PIANO MUSIC 1888-1905, Claude Debussy. Deux Arabesques, Suite Bergamesque, Masques, 1st series of Images, etc. 9 others, in corrected editions. 175pp. 9⅜ × 12¼.
(ECE) 22771-5 Pa. $5.95

TEDDY BEAR IRON-ON TRANSFER PATTERNS, Ted Menten. 80 iron-on transfer patterns of male and female Teddys in a wide variety of activities, poses, sizes. 48pp. 8¼ × 11.   24596-9 Pa. $2.00

A PICTURE HISTORY OF THE BROOKLYN BRIDGE, M.J. Shapiro. Profusely illustrated account of greatest engineering achievement of 19th century. 167 rare photos & engravings recall construction, human drama. Extensive, detailed text. 122pp. 8¼ × 11.   24403-2 Pa. $7.95

NEW YORK IN THE THIRTIES, Berenice Abbott. Noted photographer's fascinating study shows new buildings that have become famous and old sights that have disappeared forever. 97 photographs. 97pp. 11⅜ × 10.   22967-X Pa. $6.50

MATHEMATICAL TABLES AND FORMULAS, Robert D. Carmichael and Edwin R. Smith. Logarithms, sines, tangents, trig functions, powers, roots, reciprocals, exponential and hyperbolic functions, formulas and theorems. 269pp. 5⅜ × 8½.   60111-0 Pa. $3.75

HANDBOOK OF MATHEMATICAL FUNCTIONS WITH FORMULAS, GRAPHS, AND MATHEMATICAL TABLES, edited by Milton Abramowitz and Irene A. Stegun. Vast compendium: 29 sets of tables, some to as high as 20 places. 1,046pp. 8 × 10½.   61272-4 Pa. $19.95

THE RIME OF THE ANCIENT MARINER, Gustave Doré, S.T. Coleridge. Doré's finest work, 34 plates capture moods, subtleties of poem. Full text. 77pp. 9¼ × 12. 22305-1 Pa. $4.95

SONGS OF INNOCENCE, William Blake. The first and most popular of Blake's famous "Illuminated Books," in a facsimile edition reproducing all 31 brightly colored plates. Additional printed text of each poem. 64pp. 5¼ × 7. 22764-2 Pa. $3.00

AN INTRODUCTION TO INFORMATION THEORY, J.R. Pierce. Second (1980) edition of most impressive non-technical account available. Encoding, entropy, noisy channel, related areas, etc. 320pp. 5⅜ × 8½. 24061-4 Pa. $4.95

THE DIVINE PROPORTION: A STUDY IN MATHEMATICAL BEAUTY, H.E. Huntley. "Divine proportion" or "golden ratio" in poetry, Pascal's triangle, philosophy, psychology, music, mathematical figures, etc. Excellent bridge between science and art. 58 figures. 185pp. 5⅜ × 8½. 22254-3 Pa. $3.95

THE DOVER NEW YORK WALKING GUIDE: From the Battery to Wall Street, Mary J. Shapiro. Superb inexpensive guide to historic buildings and locales in lower Manhattan: Trinity Church, Bowling Green, more. Complete Text; maps. 36 illustrations. 48pp. 3⅞ × 9¼. 24225-0 Pa. $1.75

NEW YORK THEN AND NOW, Edward B. Watson, Edmund V. Gillon, Jr. 83 important Manhattan sites: on facing pages early photographs (1875-1925) and 1976 photos by Gillon. 172 illustrations. 171pp. 9¼ × 10. 23361-8 Pa. $7.95

HISTORIC COSTUME IN PICTURES, Braun & Schneider. Over 1450 costumed figures from dawn of civilization to end of 19th century. English captions. 125 plates. 256pp. 8⅜ × 11¼. 23150-X Pa. $7.50

VICTORIAN AND EDWARDIAN FASHION: A Photographic Survey, Alison Gernsheim. First fashion history completely illustrated by contemporary photographs. Full text plus 235 photos, 1840-1914, in which many celebrities appear. 240pp. 6½ × 9¼. 24205-6 Pa. $6.00

CHARTED CHRISTMAS DESIGNS FOR COUNTED CROSS-STITCH AND OTHER NEEDLECRAFTS, Lindberg Press. Charted designs for 45 beautiful needlecraft projects with many yuletide and wintertime motifs. 48pp. 8¼ × 11. 24356-7 Pa. $1.95

101 FOLK DESIGNS FOR COUNTED CROSS-STITCH AND OTHER NEEDLECRAFTS, Carter Houck. 101 authentic charted folk designs in a wide array of lovely representations with many suggestions for effective use. 48pp. 8¼ × 11. 24369-9 Pa. $1.95

FIVE ACRES AND INDEPENDENCE, Maurice G. Kains. Great back-to-the-land classic explains basics of self-sufficient farming. The one book to get. 95 illustrations. 397pp. 5⅜ × 8½. 20974-1 Pa. $4.95

A MODERN HERBAL, Margaret Grieve. Much the fullest, most exact, most useful compilation of herbal material. Gigantic alphabetical encyclopedia, from aconite to zedoary, gives botanical information, medical properties, folklore, economic uses, and much else. Indispensable to serious reader. 161 illustrations. 888pp. 6½ × 9¼. (Available in U.S. only) 22798-7, 22799-5 Pa., Two-vol. set $16.45

HOW THE OTHER HALF LIVES, Jacob A. Riis. Journalistic record of filth, degradation, upward drive in New York immigrant slums, shops, around 1900. New edition includes 100 original Riis photos, monuments of early photography. 233pp. $10 \times 7\frac{7}{8}$. 22012-5 Pa. $7.95

CHINA AND ITS PEOPLE IN EARLY PHOTOGRAPHS, John Thomson. In 200 black-and-white photographs of exceptional quality photographic pioneer Thomson captures the mountains, dwellings, monuments and people of 19th-century China. 272pp. $9\frac{3}{8} \times 12\frac{1}{4}$. 24393-1 Pa. $12.95

GODEY COSTUME PLATES IN COLOR FOR DECOUPAGE AND FRAMING, edited by Eleanor Hasbrouk Rawlings. 24 full-color engravings depicting 19th-century Parisian haute couture. Printed on one side only. 56pp. $8\frac{1}{4} \times 11$. 23879-2 Pa. $3.95

ART NOUVEAU STAINED GLASS PATTERN BOOK, Ed Sibbett, Jr. 104 projects using well-known themes of Art Nouveau: swirling forms, florals, peacocks, and sensuous women. 60pp. $8\frac{1}{4} \times 11$. 23577-7 Pa. $3.00

QUICK AND EASY PATCHWORK ON THE SEWING MACHINE: Susan Aylsworth Murwin and Suzzy Payne. Instructions, diagrams show exactly how to machine sew 12 quilts. 48pp. of templates. 50 figures. 80pp. $8\frac{1}{4} \times 11$. 23770-2 Pa. $3.50

THE STANDARD BOOK OF QUILT MAKING AND COLLECTING, Marguerite Ickis. Full information, full-sized patterns for making 46 traditional quilts, also 150 other patterns. 483 illustrations. 273pp. $6\frac{7}{8} \times 9\frac{5}{8}$. 20582-7 Pa. $5.95

LETTERING AND ALPHABETS, J. Albert Cavanagh. 85 complete alphabets lettered in various styles; instructions for spacing, roughs, brushwork. 121pp. $8\frac{3}{4} \times 8$. 20053-1 Pa. $3.75

LETTER FORMS: 110 COMPLETE ALPHABETS, Frederick Lambert. 110 sets of capital letters; 16 lower case alphabets; 70 sets of numbers and other symbols. 110pp. $8\frac{1}{8} \times 11$. 22872-X Pa. $4.50

ORCHIDS AS HOUSE PLANTS, Rebecca Tyson Northen. Grow cattleyas and many other kinds of orchids—in a window, in a case, or under artificial light. 63 illustrations. 148pp. $5\frac{3}{8} \times 8\frac{1}{2}$. 23261-1 Pa. $2.95

THE MUSHROOM HANDBOOK, Louis C.C. Krieger. Still the best popular handbook. Full descriptions of 259 species, extremely thorough text, poisons, folklore, etc. 32 color plates; 126 other illustrations. 560pp. $5\frac{3}{8} \times 8\frac{1}{2}$. 21861-9 Pa. $8.50

THE DORÉ BIBLE ILLUSTRATIONS, Gustave Doré. All wonderful, detailed plates: Adam and Eve, Flood, Babylon, life of Jesus, etc. Brief King James text with each plate. 241 plates. 241pp. 9×12. 23004-X Pa. $6.95

THE BOOK OF KELLS: Selected Plates in Full Color, edited by Blanche Cirker. 32 full-page plates from greatest manuscript-icon of early Middle Ages. Fantastic, mysterious. Publisher's Note. Captions. 32pp. $9\frac{3}{8} \times 12\frac{1}{4}$. 24345-1 Pa. $4.50

THE PERFECT WAGNERITE, George Bernard Shaw. Brilliant criticism of the Ring Cycle, with provocative interpretation of politics, economic theories behind the Ring. 136pp. $5\frac{3}{8} \times 8\frac{1}{2}$. (Available in U.S. only) 21707-8 Pa. $3.00

KEYBOARD WORKS FOR SOLO INSTRUMENTS, G.F. Handel. 35 neglected works from Handel's vast oeuvre, originally jotted down as improvisations. Includes Eight Great Suites, others. New sequence. 174pp. 9⅜ × 12¼.
24338-9 Pa. $7.50

AMERICAN LEAGUE BASEBALL CARD CLASSICS, Bert Randolph Sugar. 82 stars from 1900s to 60s on facsimile cards. Ruth, Cobb, Mantle, Williams, plus advertising, info, no duplications. Perforated, detachable. 16pp. 8¼ × 11.
24286-2 Pa. $2.95

A TREASURY OF CHARTED DESIGNS FOR NEEDLEWORKERS, Georgia Gorham and Jeanne Warth. 141 charted designs: owl, cat with yarn, tulips, piano, spinning wheel, covered bridge, Victorian house and many others. 48pp. 8¼ × 11.
23558-0 Pa. $1.95

DANISH FLORAL CHARTED DESIGNS, Gerda Bengtsson. Exquisite collection of over 40 different florals: anemone, Iceland poppy, wild fruit, pansies, many others. 45 illustrations. 48pp. 8¼ × 11.
23957-8 Pa. $1.75

OLD PHILADELPHIA IN EARLY PHOTOGRAPHS 1839-1914, Robert F. Looney. 215 photographs: panoramas, street scenes, landmarks, President-elect Lincoln's visit, 1876 Centennial Exposition, much more. 230pp. 8⅞ × 11¾.
23345-6 Pa. $9.95

PRELUDE TO MATHEMATICS, W.W. Sawyer. Noted mathematician's lively, stimulating account of non-Euclidean geometry, matrices, determinants, group theory, other topics. Emphasis on novel, striking aspects. 224pp. 5⅜ × 8½.
24401-6 Pa. $4.50

ADVENTURES WITH A MICROSCOPE, Richard Headstrom. 59 adventures with clothing fibers, protozoa, ferns and lichens, roots and leaves, much more. 142 illustrations. 232pp. 5⅜ × 8½.
23471-1 Pa. $3.50

IDENTIFYING ANIMAL TRACKS: MAMMALS, BIRDS, AND OTHER ANIMALS OF THE EASTERN UNITED STATES, Richard Headstrom. For hunters, naturalists, scouts, nature-lovers. Diagrams of tracks, tips on identification. 128pp. 5⅜ × 8.
24442-3 Pa. $3.50

VICTORIAN FASHIONS AND COSTUMES FROM HARPER'S BAZAR, 1867-1898, edited by Stella Blum. Day costumes, evening wear, sports clothes, shoes, hats, other accessories in over 1,000 detailed engravings. 320pp. 9⅜ × 12¼.
22990-4 Pa. $9.95

EVERYDAY FASHIONS OF THE TWENTIES AS PICTURED IN SEARS AND OTHER CATALOGS, edited by Stella Blum. Actual dress of the Roaring Twenties, with text by Stella Blum. Over 750 illustrations, captions. 156pp. 9 × 12.
24134-3 Pa. $7.95

HALL OF FAME BASEBALL CARDS, edited by Bert Randolph Sugar. Cy Young, Ted Williams, Lou Gehrig, and many other Hall of Fame greats on 92 full-color, detachable reprints of early baseball cards. No duplication of cards with *Classic Baseball Cards*. 16pp. 8¼ × 11.
23624-2 Pa. $2.95

THE ART OF HAND LETTERING, Helm Wotzkow. Course in hand lettering, Roman, Gothic, Italic, Block, Script. Tools, proportions, optical aspects, individual variation. Very quality conscious. Hundreds of specimens. 320pp. 5⅜ × 8½.
21797-3 Pa. $4.95

CATALOG OF DOVER BOOKS

TWENTY-FOUR ART NOUVEAU POSTCARDS IN FULL COLOR FROM CLASSIC POSTERS, Hayward and Blanche Cirker. Ready-to-mail postcards reproduced from rare set of poster art. Works by Toulouse-Lautrec, Parrish, Steinlen, Mucha, Cheret, others. 12pp. 8¼× 11. 24389-3 Pa. $2.95

READY-TO-USE ART NOUVEAU BOOKMARKS IN FULL COLOR, Carol Belanger Grafton. 30 elegant bookmarks featuring graceful, flowing lines, foliate motifs, sensuous women characteristic of Art Nouveau. Perforated for easy detaching. 16pp. 8¼ × 11. 24305-2 Pa. $2.95

FRUIT KEY AND TWIG KEY TO TREES AND SHRUBS, William M. Harlow. Fruit key covers 120 deciduous and evergreen species; twig key covers 160 deciduous species. Easily used. Over 300 photographs. 126pp. 5⅜ × 8½. 20511-8 Pa. $2.25

LEONARDO DRAWINGS, Leonardo da Vinci. Plants, landscapes, human face and figure, etc., plus studies for Sforza monument, *Last Supper*, more. 60 illustrations. 64pp. 8¼ × 11⅛. 23951-9 Pa. $2.75

CLASSIC BASEBALL CARDS, edited by Bert R. Sugar. 98 classic cards on heavy stock, full color, perforated for detaching. Ruth, Cobb, Durocher, DiMaggio, H. Wagner, 99 others. Rare originals cost hundreds. 16pp. 8¼ × 11. 23498-3 Pa. $2.95

TREES OF THE EASTERN AND CENTRAL UNITED STATES AND CANADA, William M. Harlow. Best one-volume guide to 140 trees. Full descriptions, woodlore, range, etc. Over 600 illustrations. Handy size. 288pp. 4½ × 6⅜. 20395-6 Pa. $3.50

JUDY GARLAND PAPER DOLLS IN FULL COLOR, Tom Tierney. 3 Judy Garland paper dolls (teenager, grown-up, and mature woman) and 30 gorgeous costumes highlighting memorable career. Captions. 32pp. 9¼ × 12¼.
24404-0 Pa. $3.50

GREAT FASHION DESIGNS OF THE BELLE EPOQUE PAPER DOLLS IN FULL COLOR, Tom Tierney. Two dolls and 30 costumes meticulously rendered. Haute couture by Worth, Lanvin, Paquin, other greats late Victorian to WWI. 32pp. 9¼ × 12¼. 24425-3 Pa. $3.50

FASHION PAPER DOLLS FROM GODEY'S LADY'S BOOK, 1840-1854, Susan Johnston. In full color: 7 female fashion dolls with 50 costumes. Little girl's, bridal, riding, bathing, wedding, evening, everyday, etc. 32pp. 9¼ × 12¼.
23511-4 Pa. $3.50

THE BOOK OF THE SACRED MAGIC OF ABRAMELIN THE MAGE, translated by S. MacGregor Mathers. Medieval manuscript of ceremonial magic. Basic document in Aleister Crowley, Golden Dawn groups. 268pp. 5⅜ × 8½.
23211-5 Pa. $5.00

PETER RABBIT POSTCARDS IN FULL COLOR: 24 Ready-to-Mail Cards, Susan Whited LaBelle. Bunnies ice-skating, coloring Easter eggs, making valentines, many other charming scenes. 24 perforated full-color postcards, each measuring 4¼ × 6, on coated stock. 12pp. 9 × 12. 24617-5 Pa. $2.95

CELTIC HAND STROKE BY STROKE, A. Baker. Complete guide creating each letter of the alphabet in distinctive Celtic manner. Covers hand position, strokes, pens, inks, paper, more. Illustrated. 48pp. 8¼ × 11. 24336-2 Pa. $2.50

CATALOG OF DOVER BOOKS

CHANCERY CURSIVE STROKE BY STROKE, Arthur Baker. Instructions and illustrations for each stroke of each letter (upper and lower case) and numerals. 54 full-page plates. 64pp. 8¼ × 11. 24278-1 Pa. $2.50

THE ENJOYMENT AND USE OF COLOR, Walter Sargent. Color relationships, values, intensities; complementary colors, illumination, similar topics. Color in nature and art. 7 color plates, 29 illustrations. 274pp. 5⅜ × 8½. 20944-X Pa. $4.50

SCULPTURE PRINCIPLES AND PRACTICE, Louis Slobodkin. Step-by-step approach to clay, plaster, metals, stone; classical and modern. 253 drawings, photos. 255pp. 8⅛ × 11. 22960-2 Pa. $7.00

VICTORIAN FASHION PAPER DOLLS FROM HARPER'S BAZAR, 1867-1898, Theodore Menten. Four female dolls with 28 elegant high fashion costumes, printed in full color. 32pp. 9¼ × 12¼. 23453-3 Pa. $3.50

FLOPSY, MOPSY AND COTTONTAIL: A Little Book of Paper Dolls in Full Color, Susan LaBelle. Three dolls and 21 costumes (7 for each doll) show Peter Rabbit's siblings dressed for holidays, gardening, hiking, etc. Charming borders, captions. 48pp. 4¼ × 5½. 24376-1 Pa. $2.00

NATIONAL LEAGUE BASEBALL CARD CLASSICS, Bert Randolph Sugar. 83 big-leaguers from 1909-69 on facsimile cards. Hubbell, Dean, Spahn, Brock plus advertising, info, no duplications. Perforated, detachable. 16pp. 8¼ × 11. 24308-7 Pa. $2.95

THE LOGICAL APPROACH TO CHESS, Dr. Max Euwe, et al. First-rate text of comprehensive strategy, tactics, theory for the amateur. No gambits to memorize, just a clear, logical approach. 224pp. 5⅜ × 8½. 24353-2 Pa. $4.50

MAGICK IN THEORY AND PRACTICE, Aleister Crowley. The summation of the thought and practice of the century's most famous necromancer, long hard to find. Crowley's best book. 436pp. 5⅜ × 8½. (Available in U.S. only) 23295-6 Pa. $6.50

THE HAUNTED HOTEL, Wilkie Collins. Collins' last great tale; doom and destiny in a Venetian palace. Praised by T.S. Eliot. 127pp. 5⅜ × 8½. 24333-8 Pa. $3.00

ART DECO DISPLAY ALPHABETS, Dan X. Solo. Wide variety of bold yet elegant lettering in handsome Art Deco styles. 100 complete fonts, with numerals, punctuation, more. 104pp. 8⅛ × 11. 24372-9 Pa. $4.00

CALLIGRAPHIC ALPHABETS, Arthur Baker. Nearly 150 complete alphabets by outstanding contemporary. Stimulating ideas; useful source for unique effects. 154 plates. 157pp. 8⅜ × 11¼. 21045-6 Pa. $4.95

ARTHUR BAKER'S HISTORIC CALLIGRAPHIC ALPHABETS, Arthur Baker. From monumental capitals of first-century Rome to humanistic cursive of 16th century, 33 alphabets in fresh interpretations. 88 plates. 96pp. 9 × 12. 24054-1 Pa. $3.95

LETTIE LANE PAPER DOLLS, Sheila Young. Genteel turn-of-the-century family very popular then and now. 24 paper dolls. 16 plates in full color. 32pp. 9¼ × 12¼. 24089-4 Pa. $3.50

JAPANESE DESIGN MOTIFS, Matsuya Co. Mon, or heraldic designs. Over 4000 typical, beautiful designs: birds, animals, flowers, swords, fans, geometrics; all beautifully stylized. 213pp. 11⅜ × 8¼. 22874-6 Pa. $6.95

THE TALE OF BENJAMIN BUNNY, Beatrix Potter. Peter Rabbit's cousin coaxes him back into Mr. McGregor's garden for a whole new set of adventures. All 27 full-color illustrations. 59pp. 4¼ × 5½. (Available in U.S. only) 21102-9 Pa. $1.50

THE TALE OF PETER RABBIT AND OTHER FAVORITE STORIES BOXED SET, Beatrix Potter. Seven of Beatrix Potter's best-loved tales including Peter Rabbit in a specially designed, durable boxed set. 4¼ × 5½. Total of 447pp. 158 color illustrations. (Available in U.S. only) 23903-9 Pa. $10.50

PRACTICAL MENTAL MAGIC, Theodore Annemann. Nearly 200 astonishing feats of mental magic revealed in step-by-step detail. Complete advice on staging, patter, etc. Illustrated. 320pp. 5⅜ × 8½. 24426-1 Pa. $5.95

CELEBRATED CASES OF JUDGE DEE (DEE GOONG AN), translated by Robert Van Gulik. Authentic 18th-century Chinese detective novel; Dee and associates solve three interlocked cases. Led to van Gulik's own stories with same characters. Extensive introduction. 9 illustrations. 237pp. 5⅜ × 8½.

23337-5 Pa. $4.50

CUT & FOLD EXTRATERRESTRIAL INVADERS THAT FLY, M. Grater. Stage your own lilliputian space battles.By following the step-by-step instructions and explanatory diagrams you can launch 22 full-color fliers into space. 36pp. 8¼ × 11. 24478-4 Pa. $2.95

CUT & ASSEMBLE VICTORIAN HOUSES, Edmund V. Gillon, Jr. Printed in full color on heavy cardboard stock, 4 authentic Victorian houses in H-O scale: Italian-style Villa, Octagon, Second Empire, Stick Style. 48pp. 9¼ × 12¼.

23849-0 Pa. $3.95

BEST SCIENCE FICTION STORIES OF H.G. WELLS, H.G. Wells. Full novel *The Invisible Man*, plus 17 short stories: "The Crystal Egg," "Aepyornis Island," "The Strange Orchid," etc. 303pp. 5⅜ × 8½. (Available in U.S. only)

21531-8 Pa. $3.95

TRADEMARK DESIGNS OF THE WORLD, Yusaku Kamekura. A lavish collection of nearly 700 trademarks, the work of Wright, Loewy, Klee, Binder, hundreds of others. 160pp. 8¾ × 8. (Available in U.S. only) 24191-2 Pa. $5.00

THE ARTIST'S AND CRAFTSMAN'S GUIDE TO REDUCING, ENLARGING AND TRANSFERRING DESIGNS, Rita Weiss. Discover, reduce, enlarge, transfer designs from any objects to any craft project. 12pp. plus 16 sheets special graph paper. 8¼ × 11. 24142-4 Pa. $3.25

TREASURY OF JAPANESE DESIGNS AND MOTIFS FOR ARTISTS AND CRAFTSMEN, edited by Carol Belanger Grafton. Indispensable collection of 360 traditional Japanese designs and motifs redrawn in clean, crisp black-and-white, copyright-free illustrations. 96pp. 8¼ × 11. 24435-0 Pa. $3.95

SURREAL STICKERS AND UNREAL STAMPS, William Rowe. 224 haunting, hilarious stamps on gummed, perforated stock, with images of elephants, geisha girls, George Washington, etc. 16pp. one side. 8¼ × 11.   24371-0 Pa. $3.50

GOURMET KITCHEN LABELS, Ed Sibbett, Jr. 112 full-color labels (4 copies each of 28 designs). Fruit, bread, other culinary motifs. Gummed and perforated. 16pp. 8¼ × 11.   24087-8 Pa. $2.95

PATTERNS AND INSTRUCTIONS FOR CARVING AUTHENTIC BIRDS, H.D. Green. Detailed instructions, 27 diagrams, 85 photographs for carving 15 species of birds so life-like, they'll seem ready to fly! 8¼ × 11.   24222-6 Pa. $2.75

FLATLAND, E.A. Abbott. Science-fiction classic explores life of 2-D being in 3-D world. 16 illustrations. 103pp. 5⅜ × 8.   20001-9 Pa. $2.00

DRIED FLOWERS, Sarah Whitlock and Martha Rankin. Concise, clear, practical guide to dehydration, glycerinizing, pressing plant material, and more. Covers use of silica gel. 12 drawings. 32pp. 5⅜ × 8½.   21802-3 Pa. $1.00

EASY-TO-MAKE CANDLES, Gary V. Guy. Learn how easy it is to make all kinds of decorative candles. Step-by-step instructions. 82 illustrations. 48pp. 8¼ × 11.
          23881-4 Pa. $2.50

SUPER STICKERS FOR KIDS, Carolyn Bracken. 128 gummed and perforated full-color stickers: GIRL WANTED, KEEP OUT, BORED OF EDUCATION, X-RATED, COMBAT ZONE, many others. 16pp. 8¼ × 11.   24092-4 Pa. $2.50

CUT AND COLOR PAPER MASKS, Michael Grater. Clowns, animals, funny faces...simply color them in, cut them out, and put them together, and you have 9 paper masks to play with and enjoy. 32pp. 8¼ × 11.   23171-2 Pa. $2.25

A CHRISTMAS CAROL: THE ORIGINAL MANUSCRIPT, Charles Dickens. Clear facsimile of Dickens manuscript, on facing pages with final printed text. 8 illustrations by John Leech, 4 in color on covers. 144pp. 8⅜ × 11¼.
          20980-6 Pa. $5.95

CARVING SHOREBIRDS, Harry V. Shourds & Anthony Hillman. 16 full-size patterns (all double-page spreads) for 19 North American shorebirds with step-by-step instructions. 72pp. 9¼ × 12¼.   24287-0 Pa. $4.95

THE GENTLE ART OF MATHEMATICS, Dan Pedoe. Mathematical games, probability, the question of infinity, topology, how the laws of algebra work, problems of irrational numbers, and more. 42 figures. 143pp. 5⅜ × 8½. (EBE)
          22949-1 Pa. $3.00

READY-TO-USE DOLLHOUSE WALLPAPER, Katzenbach & Warren, Inc. Stripe, 2 floral stripes, 2 allover florals, polka dot; all in full color. 4 sheets (350 sq. in.) of each, enough for average room. 48pp. 8¼ × 11.   23495-9 Pa. $2.95

MINIATURE IRON-ON TRANSFER PATTERNS FOR DOLLHOUSES, DOLLS, AND SMALL PROJECTS, Rita Weiss and Frank Fontana. Over 100 miniature patterns: rugs, bedspreads, quilts, chair seats, etc. In standard dollhouse size. 48pp. 8¼ × 11.   23741-9 Pa. $1.95

THE DINOSAUR COLORING BOOK, Anthony Rao. 45 renderings of dinosaurs, fossil birds, turtles, other creatures of Mesozoic Era. Scientifically accurate. Captions. 48pp. 8¼ × 11.   24022-3 Pa. $2.25

SOURCE BOOK OF MEDICAL HISTORY, edited by Logan Clendening, M.D. Original accounts ranging from Ancient Egypt and Greece to discovery of X-rays: Galen, Pasteur, Lavoisier, Harvey, Parkinson, others. 685pp. 5⅜ × 8½.

20621-1 Pa. $10.95

THE ROSE AND THE KEY, J.S. Lefanu. Superb mystery novel from Irish master. Dark doings among an ancient and aristocratic English family. Well-drawn characters; capital suspense. Introduction by N. Donaldson. 448pp. 5⅜ × 8½.

24377-X Pa. $6.95

SOUTH WIND, Norman Douglas. Witty, elegant novel of ideas set on languorous Mediterranean island of Nepenthe. Elegant prose, glittering epigrams, mordant satire. 1917 masterpiece. 416pp. 5⅜ × 8½. (Available in U.S. only)

24361-3 Pa. $5.95

RUSSELL'S CIVIL WAR PHOTOGRAPHS, Capt. A.J. Russell. 116 rare Civil War Photos: Bull Run, Virginia campaigns, bridges, railroads, Richmond, Lincoln's funeral car. Many never seen before. Captions. 128pp. 9⅜ × 12¼.

24283-8 Pa. $6.95

PHOTOGRAPHS BY MAN RAY: 105 Works, 1920-1934. Nudes, still lifes, landscapes, women's faces, celebrity portraits (Dali, Matisse, Picasso, others), rayographs. Reprinted from rare gravure edition. 128pp. 9⅜ × 12¼. (Available in U.S. only)

23842-3 Pa. $6.95

STAR NAMES: THEIR LORE AND MEANING, Richard H. Allen. Star names, the zodiac, constellations: folklore and literature associated with heavens. The basic book of its field, fascinating reading. 563pp. 5⅜ × 8½. 21079-0 Pa. $7.95

BURNHAM'S CELESTIAL HANDBOOK, Robert Burnham, Jr. Thorough guide to the stars beyond our solar system. Exhaustive treatment. Alphabetical by constellation: Andromeda to Cetus in Vol. 1; Chamaeleon to Orion in Vol. 2; and Pavo to Vulpecula in Vol. 3. Hundreds of illustrations. Index in Vol. 3. 2000pp. 6⅛ × 9¼. 23567-X, 23568-8, 23673-0 Pa. Three-vol. set $32.85

THE ART NOUVEAU STYLE BOOK OF ALPHONSE MUCHA, Alphonse Mucha. All 72 plates from *Documents Decoratifs* in original color. Stunning, essential work of Art Nouveau. 80pp. 9⅜ × 12¼. 24044-4 Pa. $7.95

DESIGNS BY ERTE; FASHION DRAWINGS AND ILLUSTRATIONS FROM "HARPER'S BAZAR," Erte. 310 fabulous line drawings and 14 *Harper's Bazar* covers, 8 in full color. Erte's exotic temptresses with tassels, fur muffs, long trains, coifs, more. 129pp. 9⅜ × 12¼. 23397-9 Pa. $6.95

HISTORY OF STRENGTH OF MATERIALS, Stephen P. Timoshenko. Excellent historical survey of the strength of materials with many references to the theories of elasticity and structure. 245 figures. 452pp. 5⅜ × 8½. 61187-6 Pa. $8.95

Prices subject to change without notice.

Available at your book dealer or write for free catalog to Dept. GI, Dover Publications, Inc., 31 East 2nd St. Mineola, N.Y. 11501. Dover publishes more than 175 books each year on science, elementary and advanced mathematics, biology, music, art, literary history, social sciences and other areas.